AMERICA UNBOUND

**The Franklin and Eleanor Roosevelt Institute Series
on Diplomatic and Economic History**

General Editors: Arthur M. Schlesinger, Jr., William J. vanden Heuvel
and Douglas Brinkley

1. **FDR AND HIS CONTEMPORARIES:**
   Foreign Perceptions of an American President
   Edited by Cornelis A. van Minnen and John F. Sears

2. **NATO: THE CREATION OF THE ATLANTIC
   ALLIANCE AND THE INTEGRATION OF EUROPE**
   Edited by Francis H. Heller and John R. Gillingham

3. **AMERICA UNBOUND:**
   World War II and the Making of a Superpower
   Edited by Warren F. Kimball

AMERICA UNBOUND

WORLD WAR II AND THE MAKING OF A SUPERPOWER

Edited by Warren F. Kimball

Rutgers University

St. Martin's Press
New York

E
744
A487
1992

© Warren F. Kimball 1992

First published in the United States of America in 1992

Printed in the United States of America

ISBN 0-312-07957-5

Library of Congress Cataloging-in-Publication Data

America Unbound : World War II and the making of a superpower / ed.
Warren F. Kimball.
    p. cm.
    Revised papers from a conference held at Rutgers University.
    Includes index.
    ISBN 0-312-07957-5
    1. United States—Foreign relations—1945-1989—Congresses.
    2. World War, 1939-1945—Influence—Congresses. I. Kimball,
    Warren F.
  E744.A487 1992
  940.53'2273—dc20   92-5485
                                                     CIP

To Kelly, Jake, and later arrivals

TABLE OF CONTENTS

ACKNOWLEDGEMENTS

These essays were selected to focus on the ways in which World War II contributed to the development of the United States as a superpower in the postwar era. All but one are revised versions of papers given at the conference "World War II and the Shaping of Modern America," held on the Newark campus of Rutgers University. That conference was made possible through the generous support of the New Jersey Committee for the Humanities, the New Jersey Department of Higher Education, the New Jersey Historical Commission, and Rutgers University, particularly the Dean of the Newark Faculty of Arts and Science, Dr. David Hosford. Additional support from Rutgers University came from the Newark Provost, Dr. Norman Samuels, and from two schools on the Newark campus, the Graduate School and the School of Public Administration. Special thanks to Sallie Zeiss, Jackie Kimball, and Herb Meritt for making it all run so smoothly, and to Laura Heymann at St. Martin's Press for making sense out of the garbles I sent her. I am grateful to Arthur M. Schlesinger, Jr., William J. vanden Heuvel, and Douglas Brinkley for including this collection in their excellent series.

Like so much in this era following the precipitous and unexpected collapse of the Soviet Union and its empire, occasional phrases and allusions in these chapters have been overtaken by events. For the most part, these comments bore no relation to the arguments of the authors and have been left as is. Only one chapter seemed to require a 1992 postscript, and that has been added.

Warren F. Kimball
Rutgers University, 1991

1

Introduction

Warren F. Kimball

On 8 May 1945 the United States and its allies celebrated victory over Nazi Germany; on 14 August, victory over Imperial Japan. World War II had ended, at least for the record. But wars last a great deal longer than the fighting. Whether World War II made or merely marked the transition of the United States from a major world power to a superpower,[1] the fact remains that America's role in the world around it had undergone a dramatic change. At the time World War II began in Europe in September 1939, President Franklin D. Roosevelt could not and would not advocate military intervention either in Europe against Hitler or in Asia, where Japan had been at war with China since two years earlier. He had even publicly renounced armed intervention within the Western Hemisphere—America's "backyard"—arguing that the United States should be a Good Neighbor.[2]

In less than a decade, all that had changed. By 1947, President Harry Truman could proclaim a "doctrine" that would legitimize intervention in any part of the world. Other nations had long recognized the potential of the United States (I refrain from quoting de Tocqueville). They had seen its power exercised regularly in economics, if only sporadically in politics. But World War II and the landscape it left behind prompted American leaders and Congress to conclude that they had to use the nation's strength to protect and advance its interests.

The end of the Cold War will not end the debate over the structural reasons for that transformation of American attitudes and actions. The change may have been preordained by the nature of America's political economy—if expansion and unending growth are inherent and necessary to a capitalist system. It may have been a rational reaction to the geopolitical ("real") threat to American interests posed by a pugnacious and expansionist Soviet Union. It may have been an awareness that Nazi, fascist, and Soviet practices,[3] from glorification of the state to the horrors of the Holocaust, posed threats to individual human rights so enormous that aggressive resistance was warranted.

The easy answer is to say it was a little of each. The "golden mean" is, after all, the way to win elections. But the task of historians is, as Carl Becker put it, to make sense of the past—not so as to foretell the future, but to make us sensitive to what has gone before so we can detect patterns and parallels.[4] These essays do not offer a single answer to those questions of causation, but reflect a variety of views. Still, whatever the interpretive perspective, all find World War II marking a dramatic change in the way the United States thought of its interests, ideals, and involvement in the world around it.

Both David Reynolds and Donald Cameron Watt see the process as an incremental one. Each proposes an analytical scheme to illustrate the point. Watt finds patterns of misunderstanding and ahistorical assumptions in a set of historical "generations"—a variation of thesis/antithesis/synthesis—where historical memory (and lack thereof) and historiography lead the United States to make grandiose assumptions about its own power and independence.[5]

David Reynolds suggests that, beyond the obvious economic power of the United States, there are four factors that went into America's change from being a "power" to a "superpower": the international environment, intentions, interests, and institutions. Thus, World War I briefly shocked Americans into fuller participation in world (i.e. European) affairs, although that urge soon subsided. The confused international scene did not invite U.S. participation (environment); Americans did not desire a cooperative international role (intentions); U.S. interests seemed best served by unilateral actions; and the army and the navy were drastically reduced in size (institutions). The Great Depression then prompted Americans to turn in on themselves.

That economic crisis generated economic unilateralism on the part of Roosevelt in the early thirties, yet ten years later his administration built foreign policy on the assumption that the American and international economies were interrelated. The next "historical generation," to apply Watt's taxonomy to Reynolds's argument, took economic crisis and interpreted it to mean that the United States had a "responsibility for the health of the world economy." The irony of that change must have been lost on ex-President

Herbert Hoover who had maintained that the collapse of the American economy in 1929 was due to external influences.

As the international environment altered in the 1930s with the growing threats of Nazi Germany and expansionist Japan, Americans slowly began to recast their thinking. Intervention became more necessary and more plausible once France collapsed in June 1940. Britain then survived the German air campaign of the winter of 1940-41, perhaps preparing Americans for changes to come. The shock of the Japanese attack on Pearl Harbor brought the United States into the war fully, but once in, attitudes and assumptions continued their dramatic change. During World War II, the United States developed the institutions and capabilities of a superpower, while under the spell of Roosevelt's subtle persuasion, Americans came to accept cooperative internationalism (à la Woodrow Wilson?) as the best way to avoid another war.

But the onset of the Cold War in the late 1940s made that environment of internationalism seem artificial to Americans. What had been a "difficult" Soviet Union became a challenge. What appeared to be communist victories in Eastern Europe and China, and the threat of new advances in Korea and Western Europe, prompted American leaders to return to a unilateral vision of how best to act on the international scene. As Reynolds points out, "By 1945, the U.S. government had harnessed national power to national ends." That experience was not forgotten when an atmosphere of crisis developed in the late 1940s.

David Reynolds, then, sees the effects of World War II as both transitory and long-term: transitory in that Americans again turned away from international cooperation, just as they had after World War I, and returned to an outward-looking form of unilateralism, this time under the guise of superpower leadership instead of inward-looking "isolationism"; long-term in that the United States had created institutions and embraced the intentions of a superpower.

The Munich analogy, although not mentioned, is perhaps the political glue that ties together the Cold War and World War II. The crisis that brought the United States into World War II made an article of faith out of the "lessons" of Munich (where Neville Chamberlain tried to get Hitler to accept limits on German expansion). Compromise became tantamount to a surrender of principle, while military intervention "in the cause of freedom" was elevated to a cardinal virtue.

Donald Cameron Watt finds that succeeding historical generations brought different distortions into play. The generation that rose to leadership during World War II seemed to forget the economic crisis that had preceded

the war (although that does not account for the omnipresent predictions that
depression would return as soon as wartime spending ended) as they bought
into the notion that the American economy had "won" the war. At the same
time, the "American consciousness" was imprinted with images of overwhelming U.S. military successes. The war in the Pacific was, according to
popular culture, won by the U.S. Navy and Marine Corps, while the Nor-
mandy invasion not only turned the tide against Hitler, but was presented as
an American show. (Hardly a distortion peculiar to the United States—witness British exaggerations of the importance of the desert war in North
Africa.) Thus, suggests Watt, while the preceding "generation," whose
memory went back to World War I, worked to correct the mistakes of
Woodrow Wilson, the next "generation" took on a "vision of American
omnipotence."[6] The "alleged lessons of the past" pushed Americans in the
direction of perceiving Britain as a rival and, after the war, perceiving
Western Europe as an object of American support rather than a contributor
to its own security. Watt does not question the impact of World War II so
much as to point to the misconceptions Americans took from the war.
Moreover, he argues, the problem does not originate with those who had that
war-inspired vision of American omnipotence, but with the previous "generation," which was mistakenly taken in by both the "legend of American
isolationism" and by claims that the rejection of Wilsonian solutions brought
international conflict. He goes on to suggest that the "globalism" of postwar
American leaders like John F. Kennedy was the product "of that extraordinary eighteen months [1944-45] when American money, industrial productivity and armed forces dominated and supported the victorious coalition
against Hitler and ended the war against Japan by the invocation of a
scientific revolution in the technology of total war."

That American economic strength "won" the war is a dubious claim, but
the effect of World War II in speeding up the progress of the United States
toward becoming the dominant economic power is obvious.[7] At home,
economic growth solidified the belief that government could and should
intervene in the economy. That same conviction travelled abroad as well. By
war's end, not only did the U.S. economy dwarf all others, but American
economic principles had been institutionalized in a series of international
monetary agencies. The American government found itself at the apex of an
enviable economic structure. Not only did postwar reconstruction aid help
re-create markets for American goods, but loans either reaped interest or
were contingent on concessions that tended to keep the United States as king
of the mountain. Thus, the U.S. economy benefitted at both ends: as the loans
generated interest, the principle was paid back, and borrowers had to buy

specific amounts of American goods. That system could not last forever as other nations, particularly West Germany and Japan, turned their economies around. But it took the demands of Lyndon Johnson's dual wars on poverty and Vietnam to break the American grasp. Even then, the United States remained the largest single economic power, even if it was no longer able to dictate to its rivals.

That extraordinary "system" did not spring into being by accident or conspiracy, but because American leaders consistently promoted a common vision for the world economy. They argued bitterly among themselves about how to achieve their goals and about the appropriate role of government versus that of private interests. But all agreed on two basic premises: that the United States, as the richest nation, should be capitalist to the world; and that trade restrictions should be reduced if not eliminated so that all could benefit (though it was not lost on many that American trade would benefit the most). That vision was present in some of Woodrow Wilson's thinking, and continued during the 1920s (though the role of government was different). But the vision became attainable as World War II destroyed the economies of all the major powers—save one which, in the words of Mikhail Gorbachev, "waxed fabulously rich on the war."

The first order of economic business during World War II was to redirect the economy to the war effort so as to win the war. But war seems to offer opportunities for great change, and within short order, the Roosevelt administration moved toward translating its economic conceptions into concrete plans. That thinking, as I describe, was integrally connected to the political changes in intentions and institutions recounted by David Reynolds and Donald Cameron Watt.

"Total war" and dominant, if not total, economic strength should immediately remind us of Lord Acton's aphorism about the corrupting effects of power. Warnings about the "imperial" presidency garner little support in the post-Cold War era when Americans smugly smile over having peacefully "won" the confrontation with the Soviet Union through steady pressure and a refusal to compromise.[8] But claims of a "Forty Year Peace" would come as a surprise to peasants in Korea, Vietnam, and Central America, while the real cost of the "victory" may have been the economic health of the United States. Whatever the best interpretation of the Cold War years, it is indisputable that two great crises during Franklin D. Roosevelt's time in the White House stimulated an enormous expansion of useable presidential authority. The Great Depression provided both the impetus and the justification for centralizing increasing control in the Executive Branch, but it was more than that. The power shifted even further up the line, to the Executive Office—the

White House. Even though Roosevelt made extensive use of commissions, boards, and agencies, real power and authority rested with him and his closest associates. The size of the Executive Office was small compared to the burgeoning monster that exists today, but the process had begun.[9]

The crisis of war not only confirmed that authority at home, but, as Walter LaFeber illustrates, gave Roosevelt, already inclined to gather in the reins of power, the leverage to establish personal control over foreign policy. Denied that prerogative by Congress in the mid-1930s, Roosevelt seized the initiative, which, in conjunction with enhanced powers as commander in chief, gave the President extraordinary ability to take actions that committed the United States to long-term foreign policies.[10] His denigration of the State Department prevented the emergence of any "Robert Lansings" as had appeared after World War I to challenge the president's personal rule over foreign policy, while Roosevelt's seemingly haphazard managerial style eliminated any bureaucratic challenge by disrupting the institutional channels that mandarins use so effectively to block action.

LaFeber points out that such an expansion of control as he describes did not go unnoticed or unchallenged. A number of Republican congressional voices, particularly Senator Robert A. Taft, raised warnings and questions about the danger of growing presidential power but were dismissed as partisans and tarred with the "isolationist" brush, as Roosevelt's popularity proved too widespread to confront.

Even more penetrating, though equally ineffective, were the misgivings of public commentators, ranging from *Time* magazine's Henry Luce to historian Charles Beard and constitutional scholar Edward Corwin. The latter sarcastically pointed out that Roosevelt's claim to authority from the people (open to manipulation by demagogues), and not the Constitution, appeared similar to the "leadership principle" espoused by Hitler and Mussolini. Franklin Roosevelt used World War II not only to further the growth of the "interventionist" government begun in the Depression, but also to expand the power and independence of the president in the foreign policy arena. Those who argued during World War II against Roosevelt's constant and successful campaign to gain presidential power ("discretion" was the euphemism he used) failed to convince Americans of the dangers. As LaFeber pungently puts it, the episodes of Oliver North and Watergate belie the notion that, once informed, the public reacts against excessive presidential power.

One could add that, while examinations of Roosevelt's administrative style tend to emphasize haphazardness and procrastination, the creation of an effective, powerful Executive Office dates to his era. Not only does today's Bureau of the Budget have its beginning then, but the position of

National Security Adviser (Harry Hopkins was the first to fill that role) also appeared during World War II, along with a myriad of other White House (Executive Office) functions we now take for granted. Were Charles Beard and Edward Corwin right? Did Roosevelt, consciously or not, move the nation a long way toward the same centralized foreign policy decision making that twentieth-century authoritarians espoused?

LaFeber leaves us with a dismal picture—popular presidents making use of the ever-expanding powers of the Executive Office, a compliant Congress, and a fooled and foolish public. One might add that fear (valid or imagined) is an equally strong weapon in the hands (or rather mouths) of leaders. Roosevelt effectively used, and perhaps exaggerated, the real threat of Nazi and Japanese expansion to obtain greater authority. Harry Truman and his advisers similarly employed communism and Soviet power.

LaFeber finds foreign policy in the American democracy in a precarious position, with the nation's presidency corrupted by power, its public manipulated, its elected legislators unable or afraid to confront the White House, and none willing to listen to voices that cry in the wilderness. Moreover, what about domestic liberties in an atmosphere of foreign crisis? What is clear is that, in the matter of relations with other societies, the extent of presidential prerogatives took on its modern raiment in the era of Franklin D. Roosevelt.

In a perfect world—a new world order—the military legacy of battle would be irrelevant for Americans, for the nation fights its wars only to eliminate warfare—"Perpetual War for Perpetual Peace" as one critic labelled it.[11] But if that was the public purpose of World War II (and Roosevelt commented privately to Soviet Foreign Minister V. Molotov in 1942 that peace could be expected to last only twenty-five years, later raising that prediction to fifty years when talking to Stalin[12]), the hot wars of the Cold War—from Korea through Afghanistan and Vietnam—and the post-Cold War battle in the Persian Gulf in 1990-91 all demonstrate that military lessons learned must remain subjects for study.

And that is precisely Russell Weigley's purpose. The interrelationship between military planning and political realities is driven home when Weigley, like Donald Cameron Watt and David Reynolds, points out how World War II changed in American assumptions (intentions) and transformed American military (particularly Army) thinking. The focus became preparation for war in Europe against the Soviet Union and its allies rather than defense of the American hemisphere and nation. That new approach dovetailed neatly with the "lessons" of the American Civil War, lessons that have dominated American military strategy ever since. It was no accident that Franklin Roosevelt referred to General "Unconditional Surrender" Grant when announcing that unconditional surrender would be the only terms offered Nazi Germany and Japan.[13]

The Civil War experience, where Union strength and depth were applied directly and overwhelmingly to overcome Confederate skill and initiative, was echoed by the brief experience of fighting on the western front during World War I. Once again, overwhelming strength aimed at the annihilation of the enemy's armies proved the path to victory. When the time came to formulate a plan for victory in World War II, the Americans applied those same lessons and demanded that German forces be met directly and with maximum concentration of strength. That military strategy, which called for a massive frontal assault—a second front—became a major source of dispute with the British, who preferred a more cautious series of peripheral attacks on Hitler's Europe (while Soviet armies confronted the bulk of German forces). The Americans not only won the argument, but, in defeating Hitler's forces in the West, reinforced their views. In the Korean War, the impracticality and dangers of trying to apply massive, concentrated force should have become obvious. When President Truman refused permission to extend the war to China, General Douglas MacArthur whined that the politicians were handcuffing the military—a plaint that would be echoed twenty years later in Vietnam. Moreover, it was easier to blame the politicians than to argue that the assumptions inherited from World War II were not valid in anything short of a full confrontation between the superpowers.

In the era after the Vietnam War, Army planners tried to accommodate strategies and tactics based on maneuverability and limited resources rather than rely solely on the direct application of overwhelming strength. But it may be that the war in the Persian Gulf has bolstered belief in the old formula. Massive American force, concentrated against the strength of the enemy's forces, won the day. But, as Weigley suggests in closing, the post-Cold War "peace dividend" demanded by the public means that the military cannot plan on having the size and equipment needed to apply overwhelming force in the future.

The unasked question: do both the American military and the nation's political leaders recognize that fact? Despite massive demobilization by the United States during 1945 and 1946, the experience of World War II changed American attitudes toward a large standing army, a draft, and military expenditures. All it took was the perception of a threat to restore those institutions. But the collapse of the Soviet Union and the rise of economic rivals have perhaps, refocused American thinking. Or, to use David Reynolds's categories, the changing environment (no Soviet threat and growing economic problems at home) may prompt the United States not to maintain the military institutions needed to apply overwhelming force in future conflicts. If so, will the nation recast its intentions? In a world of logic, where emotions play no role in policy, that question would be decided by a rational examination of American interests, but . . .

In addition to the institutions of massive military capabilities, one of the instruments of power for the president in the post-World War II era has been intelligence or, to be more precise, covert action. Bradley F. Smith summarizes that development in words that defy paraphrasing:

> The relative subtlety with which the war changed the government and ways of life of the American people has made it difficult for historians, and the general public, to grasp the revolutionary importance of the years 1941-1945 for the history of the United States. . . . [T]he traditional American dislike of secret intelligence and secret police systems has led people then and since to ignore, or deny, that this war inevitably moved their country into the ranks of the "normal" great powers who use such instruments as secret intelligence and covert operations to get what they want in international relations.

Intelligence historian David Kahn has pointed out that the United States was not the only society to label intelligence and covert action as distasteful, but that does not change the thrust of Smith's point.

Kahn has also pointed out that "the nation's virtually unquestioning acquiescence in the expenditure of billions of dollars and man-hours for information-gathering would not exist without the pricking, living spur of Pearl Harbor."[14] We should add to that the covert action exploits of the Office of Strategic Services (OSS) during World War II. Those activities had just as great an impact as Pearl Harbor on government leaders, and later the public, in legitimating covert operations by the Central Intelligence Agency and various military intelligence offices.

As Smith points out, the full details of that transition remain buried in the archives—archives that should and would have been opened decades ago in Britain and the United States had it not been for the mindless fears of the Cold War. Perhaps, with the end of confrontation between two nuclear superpowers, files that date back to 1941 and even earlier can be opened to the people of those two democracies. Or perhaps similar files from the now-deceased Soviet Union will be opened first, embarrassing the "democracies" into following suit.

There are few better insights into the fears of the Cold War era than the essay by Hayden Peake, himself a veteran of the CIA. Whatever Peake's assumptions, they faithfully reflect the atmosphere and actions that motivated U.S. counterintelligence and its twin, internal security policy. At its extremes, Peake's essay is either a stunning indictment of U.S. naivete, or an unintentionally revealing autopsy of American paranoia. Either way, it is worth studying as a window into the compartmented, hybrid world of counterintelligence—a world that, in the Cold War era, came to be viewed as normal; a world where accusation became tantamount to conviction, where inalienable rights were suspended in the interest of national security. Peake's reconstruction of an attitude, based in part on personal experience, delineates with great impact how that view developed out of the World War II experience.

William Korey may make academics uneasy, for he often eschews the convention of cool objectivity and adopts the first person form. But genocide and the Holocaust belong in the first person in the late twentieth century when bigots distort history to claim that Jews and other so-called *untermensch*, as Hitler termed those he hated, were not scheduled for systematic exploitation and elimination. One of the legacies of World War II for the United States should have been a deepened sensitivity toward human rights, especially the rights of persecuted minorities. But, despite the exposure of the horrors of the Holocaust, the United States proved reluctant in the postwar era to accept international proscriptions against genocide.

The reasons for that foot-dragging were many, from anti-Semitism to fears that discrimination against black Americans would come under international scrutiny. Whatever the impact of those factors, an ambiguous legacy of the war was also a sense that the United States had the right to leadership, a variation on the go-it-alone theme the United States adopted after World War I. With (super)power came the urge to tell others how to run their lives.

War is invariably unhappy and immoral in one way or another. The common phrase "the Good War" to describe World War II is both sarcastic and a bit obscene. The studies in this book focus strongly on the rise of American power during this war and the dangers inherent in such dominant strength. A sense of the United States' betrayal of its own principles hovers in the background, with World War II as the occasion of sin. But all this must be balanced with the reminder that a world, or even a Europe, controlled by Hitler and the Nazis, would have been far worse. Given what we know about the excesses of the military regime in Japan, an East Asia under its thumb is an unsettling prospect for human rights. World War II may not have been a "good" war, but it was a necessary one.

NOTES

1. As David Reynolds points out in his essay, invention of the term superpower is claimed by William T. R. Fox.

2. There were, of course, other forms of intervention. Early in the Roosevelt administration, the United States used a combination of political and economic pressures to insure the installation of a "safe" regime in Cuba. Roosevelt rejected recommendations to send in the Marines, but some thirty warships of various sizes and descriptions hovered around the island, steaming in and out of Cuban ports. The end result was the corrupt and authoritarian regime of Fulgencio Batista. See Bryce Wood, *The Making of the Good Neighbor Policy* (New York, 1961), chaps. 2-3.

3. See Les Adler and Thomas Paterson, "Red Fascism: The Merger of Nazi Germany and Soviet Russia in the American Image of Totalitarianism," *American Historical Review* 75:4 (1970), pp. 1046-64.

4. Carl Becker, "Everyman His Own Historian," *American Historical Review* 37 (January 1932), pp. 221-36.

5. Watt proposed this theory of "historical generations" using different examples in *Succeeding John Bull: America in Britain's Place, 1900-1975* (Cambridge, 1984), pp. 13-20.

6. The phrase is that of Dennis W. Brogan, as Watt points out. Brogan used the phrase in a 1952 essay titled "The Illusion of American Omnipotence," reprinted in *American Aspects* (London, 1964), pp. 9-21. William Appleman Williams in his influential essays, *The Tragedy of American Diplomacy* (New York, 1959), brought the phrase into the academic debate over American policy in the Cold War.

7. Alan Milward states that statistics suggest that the growth rate of the American economy consisted in good part of "taking up the slack which existed" from the depression. Even so, he admits that those gains "would perhaps not have been fully realizable in a less urgent situation," i.e. the war; Milward, *War, Economy and Society, 1939-1945* (Berkeley, 1977), p. 66.

8. D. C. Watt, also a contributor to this volume, has echoed LaFeber's analysis, though from a quite different perspective, labelling the American government "basically akin to the systems of monarchial rule . . . in eighteenth-century Europe"; *Succeeding John Bull*, p. 193.

9. *Inter alia* see Barry Karl, *The Uneasy State* (Chicago, 1983).

10. For additional comments see W. F. Kimball, "'Dr. New Deal': Franklin D. Roosevelt as Commander in Chief," in *Commanders in Chief: Presidential Wartime Leadership from McKinley to Nixon*, J. Dawson, ed. (Lawrence, KS, forthcoming 1993).

11. Harry Elmer Barnes used the phrase as the title for a book of essays he edited that attacked Roosevelt's prewar policies as lies and deceptions; *Perpetual War for Perpetual Peace* (Caldwell, ID, 1953).

12. Warren F. Kimball, *The Juggler: Franklin Roosevelt as Wartime Statesman* (Princeton, NJ, 1991), p. 101.

13. See Raymond G. O'Connor, *Diplomacy for Victory: FDR and Unconditional Surrender* (New York, 1971), pp. 2, 9, 51-2.

14. Comments by David Kahn, "World War II and the Shaping of Modern America," conference, Rutgers University, Newark, NJ, 4-6 April 1986.

2

Power and Superpower: The Impact of Two World Wars on America's International Role

David Reynolds

The emergence of the United States as a "superpower" was a phenomenon of the mid-twentieth century, yet it had been predicted long before. Perhaps the most distinguished prophet was Alexis de Tocqueville in 1835, who concluded the first volume of *Democracy in America* with the forecast that one day the United States and Russia would each "hold in its hands the destinies of half the world." But many others spoke in the same vein. In 1866, for instance, de Tocqueville's compatriot, the economist Michel Chevalier, urged Europe to unify in the face of the "political colossus that has been created on the other side of the Atlantic" and foresaw future armed conflict between the two continents. In 1882, Constantin Frantz, the German political commentator, considered it virtually inevitable "that the New World would outstrip the Old World in the not far distant future," while the English historian J. R. Seeley predicted two years later that within the lifetime of his students, "Russia and the United States will surpass in power the states now called great as much as the great country-states of the sixteenth century surpassed Florence."[1]

In fact, the idea that the future lay with the "world powers" became almost commonplace in late-nineteenth-century thought about international relations. For much of the century, America and Russia had been spoken of in the same breath as the two great land powers whose vast size and population guaranteed them eventual supremacy. In the last third of the century, however, America's promise seemed the greater. The Civil War had removed the possibility that the Union would disintegrate, and America's rapid industrialization closed the gap between its economy and those of Britain, hitherto the dominant industrial power, and Germany, Britain's other main rival. In 1913 the United States produced one-third of the world's manufactures, its coal output equaled that of Britain and Germany combined, and its iron and steel production surpassed that of the entire continent of Europe.[2] The trend seemed clear. Indeed, it is easy to conclude, bearing in mind America's population, natural resources, industrial might and geographical security, that "there was a virtual inevitability about the process of American expansion; that is to say, only persistent human ineptitude, or near-constant civil war, or a climatic disaster could have checked this rise to global economic (and, by extension, military) influence."[3]

That Braudelian judgment is understandable and to a large extent appropriate. In the long run there is an apparent ineluctability about America's rise to globalism. It is, after all, a characteristic of industrial as against premodern societies that "economic wealth and military power became increasingly synonymous."[4] Yet that is not the whole story. Some modern states with significant economic strength have not translated this into comparable military influence—think of postwar Japan or, more recently, Saudi Arabia. Theorists of international relations agree that the power of a state cannot be simply equated with crude capabilities such as population, gross national product, or total steel output.[5] What is striking about the history of this century is surely the relative slowness with which America evolved into a superpower, given its industrial strength by 1914.

In addition to economic power, four other explanatory concepts are suggested here to help us understand America's changing international role during the first half of this century: "environment," "intentions," "interests," and "institutions." By "environment" is meant the general pattern of international relations. This provides the context and opportunity for extending national power and influence. But a favorable environment must be exploited: there must be appropriate "intentions," a determination to bring the country's resources to bear on international events. That determination can be rooted in morality or ideology, but to be fully effective it usually also requires a concept of national "interests"—the conviction that the nation's prosperity and security depend on shaping world affairs to one's own advantage. But this can only be done if a country has the appropriate "institutions" to harness national power and project it internationally. These institutions include not only a diplomatic service and armed forces, but also a coordinated government bureaucracy.

These four concepts will be used to help explain America's rise to superpower status and the place of World War I and, in particular, of World War II in that process. The concepts function like transparencies on an overhead projector—successive overlays help us build up a more complete picture. The object is not to deny the validity of the long-run geoeconomic explanation but to build on it. The underlying "structures" of geography and economics do much to explain why America rose, but they tell us less about the timing and the form of its emergence as a superpower. And those questions about "when" and "how" are as important as "why" if we wish to understand the course and impact of the two world wars.

In 1914 the United States, although an economic giant, was a military pygmy—a largely regional power in the Western Hemisphere with negligible armed forces who showed little desire to become involved in the European conflict. But the belligerents failed to win their expected quick victory. They were obliged to mobilize their economies for an all-out war in which the industrial and financial resources of the United States soon assumed decisive importance. By 1916 the British were dependent on America for munitions, raw materials, and no less than $9 million of the $22 million per day that they needed to keep fighting.[6] The German High Command decided in January 1917 that cutting the Allies' transatlantic lifeline was the precondition of victory, and its unrestricted submarine warfare pushed a still reluctant president into war.

Woodrow Wilson was now determined to crush German militarism, but he also intended to eliminate the imperialism and armaments of the Allies, which he saw as an impediment to a new world order centered on the League of Nations. He believed that America's economic power was the instrument of international influence. As he wrote in July 1917, "England and France have not the same views with regard to peace that we have by any means. When the war is over we can force them to our way of thinking, because by that time they will, among other things, be financially in our hands."[7] His prediction apparently came true in November 1918. Wilson was able to conclude an armistice with the Germans based on his own peace aims and to impose it on the Allies by threatening that America might otherwise sign a separate peace and leave Britain, France, and Italy to fight on as best they could. Intent by now on creating a "world safe for democracy," Wilson could exploit the favorable environment provided by Europe's self-destruction and its reliance on American economic power.

But the window of opportunity soon began to close. Once the fighting stopped, the Allies were less dependent on the United States, and Wilson expended much of his now diminished influence at the Paris peace conference in securing the League of Nations. With Germany defeated and disarmed, with Britain and France expanding in the Middle East on the ruins of the Ottoman Empire, the wartime shifts in world power seemed to have been redressed and the old European order at least superficially restored.

Meanwhile, at home Wilson failed to convince Americans that it was in the interest of the United States to undertake automatic global commitments to collective security, and he refused to make sufficient concessions to break the Republicans' hold over the Senate. America's will to power, its wartime crusading idealism, evaporated in the bitter fight over the Covenant, and in the 1920s the United States refused to join either the League or its ancillary bodies.

Immediately after the armistice, Wilson and Congress started dismantling the institutions of power. Railroads were returned to private ownership, the vast government-owned shipping fleet sold off, and the wartime draft abandoned. The army, which had grown from less than 100,000 personnel in 1914 to 2.4 million by the armistice, stabilized at 130,000 to 140,000 by the mid-1920s.[8] Only the navy's status had permanently changed. The war enabled the General Board to argue for a "navy second to none," citing as justification Japan's Asian ambitions and its alliance with Britain, still the world's greatest navy. The threat of a naval race against the United States at a time of economic recession obliged the British to abandon the Anglo-Japanese alliance in 1921 and to accept "parity" with the United States. Yet throughout the interwar years America did not build up to treaty limits, and Britain, although also restricting its naval construction, remained the world's principal sea power.

Despite Wilson's failure and the dismantling of U.S. military power after the war, the president nevertheless had been right in 1917 to claim that America's new financial strength could be a powerful lever of future international influence. In 1914 America was still a net debtor nation, its trade largely financed by the City of London, and it was not until the Federal Reserve Act of 1913 that U.S. banks were even permitted to establish foreign branches. The war transformed the situation. Substantial European disinvestment and the channeling of U.S. capital into private and governmental loans to the Allies turned America into a net creditor nation of $3.7 billion, exactly reversing the amount of its debt in 1914.[9] Although Britain's total investment abroad still exceeded America's throughout the interwar period, the United States was henceforth the main source of new investment capital. During the war, J. P. Morgan and the National City Bank in particular took advantage of new federal legislation and Europe's preoccupation with war to expand their foreign operations. And in the 1920s Wall Street's new financial power was directed, with administration encouragement, into loans to restructure German finances, fund the reparations debt, and stabilize the European economy. The Dawes Plan of 1924 and the Young Plan of 1929 illustrate how the United States was now using its enhanced financial power for political ends to support a European settlement that checked France, rehabilitated Germany, and revived world trade.

Yet the institutions of U.S. financial diplomacy were crude and ineffective. In the words of Sir William Wiseman, wartime British diplomat turned Wall Street banker, in 1921: "America now sits impotent among her money bags. Her merchants and her financiers have learnt that it needs something more than cash to secure an international hegemony."[10] The federal government exerted only limited direct control over U.S. financial relations with the rest of the world. It could not dissuade Congress from insisting on the Allies' repayment of their war debts (some $11 billion), a heavy burden on international recovery and European governmental finances. Nor was it possible to restrain Congress from progressive escalations of U.S. tariffs, which made it ever harder for the Europeans to repay their debts through normal trade. And the U.S. loans to Europe, on which depended the cycle of German reparations to the Allies and Allied debt payments to the United States, did not originate from the U.S. government. They were private loans, mostly short-term—in other words, speculative capital from the overheating American economy that moved around in response to changing investment opportunities. With the collapse of the U.S. stock market from October 1929 the flow of funds dried up, and the rapid withdrawal of existing loans in mid-1931 was an important cause of the German and Australian bank crises and the British decision to go off gold.[11]

The 1930s were a period when the United States turned in on itself. The international economy broke up into loose economic blocks, centered on Britain, Germany, America, and France. Although the United States was the strongest economic power and thus the potential motor of economic recovery, it adopted insular, protectionist policies. Unlike Britain in late-nineteenth-century depressions, it did not engage in countercyclical foreign lending or significantly reduce domestic tariffs to help revive world investment and trade. In the early 1930s only two powers might have been able to alleviate the Depression. But, in Charles Kindleberger's words, "the British couldn't and the United States wouldn't." The former was "feeble, the other irresponsible."[12]

Yet the problem went deeper than intentions and institutions. It was more fundamental than an unreadiness to use economic power "responsibly" in international affairs or the inability of the Executive Branch to direct Congress and the private economy. America lacked the self-interest of Victorian Britain in the health of the world economy. The U.S. boom of the 1920s, like its late-nineteenth-century growth, was largely fueled by the continentwide, tariff-free domestic market and not by foreign demand. Britain in its heyday, by contrast, had depended on markets and raw materials around the world, and therefore needed to promote world trade and investment, especially at times of depression. "Britain's empire is abroad; America's is at home," one Chicago banker put it succinctly in 1921.[13] And the statistics bear him out. In 1928 the United States was the world's largest exporter, with 15.8 percent of global exports, yet those exports were a mere 6.3 percent of national income. Britain's exports that year amounted to 20.8 percent of its national income. Other figures tell a similar story. In 1928 the ratio of imports to national income was 5 percent for the United States and 28.8 percent for the United Kingdom, yet America was second only to Britain as the world's leading importer. And, despite an average of some $900 million per annum invested overseas by Americans in the 1920s, foreign investment was only 3.8 percent of gross capital formation, compared with about 40 to 50 percent in the case of Britain at its peak in 1870-1913.[14] The inference is clear: interest reinforced intentions as America retreated into its shell.

This insight can be extended into the military sphere as well. For security as well as prosperity the world needed America more than America needed the world. The growing challenge from Germany, Italy, and Japan to Britain and France and to the existing balance of world power evoked little direct response from an America preoccupied with chronic depression and a sharp pacifist backlash against involvement in the Great War. The prevailing opinion was that in future Europe could stew in its own juice. The peace movement was therefore able to push through a series of Neutrality Acts from 1935. These were intended to ensure that next time America's industrial, financial, and naval power would not be used to affect the course of any European war. On the contrary, by forgoing rights of trade, travel, and investment Americans would "insulate" themselves from possible entanglement in such a conflict.

In the later 1930s the Roosevelt administration tried to redirect American policy through agreements to reduce trade barriers, diplomatic initiatives to foster a European settlement, and, especially after Munich, covert material assistance to Anglo-French rearmament. But whatever the intentions, the result was little more than "pin pricks and righteous protest."[15] Naval cooperation with the British remained tentative and limited, and it was not until after war began in Europe in the autumn of 1939 that Roosevelt was able to repeal the arms embargo. Even then U.S. trade with the Allies remained on a "cash and carry" basis.

Roosevelt's problems were partly the result of public attitudes. Mindful of Wilson's mistakes he felt unable to move far in the face of strong anti-interventionist sentiment on Capitol Hill and in the country at large. As he observed in 1937, "It is a terrible thing to look over your shoulder when you are trying to lead—and to find no one there."[16] But he also lacked effective institutions for exercising presidential influence. There was no presidential staff to control the sprawling, bickering bureaucracy; all he had to show for the protracted battle over executive reorganization was the weak 1939 act that set up the executive office of the president with six assistants. Even this covered only domestic policy, and attempts at formalized coordination of external policy, such as the State-War-Navy liaison committee or the Cabinet Defense council in 1941, proved ineffectual. Similarly, after Roosevelt lost the struggle with Congress in 1937 over his attempt to "pack" the Supreme Court with pro-New Deal judges, FDR lost his hold over Capitol Hill. Essential preconditions for the New Deal legislation of the first term had been Congress's unusual receptivity to Executive wishes and the remarkable dominance and unity of the Democratic party. During the second term, normality was restored —incessant feuding between White House and Capitol Hill and chronic factionalism within the Democratic party. (Periods of firm executive leadership are the exception, not the rule, in American politics: Wilson in 1913-14, Roosevelt in 1933-35, Johnson in 1964-65, and Reagan in 1981-82 stand out in this century.)

Attitudes and institutions were only part of the story. More fundamentally, U.S. interests did not dictate large-scale intervention. For one thing, Britain was an economic rival of the United States; its "Imperial Preferences" and financial agreements impeded the revival of U.S. trade. One Anglophobe American diplomat wondered in 1936 why Britain should think "she can count on our help politically, and yet hit us below the belt commercially all over the world."[17] But there was a more fundamental consideration of self-interest. Roosevelt shared the general desire to keep out of another war and seems to have believed that a firm Allied policy with limited U.S. support would suffice to contain Hitler. "What the British need today," he wrote in February 1939, "is a good stiff grog, inducing not only the desire to save civilization but the continued belief that they can do it. In such an event they will have a lot more support from their American cousins."[18]

Roosevelt was still operating in what C. Vann Woodward, adapting Frederick Jackson Turner, called "the age of free security."[19] The term is in some ways a misnomer. In the early nineteenth century the new nation feared a British counterrevolutionary war and later struggled hard to evict the British and other Europeans from the North American continent. But after the Civil War the United States did enjoy an unusually privileged position. It was highly self-sufficient economically, protected in an era of sea power by the Atlantic and Pacific oceans and shielded in addition by Britain's own self-interest in maintaining the European balance of power. Well into the twentieth century the United States could therefore afford the luxury of low defense expenditure, relative to its vast wealth and to the outlays of more vulnerable European powers. Until the 1930s, U.S. peacetime spending on defense had usually been less than 1 percent of national income. In 1937 the figure had risen to 1.5 percent, but the comparable percentages for Japan were 28.2 percent, Russia 26.4, Germany 23.5 and France 9.1. The lowest spender of the European powers was Britain at 5.7 percent, but significantly it enjoyed geographical immunity similar in kind, if not degree, to that of the United States. Protected by water, both could avoid the necessity of large conscript armies. U.S. security might not have been totally "free," but it came at bargain rates.[20]

When the European war broke out in September 1939, therefore, the United States remained a world power in potential but not actuality. It had not translated economic strength into effective institutions of international influence, and moreover it showed an intention not to do so. That was not mere myopia. Although the wider world was increasingly affected by American action or inaction, the United States could afford to turn inward for much of the Great Depression decade because its prosperity and security seemed relatively independent of events overseas. By 1945, however, the situation had been transformed. Bearing in mind this interwar background, we can now use the four concepts of "environment," "intention," "interest," and "institutions" to explore the impact of World War II.

The two years after April 1940 saw a revolution in the distribution of world power that was more profound than any other in the twentieth century. The decisive actors were Germany and Japan, the decisive moments the spring of 1940 and the early months of 1942.

Between April and June 1940, Hitler conquered Denmark, Norway, the Low Countries and, above all, France in a mere two-and-a-half months. He succeeded where the Kaiser had just failed in 1918 to bring most of continental Europe under German control. Britain alone was left, but although it survived 1940 it was far from clear that it could continue indefinitely against blockade by sea. The German invasion of Russia in June 1941 and the successful Russian resistance provided a respite, but the chances of a durable

Eastern Front were not rated highly by Western observers until well into 1942.

By then, however, the conflict had become a truly world war. For the German successes of 1940-41 gave Japan an unprecedented opportunity to establish its own sphere of influence in Asia. The European colonial powers were unable to defend their southeast Asian possessions, and after June 1941 Russia, Japan's greatest Asian rival, could do little to intervene. Unable to obtain their aims diplomatically, the Japanese resorted to war in December 1941. Their preemptive strike on the U.S. Pacific Fleet at Pearl Harbor was the prelude to a remarkable series of combined operations which led to the conquest of Hong Kong, Malaya, Singapore, the Philippines, the Dutch East Indies, and Burma in only four months. By April 1942 India and Australia seemed in danger. Like the fall of France, this came as a devastating surprise. U.S. planners had expected the Japanese to be only a nuisance—trade raiding, some local conquests, but not much more. In fact, they had upset the balance of power in Asia as dramatically as Hitler in Europe two years before.

The United States could not remain immune from the international revolution of 1940-42. World War II was taking a very different course from its predecessor, and America's role was necessarily very different as well. After June 1940 there was no Western Front in Europe. Britain assumed a critical importance for the United States—first as the front line while a near-defenseless America rearmed, later as the forward base for bombing and then invading Hitler's Europe. But the British required massive U.S. economic and financial aid—as did the Russians from summer 1941 and the campaigns against Japan after Pearl Harbor. By 1944 the United States was producing some 40 percent of world armaments and 60 percent of the combat munitions used by the Allies,[21] in the process finally pulling the country out of the Depression and setting off a remarkable boom in consumer production as well. To defeat the Axis in this truly global war—with fronts in the Pacific, Mediterranean and, eventually, Europe—the United States also constructed a "two-ocean navy" and drafted, trained and serviced huge armed forces—12.1 million by May 1945 compared with 2.9 million in November 1918.[22]

At the end of World War I America's opportunity for world power proved only temporary, in part because of the rapid recovery of the Europeans once the fighting stopped. In 1945 Europe's predicament again eased to some extent. The Western Europeans embarked on the longest economic boom in their history and re-entered their colonies wrested back, with U.S. help, from Japan. By this time the cost of victory was all too apparent. France had been occupied and never again achieved great power status, while Britain had lost a quarter of its national wealth and was transformed from the world's second-largest creditor nation to its greatest debtor. The contraction of Anglo-French power and that of the Axis left a vacuum for the United States to fill: sharing in the occupation of Germany, dominating postwar Japan, and projecting its influence into China and the Middle East. But the United States was not the war's only beneficiary. Victory cost Russia far more—perhaps 17,000,000 dead compared with America's 323,000, a devastated country rather than a boom economy unscathed by enemy action.[23] But Russia also benefited—particularly in Eastern Europe where its control extended farther than at any time since the Napoleonic Wars.

Two great themes of this century have been Germany's double bid for continental and world power and the nationalist challenge to European empires stimulated by Japan. In World War II these themes intertwined and also intersected with a third, perhaps the greatest theme: the emergence of America and Russia as the dominant world powers. For such was the success of Germany and Japan in 1940-42 that they shattered the old order and allowed these two new superpowers to shape a new one. This new order may have been predicted for more than a century, but the extent and pace of the transition were nothing short of revolutionary.

But 1918 had also been America's moment, and the United States had not exploited that opportunity—admittedly a less dramatic one—for an enhanced world role. In 1945, however, America's "intentions" were different; there was a new will to power. To talk of a country's "intentions" is, of course, a shorthand, often a dangerous one which ignores the diversity of national opinion and bureaucratic positions, not to mention the underlying public apathy about foreign affairs which studies recurrently reveal. Nevertheless, one can reasonably claim that the war saw a profound and durable change in the broad consensus about foreign policy in the United States, a shift, to use the classic concepts, from "isolationism" to "internationalism." (It is instructive to note that at least two postwar presidents of the United States—John Kennedy and Gerald Ford—had supported and contributed to the anti-interventionist "America First" organization in 1940-41.[24]) The process was not as simple or automatic as might be suggested by Senator Arthur Vandenberg's famous remark that Pearl Harbor "ended isolationism for any realist."[25] It was the consequence not merely of events but of a protracted national debate in which the anti-interventionists were discredited and frequently vilified as "isolationists," "fascists," anti-Semites, or, at best, "illustrious dunderheads," to quote the title of Rex Stout's 1942 anthology of their "wisdom, vision and statesmanship."[26]

This did not mean that foreign policy would no longer be controversial or that U.S. diplomacy between the wars had been as "isolationist" as the internationalists' caricatures suggested. (The United States had never cut itself off from world affairs in the manner, say, of Tokugawa Japan, and the term "isolationist" was more a political polemic than an accurate definition.) But before 1940 the burden of proof had lain with those who wished to depart from the nonentanglement tradition of the Founding Fathers. Roosevelt, for instance, in 1941 felt obliged to justify U.S. naval operations in the Atlantic as merely extensions of the Monroe Doctrine. By 1945 the onus of justification was on those who argued that the United States should and could preserve its autonomy regardless of events overseas.

On an "idealistic" level the national debate focused on the concept of "one world," popularized by Wendell Willkie in what became the greatest nonfiction bestseller to date in U.S. publishing history. His account of his seven-week, 31,000-mile tour, published in April 1943, sold over 1.5 million copies in the first four months.[27] In his book the Republican presidential candidate of 1940 argued that air travel had abolished distance and that all people had to live together in the interests of peace. America's task was to eschew isolationism and imperialism and set an example of international cooperation in a world ripe for U.S. leadership. Appeals like Willkie's provided the moral context for the campaign to ensure U.S. membership in a new international organization. Sympathetic pressure groups gradually rehabilitated the reputation of Woodrow Wilson, identified U.S. repudiation of the league as a major cause of the present war, and urged that America had a providential "second chance" to secure lasting peace through collective security. The State Department mounted a massive publicity campaign to help sell the idea to the American public, while Roosevelt, remembering Wilson's failings in 1918-19, enlisted the support of cooperative Republicans such as Vandenberg. In 1945 the United States became a founding member of the new United Nations, with a permanent seat on the Security Council. This time Senate approval was overwhelming—89 to 2.

But anti-interventionism had been based not only on morality, a belief that the Old World was beyond redemption, but on necessity, the argument that the United States need not undertake foreign commitments because the "Western Hemisphere" was secure and invulnerable. Such ideas were also discredited during World War II—again partly by events and partly by interpretations of those events which became the new orthodoxy. For the first time America's "foreign-policy public" shared a set of ideas justifying international commitments as a matter of U.S. self-interest.

This new orthodoxy had three main elements (at risk of oversimplification). First, and central, was the importance of Western Europe for future U.S. security. One of the most influential exponents of this theme was the political commentator Walter Lippmann. His *U.S. Foreign Policy: Shield of the Republic*, also published in April 1943, was the "realist" counterpart to Willkie's "one world" idealistic internationalism (or "globaloney," as skeptics called it). The book sold half a million copies, as well as being popularized in condensed versions and even in a seven-page cartoon strip in the *Ladies Home Journal*.[28] In it Lippmann argued that Hitler's victories in 1940 showed that the United States could not allow a potential foe to control the industrial resources of Western Europe. In the past the Atlantic Ocean, the Royal Navy, and the balance of power had kept America inviolate. But the advent of air power and the weakening of the Europeans, particularly Britain, forced a radical reassessment, in Lippmann's view. The United States must acknowledge its membership of what he had long been calling an "Atlantic Community," and it must pay its membership dues.

Although Europe was the major concern, experience of worldwide war in the air age had inspired a truly global conception of security. If Japan could strike 3,500 miles from Tokyo against the U.S. fleet, then America's defense perimeter must be extended far across the Pacific. If aircraft could fly the South Atlantic and Caribbean, then West Africa and all of South America were inextricably related to U.S. security. The series of influential works from 1942 by "geopoliticians" such as Hans Weigert, Robert Strausz-Hupe and Nicholas Spykman, was assisted by what has been called a veritable "Copernican revolution" in cartography.[29] Conventional maps based on Mercator's projection had distorted distances and encouraged the idea of self-contained "hemispheres." A common depiction of the United States in prewar atlases centered on a "Western Hemisphere" with apparently limitless ocean disappearing on either side. But wartime cartographers, notable Richard Edes Harrison and their geopolitical collaborators promoted "air-age globalism."[30] Their new azimuthal projections, centered on various parts of the world, demonstrated that distance had indeed been revolutionized by aviation and encouraged the idea of a unified international community.

This new idea of global security was vividly illustrated by President Roosevelt in one of his most effective fireside chats on 23 February 1942. Asking Americans to study their maps as he talked, he introduced them to the truly global nature of the war and to the vital logistic links binding the United States to its new allies in Britain, Australia, China and the Soviet Union. Pearl Harbor, he argued, had disproved those isolationists who "wanted the American eagle to imitate the tactics of the ostrich," burying its head in the sand in a futile effort to ignore danger. The geography of modern global war demonstrated the error of those neo-isolationists who, "afraid that we may be sticking our necks out, want our national bird to be turned into a turtle. But," the President concluded, "we prefer to retain the eagle as it is—flying high and striking hard."[31]

The other main feature of the new U.S. thinking about "national security" was the belief that peace depended on prosperity. This belief was not new. The third of President Wilson's Fourteen Points talked of reviving economic barriers and establishing equal trading conditions, and, after the insular protectionism of the early 1930s, the State Department under Cordell Hull worked energetically for trade agreements to realize these Wilsonian goals. But Congress and the White House were lukewarm and Hull's achievements limited. It was not until the war that Wilsonian economics became official orthodoxy. By 1942 the State, Treasury, and Commerce departments gave priority to promoting world economic growth and re-creating an international economy based on convertible currencies, stable exchange rates and nondiscriminatory trade.

Clearly it was in America's narrow self-interest to break down commercial and financial barriers to trade such as Britain's Imperial Preference. Now the world's strongest economy, it was best able to profit from an open market. And although postwar exports still ran at less than 10 percent of the total GNP, certain key sectors relied heavily on foreign markets. In 1947, nearly 20 percent of U.S. coal and steel was exported, half U.S. wheat, and 10 percent of the total output of General Motors.[32] Wartime demands also made the United States less self-sufficient in crucial raw materials. Having been a leading exporter of lead and zinc before the war, America was importing 35 percent of its consumption of each in 1943, and by 1948 it was a net importer of petroleum for the first time since the late 1910s.[33] Although their fears were exaggerated, postwar U.S. policymakers showed an understandable concern for access to markets and raw materials.

But prosperity was not seen as a zero-sum game. Increased trade would benefit all nations, encouraging economic growth and reducing the commercial rivalries that, it was argued, lay at the root of war. "Nations which act as enemies in the marketplace cannot long be friends at the council table," as Assistant Secretary of State Will Clayton put it in May 1945.[34] Growth was also expected to alleviate conflicts within as well as between nations, by reducing pressure for radical change. It was hoped that "the politics of productivity"[35] would replace the politics of revolution as well as the politics of war.

By the summer of 1945 the term "national security" (popularized by Walter Lippmann) had become something of a commonplace in Washington.[36] The independence of Western Europe, the extended air defense of the United States, and the revival of a prosperous world economy—these were the main characteristics of America's new self-interested "internationalism." And at the same time the United States was developing new institutions to ensure that U.S. capabilities matched its defined "interests."

In Europe the accent was on diplomacy. This time the United States took an active and continuing share in the planning and negotiations for a European peace settlement, not bowing out as after 1919. The lesson of two world wars was that Europe was too important to be left to the Europeans. In particular, the future of Germany was of fundamental significance for the United States. On the one had, it must not be allowed to become a great power again, nor must its industrial resources fall into the hands of a potential foe.

On the other hand, those resources were essential for the economic recovery of Western Europe, still one of the powerhouses of the world. These contradictory concerns about Germany as both a potential military threat and a potential economic benefit provoked substantial intragovernmental argument in Washington in 1946-47 and growing friction with the Soviet Union. But in 1944-45 it was hoped that compromise could be reached through great-power collaboration under the auspices of the United Nations. For Roosevelt, America, Britain, and Russia were to act as judges and "policemen" of Europe.

The "institution" of global security was a new military establishment centered on air power. This did not happen immediately: an independent U.S. Air Force was not created until 1947 after an intense bureaucratic battle between admirals and airmen. But by 1944 the U.S. Navy had accepted that the battleship era was over. It based its claim for a leading role on "sea-air power"—the aircraft carrier—while the embryonic air force insisted that the new long-range bomber (the B-36) should have pride of place in future budgets. The airmen's case was strengthened by the efficacy of the new atomic bomb dropped on Hiroshima and Nagasaki in August 1945 and by the fact that autumn aviators such as Generals Spaatz, Arnold, and LeMay were already talking of an "air-atomic" strategy requiring a seventy-group air force.

But the American eagle, in Roosevelt's words, could only "fly high and strike hard" if it had safe perches around the globe. Since the mid-1930s Roosevelt had been assiduously acquiring Pacific and Atlantic islands for naval and air bases to enlarge America's defense perimeter and in 1940 negotiated rights on eight British possessions in the Western Atlantic and Caribbean in return for fifty old U.S. destroyers. By 1943 the policy was being systematized. The Joint Chiefs of Staff drew up plans for a grid of bases from the Philippines to the Azores that would provide defense in depth and would enable the United States to strike fast and hard at any enemy.

Supplementing these were transit and landing rights negotiated with private airlines and foreign governments which would allow bases to be reinforced promptly in any emergency.[37]

Air power from bases on land and sea was envisaged as the guarantor of U.S. security in the air-atomic age, deterring attack or, in the event of war, retaliating quickly while keeping the enemy at arm's length. Despite changes in the balance of power and the technology of war, the United States would thereby still be able "to fight our wars, if they be necessary, in someone else's territory."[38]

The underlying objective was to prevent war breaking out. Here new economic institutions were intended to play a significant part. One major change from the 1920s was the acknowledgment of federal government responsibility for foreign economic policy. This would no longer be left to private interests, particularly bankers, acting with the blessing of Washington. The monetary crisis of 1929-31 had shown the folly of that. As Henry Morgenthau, Treasury Secretary for nearly all of Roosevelt's presidency, remarked in 1946, his primary goal while in office had been to "move the financial center of the world from London and Wall Street to the United States Treasury and to create a new concept between the nations of international finance."[39]

That "new concept" testified to another fundamental change from the 1920s: the acceptance of American responsibility for the health of the world economy. Since 1942 U.S Treasury officials, led by Harry White, drafted and negotiated plans for new world financial institutions which would help reflate world trade through increased liquidity. These were approved at the Bretton Woods conference in July 1944. The International Monetary Fund in particular was to assist nations in overcoming their balance of payments problems through short-term loans, and 36 percent of the Fund's original $8.8 billion resources were provided by the United States.[40] These new financial institutions were intended as a framework for gradual reversion to multilateral trade once the immediate period of postwar reconstruction was over. In this way the U.S. government began to acknowledge its "responsibilities" in the international economy.

Industrial power and world influence had been gradually shifting toward the United States throughout the twentieth century, but I have suggested in this brief sketch that World War II saw a very rapid acceleration of the process. During the crisis years 1940-45 America developed an enhanced awareness of its global reach and a new conviction that its own self-interest required a greater managerial role in world affairs. At the same time the capacity of the federal government to harness national power and to use it internationally was greatly enlarged.

This is necessarily a very schematized interpretation intended to highlight broad changes in America's international role. It is therefore appropriate in conclusion to note briefly a few qualifications which help to blur the sharp edges of the silhouette.

The previous account may, for instance, suggest an excessively "rationalist" view of foreign policymaking—that a nation state can be conceived of as analogous to a rational human being.[41] He reacts to major crises by adapting his philosophy, reassessing his personal interests, and finding more appropriate means to achieve them. In other words, "environment" changes "intentions" and "interests" which in turn affect "institutions." Of course, that belies the reality of human as well as social life: the dynamics of change are more complex, its directions more erratic.

For example, institutions may create interests as much as the reverse. The debate about air power illustrates this. To establish themselves as a separate service the airmen exaggerated the wartime effectiveness of strategic bombing and the contribution of the atomic bomb to ending the war against Japan.[42] On a more general level, different parts of the federal government tended to stress different clusters of "national security" ideas in line with their own bureaucratic interests. The U.S. Treasury emphasized the goals and institutions of economic recovery, while the JCS focused on military measures, including a demand for universal military training. This reminds us that it may be misleading to refer to the new wartime ideas about "national security" as a unified "doctrine" or "concept."

But my outline needs to be modified in another way. We have to look forward as well as back if we wish to appreciate the true significance of World War II, for the immediate postwar period saw a reduction of U.S. power and influence reminiscent in kind, if not degree, to that after World War I. The armed forces were cut from 12.1 million to 1.6 million in two years. In the same period America's "international expenditure" (defense, foreign military aid, foreign economic aid) dropped from 88 percent of the federal budget to 51 percent and from 39 percent of GNP to 8.43 percent.[43] Domestic preoccupations were again paramount—getting the boys home, combatting inflation, coping with pent-up labor discontent—and between April 1947 and August 1948 the draft was abandoned. There was a tendency to assume that the new international institutions, such as the United Nations and the International Monetary Fund, backed by great-power cooperation, would provide the necessary framework for peace and prosperity. The

Russians were initially seen as difficult rather than dangerous, the weakness of Europe underestimated.

What really confirmed the wartime shift in America's role was the Cold War. By 1947 "one world" internationalism was discredited and the Soviet Union regarded as the new "totalitarian" threat to peace, capitalism, and democracy. This "threat" took various forms: the menace of communism in an impoverished Western Europe from 1946 to 1947; the imbalance of conventional forces in Europe in 1948; the "fall of China" and the loss of atomic monopoly in 1949; and then the outbreak of war in Korea in 1950 that, it was feared, presaged war in Europe by 1952.

The Cold War gave a focus for America's new notions of "national security"—its specific aim became the containment of Russian power and, increasingly, of international communism as a whole. In the process, the "institutions" changed: diplomacy and economic aid gave place to military power, with the development of large land forces again from 1950. The first serious efforts were also made to coordinate the nation's external policies. The year 1947 saw the creation of the Central Intelligence Agency, the National Security Council, and a "unified" Department of Defense. As in 1940-45, the dynamics of policy change were complex. Up to a point the United States was reacting to a new and unexpected situation caused by the wartime extension of Soviet influence. But that expansion was unacceptable in part because of the greatly enlarged definition of U.S. security needs. Institutional self-aggrandizement was again an element, encouraging airmen and later soldiers to exaggerate the Soviet "threat."

But what one can say in general is that cold war and world war have to be taken together in understanding the revolution in America's international role in the 1940s. In retrospect, the decade can be seen as a dual crisis, with the second phase being viewed as a possible replay of the first unless the "lessons of the part" were heeded.[44] Together they form the context for America's emergence as a superpower.

Nevertheless, our attention to World War II is surely warranted. The expansion of Russian power was a direct consequence of that conflict, and the "Soviet threat" gave a specific referent to ideas about peace and security formulated in wartime. By the end of the war the United States was undoubtedly a "superpower" on the criteria used by William Fox, who probably coined that term in 1944. For him "superpower" meant "great power plus great mobility of power."[45] By 1945 the U.S. government had harnessed national power to national ends, creating a permanent naval and air power establishment and essaying for the first time a U.S. foreign economic policy. This revolution was grounded in novel ideas about how national security was related to world peace, political stability and capitalist prosperity. The development of the U.S. Navy and the Army Air Forces, linked to a network of bases, gave the United States "great mobility of power" for influencing and responding to a greatly changed world order, in which the powers of Europe, hitherto the creators and sustainers of the modern international system, had been displaced. The remarkable economic growth of the United States may constitute much of the long-term explanation for its rise to globalism, but America's transformation from power to superpower was very much the consequence of World War II.

This account of when and how the United States became a superpower may also help us understand the problems it has faced in trying to play that role since the 1940s.

First, the international environment of the 1940s was artificial: America's dominance was extreme because so much of the developed world had been ravaged by a war from which the United States, uniquely, had prospered. Immediately after 1945 the United States produced about half the world's manufactured goods and held half the world's currency reserves. By 1970 these proportions had dropped to one-third and one-sixth, respectively.[46] In the 1940s and 1950s the United States had the industrial and financial strength to assume global obligations and to sustain the security and prosperity of friendly nations through troops, economic assistance and development aid. Commitments such as NATO, the Marshall Plan, and the Alliance for Progress all depended on America's ability to keep on exporting capital. By the 1970s, with worsening trade performance and widening budget deficits, this was no longer possible on the same scale, as the 1971 decision to end the Bretton Woods gold-dollar convertibility demonstrated. Since then, successive administrations have intermittently tried to reduce America's overseas burdens, but with limited success. In the Reagan era the situation worsened with the administration's massive budget deficits. In the mid-1980s the United States became a net debtor nation for the first time since before World War I, importing rather than exporting capital in order to cover its trade and budget deficits, a reversal of its recent role which has alarming implications for the health of the world economy.

This essay has argued that there is no *immediate* correlation between changes in a country's economic strength and shifts in its external policy; the effects of America's debtor status may take years to make themselves felt. But it is clear that the United States became a superpower at a time when every other country—even its main rival, the Soviet Union—was in a different league. This has made it harder to adapt to a world very different from that of the 1940s, entailing the reduction of burdens, the extension of

Soviet influence, and the limits of American capacity to shape the actions of its clients.

The late emergence of the United States as a superpower has also posed problems for the domestic management of external policy. Here the American experience was very different from that of much of continental Europe, where the national security state had long been in existence, since the era of "enlightened despotism" in the eighteenth century. The institutions of strong national governments—effective taxation, enlarged bureaucracies, standing armies, and the official promotion of strategic industries—were gradually created by European monarchs in the interests of defense and internal security.[47] Subsequently, most of these autocratic governments were gradually forced to concede domestic liberties to their subjects, but in many cases not until the twentieth century.

In the United States the pattern was reversed: democratization preceded statebuilding. The legacy of 1776 was a reaction against anything that purported to be a strong central government: under the constitution of 1787 the powers of the federal government were divided and balanced, the rights of the individual states safeguarded. By the 1830s local autonomy was reinforced by the prevalence of democracy for most white adult males, not just in local elections but in choosing their head of state (inconceivable in Europe). This combination of extremes—highly developed democratic politics without a concentrated governing capacity—made early America the great anomaly among western states.[48] In the era of "free security" there was no external threat to impel statebuilding in the European sense. Not until the twentieth century was a serious attempt made to create stronger institutions of national government, intermittently in the dual crises of the 1940s (world war and cold war), the era in which national security seemed seriously at issue for the first time.

Thus, unlike most of Europe, the United States was a democracy long before it became a state, let alone a superpower.[49] Yet, since the 1940s, it has been trying to exercise that superpower role through democratic and antistatist institutions. These may be suited, perhaps, to its own domestic needs as a vast, continent-size complex of interest groups, but they are at odds with the historical experiences of most other countries who have risen to the rank of great powers.

NOTES

For helpful comments on the original version of this essay, the author is grateful to Dr. J. A. Thompson (Cambridge), Professor Paul Kennedy (Yale) and to members of the conference.

1. Alexis de Tocqueville, *Democracy in America*, ed. J. P. Mayer (New York, 1969), p. 413; Michel Chevalier, "La guerre et la crise européenne" ["The War and the European Crisis"], *Revue des Deux Mondes*, 1 June 1866, pp. 784-5; Constantin Frantz, *Die Weltpolitik unter besonderer Bezugnahme auf Deutschland [World Politics with Particular Reference to Germany]* (Osnabruck, reprint ed., 1966), vol. I, p. 89; J. R. Seeley, *The Expansion of England* (London, 1884), p. 301.

2. A.J.P. Taylor, *The Struggle for Mastery in Europe, 1848-1918* (London, 1954), p. xxxi.

3. Paul M. Kennedy, "The First World War and the International Power System," *International Security* 9 (1984), 35.

4. Robert Gilpin, *War and Change in World Politics* (Cambridge, England, 1981), p. 124.

5. For example, Joseph Frankel, *International Relations in a Changing World* (Oxford, 1979), especially pp. 100-5.

6. See Kathleen Burk, *Britain, America and the Sinews of War, 1914-1918* (Boston, 1985), p. 81.

7. Woodrow Wilson to Colonel House, 21 July 1917, in Arthur S. Link, ed., *The Papers of Woodrow Wilson*, vol. 43 (Princeton, 1983), p. 238.

8. U.S. Department of Commerce, Bureau of the Census, *Historical Statistics of the United States: Colonial Times to 1970* (Washington, D.C., 1975), p. 1141.

9. Mira Wilkins, *The Maturing of Multinational Enterprise: American Business Abroad from 1914 to 1970* (Cambridge, MA, 1974), pp. 29-30.

10. Sir William Wiseman, memo for Foreign Office, May 1921, Wiseman papers 1/4/110 (Sterling Library, Yale University, New Haven, CT).

11. David S. Landes, *The Unbound Prometheus: Technological Change and Industrial Development in Western Europe from 1750 to the Present* (Cambridge, England, 1969), pp. 371-72. In recent years, however, economic historians have also employed "endogenous" explanations as well, for example, T. Balderston, "The Beginning of the Depression in Germany, 1927-30: Investment and the Capital Market," *Economic History Review* 36 (1983), pp. 395-415.

12. Charles P. Kindleberger, *The World in Depression, 1929-1939* (Berkeley, 1973), pp. 292, 303. For a recent modification of this argument see David A. Lake, "International Economic Structures and American Foreign Economic Policy, 1887-1934," *World Politics* 35 (1983), pp. 517-43.

13. David M. Kennedy, *Over Here: The First World War and American Society* (New York, 1980), p. 345, quoting C. H. Crennan.
14. John Braeman, "The New Left and American Foreign Policy during the Age of Normalcy: A Re-examination," *Business History Review* 57 (1983), pp. 82-86; cf. L. J. Williams, *Britain and the World Economy, 1919-1970* (London, 1971), p. 67.
15. James MacGregor Burns, *Roosevelt: The Lion and the Fox, 1882-1940* (New York, 1956), p. 385.
16. Quoted in Gloria J. Barron, *Leadership in Crisis: FDR and the Path to Intervention* (Port Washington, NY, 1973), p. 22.
17. J. Pierrepont Moffat to Norman Davis, 7 October 1936, Davis papers, box 41 (Library of Congress, Washington, D.C.).
18. Franklin D. Roosevelt to Roger Merriman, 15 February 1939, quoted in David Reynolds, *The Creation of the Anglo-American Alliance, 1937-41: A Study in Competitive Co-operation* (London, 1981), pp. 43-44.
19. C. Vann Woodward, "The Age of Reinterpretation," *American Historical Review* 66 (1960), p. 3.
20. Quincy Wright, *A Study of War* (2 vols., Chicago, 1942), I, pp. 666-72, Appendix XXII, especially tables 58-59.
21. Alan S. Milward, *War, Economy and Society, 1939-1945* (Berkeley, 1977), pp. 67, 70.
22. *Historical Statistics*, p. 1141. Total U.S. population in 1918 was about 105 million, in 1945 about 140 million. (Ibid., p. 8.)
23. Figures from Milward, *War, Economy and Society*, p. 211.
24. Justus D. Doenecke, *Not to the Swift: The Old Isolationists in the Cold War Era* (London, 1979), p. 21.
25. Arthur H. Vandenberg, Jr., and Joe A. Morris, eds., *The Private Papers of Senator Vandenberg* (Boston, 1952), p. 1.
26. Rex Stout, ed., *The Illustrious Dunderheads* (New York, 1942).
27. Wendell Willkie, *One World* (New York, 1943); Ellsworth Barnard, *Wendell Willkie: Fighter for Freedom* (Marquette, MI, 1966), p. 412.
28. Walter Lippmann, *U.S. Foreign Policy: Shield of the Republic* (Boston, 1943); Ronald Steel, *Walter Lippmann and the American Century* (New York, 1980), p. 406.
29. Alan K. Henrikson, "America's Changing place in the World: From 'Periphery' to 'Centre'?" in Jean Gottmann, ed., *Centre and Periphery: Spatial Variations in Politics* (London, 1980), p. 83.
30. Alan K. Henrikson, "The Map as an 'Idea': The Role of Cartographic Imagery during the Second World War," *The American Cartographers* (1975), p. 24.
31. *The Public Papers and Addresses of Franklin D.Roosevelt*, comp. Samuel I. Rosenman, vol. 11, 1942 (New York, 1950), pp. 105-17, especially 107-8. Alerted by the White House, many U.S. newspapers had printed large maps to help radio listeners follow the President's talk.
32. Thomas G. Paterson, *On Every Front: The Making of the Cold War* (New York, 1979), p. 78.

33. Alfred E. Eckes, Jr., *The United States and the Global Struggle for Minerals* (Austin, TX, 1979), pp. 122, 147.

34. Paterson, *On Every Front*, p. 71.

35. The phrase coined by Charles S. Maier in "The Politics of Productivity: Foundations of American International Economic Policy after World War II," *International Organization* 31 (1977), pp. 607-33.

36. See Daniel Yergin, *Shattered Peace; The Origins of the Cold War and the National Security State* (London, 1977), pp. 194-95.

37. Melvyn P. Leffler, "The American Conception of National Security and the Beginnings of the Cold War, 1945-48," *American Historical Review* 89 (1984), pp. 349-56.

38. Gen. Charles H. Bonesteel, 28 August 1945, quoted in Michael S. Sherry, *Preparing for the Next War: America's Plans for Postwar Defense, 1941-45* (New Haven, 1977), p. 205.

39. Letter to President Truman, March 1946, quoted in David Rees, *Harry Dexter White: A Study in Paradox* (London, 1973), p. 138.

40. Richard N. Gardner, *Sterling-Dollar Diplomacy in Current Perspective: The Origins and Prospects of Our International Economic Order* (New York, 1980), pp. 112-3.

41. Ernest May has suggested "proclivities" as a more appropriate word than "intentions." See Ernest R. May, ed., *Knowing One's Enemies: Intelligence Assessment before the Two World Wars* (Princeton, 1986), p. 503.

42. Gregg Herken, *The Winning Weapon: The Atomic Bomb in the Cold War, 1945-1950* (New York, 1981), pp. 209-10.

43. Robert A. Pollard, *Economic Security and the Origins of the Cold War, 1945-50* (New York, 1985), pp. 256, 258.

44. Ernest R. May, *"Lessons" of the Past: The Use and Misuse of History in American Foreign Policy* (New York, 1973), pp. 49-51. For the elision of World War II in recent historiography about domestic change in twentieth century America, see Gerald D. Nash, *The Great Depression and World War II: Organizing America, 1933-45* (New York, 1979).

45. William T. R. Fox, *The Superpowers* (New York, 1944), p. 21. It is worth noting that Fox included Britain with the United States and Russia among the "superpowers" in this work. For Fox's claim to have invented the term see his article "The Super-powers Then and Now," *International Journal* 35 (1980), 417-36.

46. See Paul Bairoch, "International Industrialization Levels from 1750 to 1980," *Journal of European Economic History* 11 (1982), 301-2; Benjamin J. Cohen, "The Revolution in Atlantic Economic Relations: A Bargain Comes Unstuck," in Wolfram F. Hanrieder, ed., *The United States and Western Europe: Political, Economic and Strategic Perspectives* (Cambridge, MA, 1974), p. 127.

47. See E. N. Williams, *The Ancient Regime in Europe: Government and Society in the Major States, 1648-1789* (Harmondsworth, England, 1972), pp. 32-4.

48. Stephen Skowronek, *Building a New American State: The Expansion of National Administrative Capacities, 1877-1920* (New York, 1982), p. 8. A fascinating study. Elsewhere I have noted the parallels in this respect between America and Britain, both essentially "liberal" polities. See David Dimbleby and David Reynolds, *An Ocean Apart: The Relationship Between Britain and America in the Twentieth Century* (New York, 1988), especially, ch. 2 and conclusion.
49. See Zara Steiner, "Decision-making in American and British Foreign Policy: An Open and Shut Case," *Review of International Studies* 13 (1987), p. 16.

3

U.S. Globalism:
The End of the Concert of Europe

Donald Cameron Watt

In the process of calling public attention to the patterns they perceive in the past, historians have to invent labels for them, labels that will strike the attention of their audience and hold that attention. The labels that the events of the past bear will recall, to those who see them, the previous occasions on which historians have used similar labels. This practice of inventing labels is obviously useful, but it carries with it three great dangers. The first is that it is only too easy to mistake labeling something for understanding it; the second, which follows, is that the label becomes the thing itself, and the reality is lost; the third, perhaps the most dangerous, is that since history is concerned with the one-way passage of time, and we notice time mainly by the changes and the rates of change coming with that passage, the labels will remain unchanged and we shall miss the changes for focusing on the labels.

The concept of U.S. globalism is just such a label and carries with it just such dangers. Was the United States really a global power in 1945? If so, then how did Americans and American policymakers perceive the globe? They were profoundly uninterested in Africa and remained so, with the exception of the Congo, until the 1970s. Southeast Asia, excepting Indonesia, was a British concern. The American Joint Chiefs of Staff were concerned that Britain should remain the leading power in the Middle East and the Indian Ocean. Some oilmen might disagree, but they were still only of limited influence. The rise of Israel was to make the fate of one part of the Middle East a perennial American election issue. But America was to refuse to join the 1954 Central Treaty Organization which made Britain, Turkey, Iraq, Iran, and Pakistan allies. Apart from the brief episode of the Eisenhower Doctrine and the 1958 intervention in the Lebanon, the United States only began to play the major role in the area in the 1970s.

Nor was the United States inclined toward global involvement in Europe at the end of World War II. President Franklin D. Roosevelt did not want the supply lines to the American zone of occupation in Germany to run through France, which he believed would be in a state of civil war after the war. France, he said, was a British responsibility. The United States refused to get involved in the fate of southeast Europe before 1947, for fear of being dragged into the Anglo-Soviet clash in that area that the Joint Chiefs of Staff and the State Department anticipated. If one is to talk of the United States as a global power, one must qualify the term global, begin earlier, and end later than the years of World War II.[1]

The United States first became conscious of its position in the world in the 1880s and 1890s. To some, particularly the farmers of the Midwest and the South, selling their corn and meat in a world market on money borrowed on a world market was a highly unwelcome experience. The great Populist campaign of 1892-1900 for bimetallism was essentially one designed to isolate the U.S. economy from that of the world and the tyranny of the gold standards. The two demons in Populist rhetoric were the Jews and the British. To them were added all the new East European migrants who flooded into the cities and provided the city machines with the voting fodder they needed: the Bohunks, Polacks, Litvaks, Yids, Wops and other assorted pejoratively named substitutes for the Irish, English, German, and Scandinavians of the earlier period of immigration.

To others, those years brought both ambition and anxiety. The extraordinary rate of industrial development in the United States and the massive growth in the iron and steel production figures inspired in them a consciousness of America's emergence as a possible world power. But a world power needed trade and markets which the European colonial powers and czarist Russia seemed determined to gain control of for themselves. Worried by the competitive doctrines of Social Darwinism and warned or encouraged by the writings of Admiral A. T. Mahan, America's rulers, cheered on by a vociferous section of the American press and public, declared an Open Door policy, expelled Spain from the Caribbean and the Philippines, hijacked the route for a Panama Canal, intervened with strength and moderation to bring an end to the first Moroccan crisis and the Russo-Japanese War, and embarked on the construction of a world navy. The European powers were rudely enlightened as to the presence of a new active power whose wealthy citizens sent their sons to Oxford, Heidelberg, and the Sorbonne and their daughters to marry into European nobility. European ambassadors clustered around Theodore Roosevelt during his presidency as around the Court of St. James's or the Hofburg in Vienna. America was, before 1914, one whose friendship was sought and whose resources were investigated.

America, however, was not a member of the Concert of Europe, that organization whose demise, properly speaking, occurred irremediably in July 1914 with the outbreak of World War I. At its best it was an association of the most powerful states of Europe that over the last four decades before 1914 had come to accept a series of ground rules governing their conduct toward one another and toward those parts of the world that did not belong to the Concert. They did not always observe those rules, but when they did not, everyone, themselves included, recognized that the rules had been broken. These rules taken together composed the basis for a kind of informal consensus politics, by which the expansion of European power—at the expense of the two disintegrating empires of Ottoman Turkey and Manchu China—and the partition of Africa were regulated without war. There were signs in the tentative Anglo-German agreements reached in the last years before the war that the division of the declining empires of Spain, Belgium, and Portugal might have suffered the same fate. But like the Anglo-French-Italian agreement of 1906 on the partition of Ethiopia, these agreements were not, in fact, implemented. The internationalist element developed with the extension of French control in Morocco by international agreement and the internationalization of the Macedonian question in 1902.

This system broke down irretrievably in 1914. Up to a point, Theodore Roosevelt had accepted it. Woodrow Wilson, it is clear, did not. International law he understood, as his constant emission of notes of protest in the period of American neutrality from 1914 to 1917 shows. But he neither understood nor accepted the notion of normal rules and conventions of international "customary law," as it is now called. As the conservative he in so many respects was, he believed in the regulation of behavior by law, including the behavior of special interests and powers, in the interests of the general mass of the people whom he claimed to represent. But in spirit and in beliefs he was a radical reformer. His aim, even during the period of American neutrality, was to change the international system so as to limit the use of power in ways he regarded as illegitimate. To show he refused to share the British and French belief that they were defending the prewar system against German violation of it, he proposed to use the power war gave him as much to reform and limit British and French behavior as that of Germany. He was, unfortunately, ill equipped both intellectually and experientially to exercise that power. He was alien to the true legal conservatism of his Republican critics, Henry Cabot Lodge, Charles Evans Hughes, and the reservationist wing of the Senate. His ideas were largely based on those of British radical critics of the prewar system as communicated to him via Colonel House's contacts in the U.S. Embassy in London. And when he set sail for Paris, with a Republican Congress successful in the 1918 midterm elections, he was completely unprepared for conference diplomacy between equals. The draft treaty, and the covenant of the proposed League of Nations were British drafts. The conference secretariat was organized by the secretary to the British cabinet. Wilson found himself faced with his equals in political standing and his superiors both in their command of the skills of conference diplomacy and negotiation and in the support they enjoyed from their own electorates. The one attempt he made to appeal to the people of Europe over the heads of their elected representatives, in the case of Italian claims on Fiume, was a miserable failure. American power was unquestioned, but the German appeal for an armistice in November 1918 had made it unusable. He returned to America with a treaty and a covenant that he could not carry through Congress, having broken with Colonel House, the only negotiator of any real talent on his staff.

The covenant as written continued the nineteenth-century European Concert's distinction between states with full rights and those regarded as unqualified, although being couched in Wilsonian terms it talked of "peoples" rather than states. These distinctions were enshrined in the mandates system, which, borrowing from the more enlightened theories of colonial development as preached by Britain, France, and the Netherlands, divided colonial territories into A, B, and C class mandates according to the degree of approach to self-governing, "civilized," status the individual territories were judged to have attained. To that extent the basic divisions drawn by the concert system between "civilized" and other states were universalized, though the only beneficiaries were the former subject peoples of the German colonial and the Ottoman empires. The United States, however, was not interested. America temporarily turned away from Europe, its expansionist energies funneled briefly into conflict with Britain in Latin America and the Middle East and with Japan in the Pacific.

The 1920 election brought into power Charles Evans Hughes, a Republican secretary of state of profoundly conservative internationalist views. The Washington treaties of 1922 demonstrated Hughes's skill and fairness in the settlement they brought to the Pacific, the Far East, and to Anglo-American competition at sea. His shocked condemnation of the Geneva protocol of 1924 as one that, if realized, would force the United States to treat the League of Nations as a hostile coalition demonstrates his profound hostility toward the supranational. But under his guidance and that of his successors, especially Henry Stimson, America reentered the international system, took an active part in the World Disarmament Conference, underwrote much of the Franco-German settlement on reparations, and edged toward accommodating the American position to the peace-keeping clauses of the League covenant and toward acceding to the World Court. Public opinion, both in the country and in Congress, was a long way behind them but following steadily under the pressure of the American peace and disarmament lobbies. It was the collapse of the American economy in the last years of Hoover's presidency and the outbreak of conflict in Manchuria and Shanghai that defeated this movement and took America away from involvement in the external world.

The years from 1933 to 1938 found America's economy stagnated, and the country's woes preoccupied its politicians. By the devaluation of the dollar and the destruction of all attempts made to stabilize world raw material prices in the summer of 1933, Franklin Roosevelt made good the promise made in his inaugural speech that he would attempt to lift America's economy without waiting for the revival of the world economy. Since his method was to close down those parts of the American economic system that depended on world markets by paying farmers to plough in their surplus wheat, cotton, and tobacco acreage, it is hardly surprising that he failed. The level of American economic activity in 1939 was much the same as that of 1933. But the effect of Roosevelt's action and that of Congress in passing high tariffs was to fragment the rest of the world's trading and financial systems. Britain, trading widely in sterling, managing the pound, and encouraging the market toward Commonwealth-produced raw materials by what was by American standards a remarkably moderate level of protectionism, fared remarkably well. France went from crisis to crisis. Germany took refuge behind a totally managed economy and a spreading system of barter agreements almost on Soviet lines. Japan was driven to contemplate expanding its markets by force and Japanese heavy industry became a client of the Army and Navy. Most of the world's gold supply lay sterilized in Fort Knox. There was very little that was global about Roosevelt's first term or the first two years of his second.

American opinion was remarkably well informed about the events which were to drag Europe and the Far East into World War II. A generation of foreign correspondents who had cut their teeth in France in 1917-18 and learned their craft during the allegedly isolationist twenties saw to that—aided by the new media of radio and newsreel. But for American opinion, international politics was a spectator sport. Those who had led the internationalist pressure groups of the 1920s were now prominent in isolationist groups intent on rewriting America's neutrality laws. In 1938 they failed by one vote to pass an amendment through the lower house of Congress which would have taken from Congress even the right to declare war.

How then to explain the extraordinary expansion of American power and American vision between 1938, the year of the Ludlow amendment, and 1948, the year in which Congress confirmed the European Recovery Program and entered into the conversations which were to lead, the following year, to the signature of that permanent, "entangling alliance," the North Atlantic Treaty?

There is one very popular school of history writing which would find this question simply absurd. Believing history, a matter of great, long rolling impersonal waves and trends that move inevitably from one century to another, they would argue that the developments of these ten years were inevitable, the product of America's wealth of resources and population and relative invulnerability to war in Europe, and even that America's "rise to globalism," as one American historian has called it, was predestined.[2] But this kind of history is born of the paradox that once events have happened, their causes can be recognized and their occurrence seems inevitable, while up to the moment of their occurrence, it seemed that those who took part in them had a free choice and that only in very general terms was their outcome predictable. Few people live their lives nowadays on the basis that the future is predictable, and those that do usually end up on Skid Row, irretrievably in debt to the bookies. It is only on the very broad basis of statistical analysis used by actuaries in insurance companies—and bookmakers and casino owners—that human behavior is predictable.

No one in 1938 could have predicted the events of 1948; many were unable or unwilling even to predict the events of 1939, a mere year ahead. There was a strong current of thought, nowhere clearer than in Nazi Germany and the Soviet Union, that said that the democracies of western Europe, having won themselves freedom from war by sacrificing Czechoslovakia in September 1938, would yield again when Nazi Germany picked a quarrel with its next victim, Poland, Romania, or wherever. Cordell Hull was of this opinion until 3 September 1939, the day Britain and France declared war on Germany.

Yet the change already had begun, even before the year 1938 had ended. The British government and people, having survived the year without a war and seeing no end to Hitler's ambitions and demands, were pressing forward their rearmament program. Hitherto, the preservation of British financial strength, and the overseas trade drive on which this rested, had priority over the cost of rearmament. From the opening of 1939 those restrictions were removed. To the increasing alarm of the guarantors of Britain's finances, priority was given to rearmament against Hitler. The rate of British aircraft production was rapidly overtaking that of Nazi Germany. From April 1939 onward the British public was resigned to war. The volunteer Territorial Army was doubled in size in April. In May full-scale conscription was introduced. On 3 September, after Hitler had signed a pact with Stalin and attacked Poland, Britain formally declared war on Germany. World War II, at least as Europeans reckon, had begun.

It was to be another two years and three months before the Japanese attack on Pearl Harbor brought America into the war. It is worth while to reflect for a moment on this difference. The British people went to war mainly for reasons connected with the underlying concepts of the former Concert of Europe. They declared war against Hitlerian Germany because in their view there could be no peace in Europe unless there was some consensus as to what constituted "civilized behavior" between states. They went to war in defense of a system of international relations based on the concepts embodied in the covenant of the League of Nations, one of which was that the defense of international order is the business of all the members of that order. Their inactivity in the Manchurian issue and their failure to push economic sanctions against Italy during Mussolini's attack on Ethiopia showed that that concept of order was essentially limited both by realism as to where and how force could be exerted and by the old nineteenth-century distinction between international politics within Europe and international politics elsewhere. Thus, although by 1939 the League of Nations was a virtual fiction, and most of the smaller nations of western Europe had retired into the premature neutralism of the Declaration of Copenhagen, the reasoning that led Britain into war in 1939 was still centered on Europe and on Europe as the center of the international order.

It is vitally important for the understanding of the process that led up to the Japanese attack on Hawaii in December 1941 to realize that Franklin Roosevelt and much of his administration shared this Eurocentric approach. In the months after Munich, Roosevelt had come to see Nazi Germany as the main threat to the security of democratic America, and Britain and France as the shields against German expansion. By the end of October 1938 he was conveying clandestine assurances to Britain's prime minister Neville Chamberlain that no matter what America's new neutrality legislation might say, Britain could count on access to American heavy industry in the event of war. America's frontier was on the Rhine. In 1939 Roosevelt was lured into attempting to persuade Congress to repeal the neutrality legislation, an appeal that, given the entrenched strength of the isolationists, was bound to fail. But he pressed ahead with other contacts, negotiating for U.S. bases in the British West Indies and acting in July 1939 to take over from Britain the main weight of containing Japan in the Pacific. The collapse of France in June 1940 gave him some months of desperation, made stronger by the need to run again for election by a divided and uncertain American electorate. But as British resistance to German air power and the first British (and Greek) defeats of Italy restored his optimism, he resumed the same policy. "Destroyers for Bases" and, finally, Lend-Lease answered Churchill's plea to "give us the tools and we will finish the job." At the same time, his neutralization of the western half of the Atlantic curtailed and limited the effectiveness of German U-boat warfare against Britain's vital supply lines.

It was part of his vision of British strength that he was convinced that a Japanese blow at the source of much of Britain's remaining wealth, the tin and rubber of Malaysia, would constitute a desperate threat to Britain's ability to restrain Hitler in Europe. His Pacific policy was therefore based on the need to restrain Japan by economic pressure. It was a doctrine he had first mooted in his much misunderstood "quarantine speech" of October 1937. He discussed it with the British ambassador in December of that year at the time of the Japanese attack on the USS *Panay*. He had referred to it in his address to Congress in January 1939. The British had always expressed anxiety that faced with economic strangulation, Japan might choose to escalate the conflict. By January 1941, however, the British government no longer cared. Warnings such as that given by the British ambassador to Japan were ignored. Whether Churchill hoped that a Japanese attack would bring the United States into the war, we may never know. We do know that he suppressed with contumacy the ambassador's final report, which argued that a different diplomatic approach could have avoided Japan's decision for war in November 1941.[3] America's entry into the war only confirmed, however, the Eurocentric approach of Roosevelt and his closest advisers. Plan "Dog," adopted in the winter of 1940, put Europe and the defeat of Hitler first. To that view, despite all the stresses and strains that followed, the Roosevelt administration remained true to the day of his death. It was followed within the month by Hitler's suicide and the meeting of Soviet and American troops in the middle of Germany—a meeting point from which it took the superpowers forty-five years to withdraw.

If President Roosevelt's globe had been centered, like Mercator's projection, on the Greenwich meridian and Europe when war began, it had changed very much by the time of his death. Roosevelt had already put his signature to the vague echoes of Wilsonian globalism in the Atlantic Charter, a document that, it is often forgotten, was mainly of British rather than American drafting. Like Wilson before him he approached the question of the postwar order with as much determination to reform his allies as he did to remodel his enemies. Like Wilson he hid this determination to use American strength behind a cloud of "universaholic" rhetoric. But the secret plans which he put to his Project M team for large-scale movements of population and for the wholesale remodeling of agriculture in Southeast Asia show a tougher and more imperialist approach than Wilson ever envisaged. And his scheme for the Four Policemen, which would make Britain, the Soviet Union, and China the enforcers of peace in the four corners of the world, was entirely un-Wilsonian. Roosevelt shared Wilson's belief that large parts of the global population were too immature to be able to sustain self-government. The substitution of trusteeship for the Mandate system was little more than a terminological adjustment designed to make it easier to talk Congress into accepting important areas in the Pacific and the Caribbean. And before his death he had so weakened in his opposition to French colonialism as to accept their ultimate return to Indochina. Elsewhere he sought to raise India to statehood and China to equal status with the Big Three. As for Europe, that was Britain's problem, especially France and southeast Europe. Poland only worried him during the 1944 elections, Yugoslavia hardly at all. He shared Britain's determination to keep the Soviet Union out of the Italian peace settlement and the Mediterranean. Where the Middle East was concerned he was tempted by the oil of Saudi Arabia at a time when his secretary of the interior feared American oil was being exhausted. But otherwise he left it to Britain.

Which brings us to consider the long term effects of the experience of World War II on the United States. The first and most important effect was that the end of the war in 1945 left the United States by far the richest, wealthiest, and most powerful nation-state in the world. In the four years from December 1941 to September 1945 it had been able to fight a two-ocean war as well as to finance a substantial part of the war effort of its two main allies, Britain and the Soviet Union. The effort had not left the United States bankrupt or destroyed its economy as it had those of its two main allies. It had needed little or no rationing or restriction of domestic consumption. In the four years of war the United States sustained a consumer goods boom on an unprecedented scale. It was this consciousness of wealth and of upward social mobility among the previously relatively depressed minorities with which Americans finished the war. Nothing seemed beyond American strength, financial power, organization, or engineering genius.

Seen from the vantage point of the last decade of the twentieth century, what is most striking is the extraordinary lapse of memory that the five years of economic growth from 1941 brought with them. America seemed totally to have forgotten the ten years of industrial and agricultural depression and stagnation to which the U.S. economy had plunged between 1929 and 1939: the dole queues, the apple sellers, the dust bowls, and the bitter industrial warfare of the mid 1930s. Rather, more deliberate action hid from them the role British capital and British war purchases had played in priming the pump in the years 1939-40, years in which two-thirds of Britain's capital investments in America had been sold at giveaway prices to the benefit of America's heavy industries and American agriculture. Equally hidden was the role European refugees and British scientists had played in the development of the bombs which had brought the war in the Pacific to an end. In American eyes the wealth, the power, and the scientific achievement were the evidence, if not the explanation for and justification, of victory. To a large extent they were, but by no means entirely.

The period of experience which left the deepest imprint on American consciousness was the years of victory, 1944 and 1945, a period of overwhelming and ubiquitous American military strength. The war in the Pacific was fought by the U.S. Navy and Marine Corps, with some help from the U.S. Army Air Force. The efforts of the British and Indian armies in Burma were constantly denigrated for reasons of anticolonialism or pro-Chinese philosophy. The Indian army was dismissed as mercenaries. Forgotten was the record of the U.S. Army in the Philippines in 1942 against the flower of the Japanese army. Forgotten too were the experiences of jungle warfare against the Japanese in Guadalcanal and in New Guinea where much of the fighting on the ground was carried out by the Australians. The U.S. Army seemed determined to forget, and its failure to develop any doctrine of jungle warfare was to become painfully and disastrously obvious in Vietnam twenty years later. The contrast with British application in Malaya in the 1950s against communist guerrillas and in the 1960s against the Indonesians, of the lessons learned so painfully in Malaya and Burma from 1942 to 1945, is very striking. The U.S. Army remembered only the war in Europe.

To discuss fully the impact of the experience of war on the whole range of U.S. society would require a decade of single-minded research by an army of historians. But there is a need to discuss the impact of the war on three generational groups of America's elites, those who already exercised power in 1944, those for whom the years 1944-45 were crucial, and those leaders of the 1960s and after who had been young officers between 1943 and 1945. Each experienced the global nature of American power, but for each the globe had a very different shape and their visions of it were formed by a very different experience.

The first group, from the president downward, already enjoyed authority when America entered the war. What they now found was that their authority suddenly seemed extended, even to the point of being limitless. The experience, however, was one that they found unnerving, for it seemed to repeat closely what they had experienced either vicariously or directly at the end of World War I. They had been there before, so they believed. And, in common idiom, they had "blown it." Faced with the responsibilities of world leadership America had stammered gracelessly and withdrawn. This phraseology, from Samuel Adams's best-selling *Epic of America* (1940), summarized the anxieties and the guilt of the generation that had fought in 1918 on the battlefields or in 1919-20 on the electoral hustings. A retrospective obsession with the so-called lessons of the past, especially from 1918 to 1920, appears to have dominated much of their thinking from Roosevelt downward. It dictated the doctrine of unconditional surrender, the product of a State Department group lead by Norman Davis, a veteran of the U.S. delegation to the Paris Peace Conference. It gave the Allies Lend-Lease instead of war debts. It determined them on the establishment of a new substitute for the League of Nations, of which both the United States and the Soviet Union would be members. It provided their thinking on Germany's future with its nightmares of a new revanchist Germany, fueled by a new nationalism and faced by a new return to isolationism of the 1920 kind, or rather what it believed to be the pattern of 1919-20. Like so much of what passes for the lessons of history in the United States, the history, lacking any guidance from professional historians, was oversimplified and misunderstood by the politicians who appealed to its lessons. It was noticeable that whereas Britain drafted its most senior historians into the Foreign Office's political intelligence section, which represented a direct succession to the Political Intelligence Department of World War I and indeed included some of the same men who had served in that earlier organization, American historians seemed to have served exclusively in the Office of Strategic Services, where most of their reports and analysis seem to have gone largely unread by the policymakers. Thus, Sir Charles Webster, whose analysis of the Congress of Vienna inspired the British management scheme for the Paris Peace Conference, introduced essential modifications to the early British approach to the problems of a successor to the League of Nations, modifications which represented a decisive departure from Roosevelt's conception of a world dominated by the four superpowers: America, Britain, China, and the Soviet

Union. No American historian came within miles of such influence on the State Department, let alone on the president.[4]

The other major influence on American planning for postwar security also harked back to the alleged lessons of the past. This was the determination to dismantle what remained of European and British economic and financial dominance outside Europe. The particular targets were the sterling area and the Ottawa system of imperial tariff preference; minor, but none the less important, areas of attack were the remaining positions of British strength in Latin America, especially in Brazil, Chile, Venezuela, and the Argentine, the British system of Imperial air communications, and the British investment dominance in Australia. Access to Middle Eastern oil and the repeal of the 1928 Red Line agreement were also at issue. These were all issues which had bedeviled Anglo-American relations between 1918 and 1920, with the exception of the question of international civil air routes. In the Treasury and State departments, especially in the area desks responsible for U.S. relations with Latin America and the Middle and Far East, and in the views of Cordell Hull and Sumner Welles, Britain's system of economic and financial empire represented the same major threat to peace as Charles Sumner, J. L. Hobson, and the anti-imperialist writers of the 1890s and 1900s had agreed it to be. In their thought the Concert of Europe, with its secret diplomacy, its rules and conventions governing relations between states and powers, was inextricably intermingled with the whole concentration of events which had led to the outbreak of two Anglo-German wars in thirty years; in the first of these American money and American lives had been spent and spilt in the service of British imperial interests. They were determined that this should not happen again. If the laying of the ghost of German revanchism was a major priority with them, so was the ending of that British Empire-envy of which and competition with which had fueled German nationalism and revanchism alike. It was not for democracy that the world had to be made safe so much as for the American version of democracy. It used to be said that in Washington war was being waged with five enemies in descending order of priority: with the army or navy, with the Republican party, with the British, and thereafter with the Germans and the Japanese. For many of Roosevelt's political appointments, for many of the career officers in the State Department, the armed forces, the Treasury, the Departments of Commerce and of the Interior, and for Office of Strategic Services country teams, it was the third of these which occupied most of their time and thoughts in the interests of the United States, in the interests of American democracy, and in the interests of peace as they conceived them. They were however not the only, not even the most powerful of the factions—they were by no means a united faction anyway—concerned with the formulation of American policy. But they were the most persistent, and in their identification of American nationalist perceptions with the ideological element on the Allied side of the anti-Nazi coalition they resonated with the instincts of the American people as expressed in Congress, in the American press, and in the media, including Hollywood.

In this they did not differ from the second group, those who came to command in 1943-45, who were to provide much of the political leadership of the United States in the 1950s. For purposes of shorthand, of labeling, one may describe this as the Eisenhower generation. These men came to their own in coalition warfare, in a coalition dominated by the power and wealth of the United States. In December 1944, for example, Eisenhower commanded eight armies in battle on the western front: five American, one British, one Canadian, and one French. His command structure was integrated and, with the exception of the commanders and staffs of the individual armies, he had ruthlessly eliminated those who let nationalist hostility to their allies affect the efficient operation of his command. Those who worked in this structures (and in similar combined structure under General Marshall and the Combined Chiefs of Staff in Washington, in the Shipping Control boards, controlling the Atlantic convoy systems, in the raw material control boards, in the purchase of war materials in the United States) established networks of personal trust and confidence that not only made a reality of the coalitionist rhetoric of the various heads of government of the victorious coalition, but continued the concepts of alliance and cooperation into the 1950s. This was the generation that built the European Recovery Programs, that established and reformed the North Atlantic Alliance system, that rallied to the support of the American forces under the flag of the United Nations in Korea, and that laboriously rebuilt the structure of the western alliance after the shock of Suez in 1956. They are as significant on the American side of the Alliance as on the European.

The important element in the analysis of this group's attitudes and policies in the 1950s is that the experience of 1943-45 with its rapid and overwhelming growth in American strength was the first major element in their practical political experience. Seen from the standpoint of London, Paris, Brussels, or Oslo, they are no less nationalist than their predecessors. Much of their behavior toward British, French, and European interests in the 1950s can hardly be regarded as amicable. But the antagonisms and the antipathies took place within a family relationship. The comparative ease with which the Anglo-American relationship survived the brief interposition of American forces between the Anglo-French maritime expedition approaching Suez in

1956 and their objectives, and the way in which the United States had taken the podium at Lake Success to harry and humiliate the British prime minister and foreign secretary is an extraordinary witness to the strength of the coalition syndrome among the governing elites on both sides of the Atlantic.

As historical work on the 1950s proceeds, with the steady opening of the European and American archives to research, one is struck by the degree to which the relative strengths of the European and American sides of the coalition differ from the subjective images of that relationship entertained by the leaders and publics of the coalition nations. To give only one example: Both in his brief career as Supreme Allied Commander of the NATO forces and in his career as president, Eisenhower's attitude toward his European allies was governed by an assumption of American dominance that is quite out of kilter with reality save in two areas, that of American naval dominance of the Atlantic and Pacific oceans and that of the American lead in the developing technology of nuclear warfare. The American contribution to the defense of the European front against a possible Soviet land invasion was on much the same scale as that of the Netherlands and considerably less than the ground forces of Britain, France, and the remilitarized and Europeanized army of the Federal German Republic. Indeed, that limited military commitment allowed President Lyndon Johnson to become involved in Vietnam in the 1960s at a level which would have been quite impossible without a political withdrawal from Europe. Indeed, until the Korean War had broken out there had been no intention of committing American ground forces to the defense of Europe at all, and the commitment made immediately thereafter was intended to be merely a temporary bridging commitment to persuade Germany's former victims to accept Germany as a major military member of the coalition.

This being said, it is extraordinary to find in the American records covering the formation of the Brussels Treaty Organization and the North Atlantic Alliance and thereafter a continuous carping denigration of the degree of European commitment and achievement and a continuous insistence on a degree of European integration across national boundaries that went far beyond anything that the American member of the alliance envisaged or, had it been envisaged, would have had the remotest chance of carrying through Congress. It is my contention that this psychological subjective disparity, this curious double standard which American records and much of the American historical studies so far written on the basis of these records display, represents a perpetuation of the assumption of supremacy which was entirely justifiable in terms of the experiences of 1944-45.

This factor can perhaps be overestimated. Much of current American attitude to the alliance arises from the deliberate decision taken in 1947-49 to justify the American commitment, first to the economic and then to the military defense of Europe in terms of an expiation for the sins of 1918, as an act of American grace rather than a definite continuation of Roosevelt's view that the major threat to American security came from central and eastern Europe and that the main line of defense to this lay in maintaining and defending the independence of the coastal nations of the eastern Atlantic. If the American commitment to Europe was an act of grace then it could have been withdrawn if the European nations did not behave in ways that could be perceived as acknowledging that act. This line of thinking, which at one time used to be associated with the annual congressional resolutions on the withdrawal of U.S. troops from Europe submitted by then Senator Mike Mansfield, is still very firmly embedded in American political mythology. Its origins lie not with the generation whose conviction of American strength (the illusion of omnipotence as that most acute of British writers on America, the late Dennis Brogan called it) was based on the experience of 1944-45. They lie with their predecessors whose obsession with the legend of American isolationism in the 1930s led them to feel that congressional isolationism could only be overcome by an appeal to American guilt feelings.

The last elite is the generation that came into power in the 1960s and 1970s, that generation which experienced World War II as young officers and other ranks. Two presidents, John F. Kennedy and Richard Nixon, the one Bostonian Irish, the other small-town Californian, can be used to exemplify their generational group. Both served in the Pacific, both found themselves heavily engaged in Southeast Asia, and both found themselves in direct confrontation with the Soviet Union, yet each was to show an undue, unexpected concern for the health and continuance of the European-Atlantic alliance. The impact of the wartime experience is much clearer in the case of the Kennedy administration, with its evocation of World War II rhetoric and idealism, with its obsession with the military vocabulary of World War II (advisory groups becoming "task forces" and so on), and with the assurance of the young battlefield platoon or company commanders, suddenly free of the unrealistic and outdated concepts of their army or fleet commanders intent on winning the last war but tied by the drill book and approved military regulations. Consider for a moment the style of the Kennedy administration with its continuous improvisation, its disrespect for the staff structures of the Eisenhower presidency, its restless and relentless reshuffling of personnel, its evaluation of its own appointees entirely in terms of their ability to improvise under stress, to come up with new ideas, to play the game two moves ahead of their opponents, and yet their own limiting and inhibiting conservatism to the ideas of their own peer group. Kennedy's much advertised disappointment with Secretary of State Dean Rusk and Dean Acheson, his too ready acceptance of the CIA at its own evaluation, the restless interventionism displayed everywhere from Laos to West Irian, from the Bay of Pigs to the Congo, from the Yemen to Algeria, the belief in instant social engineering, the conviction that the leaders of the new emergent Group of 77 would share his own evaluation of the United States as a revolutionary force, and his total failure with the older generation of European leaders—President de Gaulle, Konrad Adenauer, even with men such as Paul Henri Spaak who shared much of his ability to use and to be aroused by Wilsonian rhetoric—all mark him and his generation as the product in youth of those extraordinary eighteen months when American money, industrial productivity, and armed force dominated and supported the victorious coalition against Hitler and ended the war against Japan by the invocation of a scientific revolution in the technology of total war. They shared too the assurance that victory could be achieved without real (as opposed to rhetorical) sacrifice in which none of their European allies—totally mobilized, totally conscripted, rationed to the minimum necessary to preserve the health of the productive and fighting sections of society, and conscious of the destructiveness of ordinary, conventional, pre-Hiroshima warfare—could ever partake. Where they felt uncertainty, as Richard Nixon clearly did, it was the product of personal psychological circumstance rather than of the shared experiences of their own peer group.

Their globalism was that of their own age group in Britain too, the globalism of young men who at the stroke of some minor bureaucrat's pen might find themselves translated anywhere, from Anchorage to Antarctica, from the ice cold of the Murmansk convoys to the steaming heat of Miyitkyina or the jungled shores of Mindanao; only Britain and the United States fought a truly global war in the years 1941-45. Apart from a few commerce raiders and the doomed men of the German U-boat flotillas, Germany's war effort was confined to the triangle formed by Leningrad, Cairo and the Atlantic coastline. The appalling losses of the Soviet Union were confined to the European fronts from central Europe to the Murmansk-Moscow-Stalingrad-Caucasus line. Apart from the unhappy Italian "volunteers" who fought on the Soviet front, Italy's war was confined to the shores of the Mediterranean. Japan's forces broke into the Indian ocean only once. Their Pacific war was only one of the fronts on which American and British forces were engaged. France's few "free" forces fought battles scattered very widely, from Indochina to Syria and the frontiers of Chad. But one is talking only of a handful of scattered units. Major participation by French forces in the war was confined to the first and last year of the war and to battlefields in France and Italy. Only Britain and America fought a global war. Despite the strains and stresses, the impatience, the prejudices, the misunderstandings and the occasional accusations of betrayal which are part of the process by which America succeeded to Britain's one-time position as the sole genuinely global power, neither Britain nor the United States could long escape the necessity for cooperation, nor that this cooperation could always be based not on the common language which in Churchill's jest divided the two powers, not by the common heritage of common law, but by the shared experience of global power and position. It is hardly surprising, therefore, to find President Kennedy sometimes preferring Macmillan's advice to that of his own advisors or Nixon and Secretary of State Henry Kissinger operating on the same wavelength as Prime Ministers Harold Wilson and James Callaghan. Even that most unlikely and tenuous of partnerships, that of civil rights leader Andrew Young with British liberal David Owen in Africa becomes comprehensible once this basic parallelism of experience is considered.

In the Concert of Europe, Britain always played an uneasy role, at once the object of European envy and hostility and the ally sought by one faction against another. Like America, Britain swam in and out of isolationism. Like America, its people were as much concerned with what was going on in Buenos Aires as in Brussels or Berlin. And, like America today, British opinion tended to judge the international behavior of the other powers on a moral scale that ranked nations from uncivilized pariahs and thoroughly dangerous but long term opponents to members of the family. That moral scale assumed the desirability of certain kinds of international behavior and the total unacceptability of to international affairs that Britain declared war on Germany on 3 September 1939 and made Hitler's "limited war" into World War II.

NOTES

1. Eduard Mark, "American Policy towards Eastern Europe and the Origins of the Cold War, 1941-1946: An Alternative Explanation," *Journal of American History* 68, no. 4 (1981), pp. 313-36; Geir Lundestad, *The American Non-Policy Towards Eastern Europe, 1943-1947* (New York, 1975).
2. Stephen Ambrose, *America's Rise to Globalism: America Foreign Policy since 1938* (New York, 1988).

3. See S. Oki Ogbi, "The Pacific War Controversy in Britain: Sir Robert Craigie versus the Foreign Office," *Modern Asian Studies* 17, no. 3 (1983); D. C. Watt, "Senso kaihi wa keno de attake: Kure-gi-nokoku to seisaku kettei eri—to no hanno" ["Could War in the Far East Have Been Prevented in November 1941?" Sir Robert Craigie's final report on his embassy to Japan and the reactions of the British foreign policymaking elite], in Akira Iriye and T. Aruga, eds., *Senkanki no Nihon gaiko* [Japanese Foreign Relations During the War] (Tokyo, 1984).

4. See D. C. Watt, "Every War Must End: Planning for Post-War Security in Britain and American in the Wars of 1914-18 and 1939-45: The Roles of Historical Example and of Professional Historians," *Transactions of the Royal Historical Society* 28, 8th ser. (1978).

4

American Empire, American Raj

Walter LaFeber

In 1943 the most distinguished, and perhaps most influential, expert on the
U.S. Constitution, Professor Edward S. Corwin, pinpointed how Franklin D.
Roosevelt had gathered power into the White House after World War II had
erupted. Such an observation was not news. The news lay in Corwin's noting
the Labor Day speech of 1942 in which Roosevelt had truly revealed, in
Corwin's view, his disdain for constitutional limits by announcing that after
the war was won, "the powers under which I act automatically revert to the
people—to whom they belong." Corwin acidly commented that Roosevelt
seemed to believe that he "derives his war powers *directly* from the people,
and not via the Constitution, a doctrine closely akin to the leadership
principle which our armed forces are combating today in the four quarters
of the globe."[1]

Corwin was not alone in warning that unless Americans took great care,
they might end up accepting under another name "the leadership principle"
they hated in Germany and Japan. The danger revolved around a centralized
government dominated by a president who, due to his immense personal
popularity and control of the broadcasting media, could exert ex-
traconstitutional powers until he fatally weakened the basic document itself.
The executive would then become, as recent scholars have phrased it, a
"plebiscitary Presidency," in which the president exploits mass communications to bypass both constitutional and congressional restraints—even the
restraints of the party system—to rule. The leading scholar on this problem,
Theodore Lowi, believes that FDR's "legacy can be summed up in a single

concept, the *plebiscitary* presidency. He set its foundations and determined its initial directions."[2] Forty years after Roosevelt's death, a Pulitzer Prize winning columnist, Robert Samuelson, saw the legacy from another perspective: "We postwar Americans—about 70 percent of us were born after 1939—cannot easily appreciate how much our attitudes and discontents descend from the war. In 1939 America was deeply divided over the roles of government, business, and labor. By 1945 a new social consciousness was emerging." Because of a blend of "New Deal ideology and wartime pragmatism," Samuelson noted, the "Government's role as our final social umpire [now] seems utterly natural." The question of the President's power in that governmental "role" is not discussed in this context even by an observer as perceptive as Samuelson.[3]

Yet surely the "social consensus" of 1945 was shaped most especially by Roosevelt. Even Ronald Reagan admits to his New Deal roots, and if imitation is the sincerest form of flattery, Reagan repeatedly flattered Roosevelt with his use of mass media, including the lunch-side Saturday radio address that enabled the president to go over the heads of Congress to present his case forcefully and directly to the American people. Aside from a few academicians such as Lowi, we have not been able to formulate and raise the fundamental questions about Reagan's command of the present "consensus" in the way that Corwin and others did about Roosevelt's command, even in the middle of a great war.

Certainly debate over presidential powers was not lacking from 1943 to 1945, despite the exigencies of the war and despite the immense popularity of FDR. A number of reasons help to explain the extent and passion of this debate. For one, it occurred amid a growing realization that the United States would be the postwar superpower and, as Roosevelt told Stalin directly, that the United States would necessarily be interested in affairs around the globe. A second reason for the distinctive debate was that its major participants included Corwin, Walter Lippmann, Charles Beard, Robert Taft, James Forrestal, and Senator Arthur Vandenberg who, regardless of what one might otherwise think about them, cannot be accused of either insensitivity to power or lack of passion in dealing with the problem of power. A third reason was the belief on the part of Corwin and other close observers that the New Deal had created the new presidency. War had only reaffirmed already-held executive powers and had added a few more, although a significant more because, some feared, following the war the United States might well be involved in a number of new conflicts to maintain the status quo created by the old wars.

This point needs underlining. President Roosevelt dropped the famous remark in 1943 that "Dr. Win-the-War" had replaced Dr. New Deal. Henry Luce's *Time* magazine, with obvious relief, ran an obituary under its "Milestones" column in January 1944:

> Death revealed. The New Deal, 10, after long illness; of malnutrition and desuetude. Child of the 1932 election campaign, the New Deal had four healthy years, began to suffer from spots before its eyes in 1937, and never recovered from the shock of war. Last week its father, Franklin Roosevelt, pronounced it dead.[4]

But Luce, the devout son of missionary parents, might well have feared a resurrection, for if the publisher believed the New Deal to be dead, why did he, with great fanfare, serialize in *Life* magazine Beard's attack in his book *The Republic* on the New Deal and especially on presidential powers? In retrospect, scholars can conclude that after the early 1940s there were going to be no more New Deals in an American society growing conservative. But that was not so clear at the time. In early 1945, FDR called for a second Bill of Rights. Critics quickly noted that the first Bill of Rights prevented government intervention against individual rights, while Roosevelt's bill asked the government to intervene directly to ensure such rights.[5] But presidential (that is, Roosevelt's) prerogatives could well be dramatically expanded even more by the post-1938 powers that had been created to conduct foreign policy. These powers not only included a highly charged commander in chief capacity, but also though the 1939 Reorganization Act, in which the president had obtained vast powers to control or circumvent his bureaucracy and opponents in Congress and the media that might try to use that bureaucracy to block the president's programs.

Meanwhile, White House publicists worked to inflate executive powers further. When a Hadley Cantril poll asked Americans whether the president could "make some important decisions before consulting Congress," 78 percent of the respondents said he certainly could do so. One White House official, however, expressed concern over such a low figure and pushed Harry Hopkins to authorize a public relations campaign so Roosevelt could act "in the same way that a Commanding General in the field does."[6] The Office of War Information published a widely distributed pamphlet in 1942 giving one of the most spread-eagle views of presidential power. Luce and other Roosevelt opponents had good reason to fear that the end of the New Deal meant not the diminution of Roosevelt's prerogatives but perhaps a significant increase, and an increase based, moreover, on public support generated by the administration's own propaganda organs.

The arguments for a strong presidency received significant support from Walter Lippmann's influential columns. The highly respected journalist feared a rerun of 1919 when "an insolvent foreign policy" had created severe "domestic division." He even argued in his widely read book of 1943 that "since 1899 American foreign relations have never . . . been solvent. Accordingly the nation has been deeply divided throughout this period." Clear thinking and strong leadership were required, Lippmann argued, for the war had taught that "we have to defend two-thirds of the surface of the globe from our continental base in North America."[7] That big a beat required a policeman with long strides or a visionary leader who could stabilize the world through nonmilitary means. Throughout the 1930s and the early war years, Lippmann never had a problem keeping his enthusiasm for Roosevelt under rigid control, but on 7 April 1945, the journalist wrote a remarkable column that lauded both FDR's wartime leadership and his "cool, objective realism about what really matters most" that had made him "quite the equal" of Stalin and Churchill. Lippmann wanted to "explode the myth" that FDR and his advisers "have been amiable weaklings, suckers, and Santa Clauses." The case had to be made not only out of justice to the president, but also "for our own sakes in the trying days to come. We have power. We have wealth." However, these would be worthless "if we lack self-confidence," by which Lippmann clearly meant confidence in powerful presidential leadership.[8]

In that and other columns, Lippmann's long-held desire for powerful presidents overcame his lack of confidence in Roosevelt as a person. FDR, moreover, seemed to be making deals that fit into Lippmann's widely publicized plan for well-delineated spheres of influence after the war. In a 1950 oral history interview, Lippmann cited "supersecret press conferences" with FDR and then denied that the president ever believed "he could charm Stalin into agreeing with him. . . . Roosevelt was a cynical man. He distrusted everybody. What he thought he could do was outwit Stalin, which is quite a different thing." FDR, however, did not live long enough to carry out his plans. Lippmann's second book, *U.S. War Aims*, which appeared during the conflict, blasted one-worldism, but came out, as he recalled, "as Roosevelt was nearly in his last phase, and Truman, of course, never read a book."[9] That cut at Truman in 1950 perhaps revealed Lippmann's frustration that such a strong president as Truman could follow so many policies that, in the columnist's view, were so inept. From Woodrow Wilson through Lyndon Johnson, Lippmann was never able to reconcile presidential power, which he loved, with the strong presidents' policies that he so often attacked.

Lippmann's view of presidential power did become ascendant, but his plea for spheres of influence ran against the American grain. In 1944 and early 1945 the belief grew among close observers that the European balance of power was to be replaced by a collective security system ensured by a world organization. As commander in chief, the president was to watch over the U.S. military forces committed to the new United Nations as well as the supposedly smaller number of troops needed to work the Atlantic and Pacific bases that protected North America.[10]

Debate quickly erupted after the UN plans appeared in 1943 and 1944 over the question of whether the president could extend his constitutional powers in the new postwar world. Many legal and foreign policy experts had no doubts. In a widely noted book, a respected lawyer and assistant secretary of state, James Grafton Rogers, compared the "new adventures" around the earth to U.S. pioneering of "the economic and political problems of territorial expansion in such places as Missouri and Nebraska." To avoid the global equivalent of a Missouri Compromise crisis, Rogers argued that the new United Nations should "employ armed force, if needed, to police the nations," and that in this framework the president enjoyed wide prerogatives in ordering the troops around the globe. The president's great powers, Rogers decided, and even the powers of Congress, "are not to be found precisely expressed in the Constitution but are . . . more in the nature of things." In any case, "history shows that our fortunes in foreign affairs are committed into the hands of the Presidents we elect. The checks retained rest in a majority of the two Houses of Congress, which have some powers but have exercised them little,"[11] or so argued Rogers, one of the country's leading legal minds in 1945. The president's power to move troops, perhaps even to start wars, were apparently to be as constitutional in cases involving, say, Southeast Asia as they had been when used by James K. Polk in Texas in 1846.

Rogers's brief received strong support from six other leading international lawyers, including Philip Jessup, James Shotwell, and Quincy Wright. This group argued in the *New York Times* and elsewhere that the president could send U.S. forces into action as part of a UN police force. Such action "would not change the situation from that which has always prevailed. The President has always had the power under the Constitution to use force," even when "such actions . . . sometimes preceded war." The authors cited as evidence the U.S. "interpositions" in Mexico, Haiti, Nicaragua, "and other places." They carefully specified that Congress must agree to the UN Charter and be kept informed during crises, but otherwise it was clear that in their view the U.S. entry into the UN opened exciting possibilities for extensive presidential activities. In an editorial, the *New York Times* endorsed the letter and indeed even went beyond it, arguing that the president should be able to respond quickly to international attacks ("A German attack on France or a Japanese attack on China would actually menace us today as much as an attack on Mexico a century ago"). But the executive also should be able to follow a policy of deterrence; the UN proposals "would authorize [the President] to keep us out of war by joining with other nations in measures that would discourage aggression or stop it in its tracks."[12] As U.S. foreign policy became more imperial (in the sense of becoming of exceptional size), so, too, did presidential powers.

Not all lawyers with access to the media agreed. In August 1943, Walton Hamilton, a Yale Law School professor, wrote "The Ever-Growing Power of the Presidency." Amid patriotic articles entitled "Bombing a Path to Berlin," and "We Must Not Fail the World Again," Hamilton sounded almost un-American. He argued that "the Presidency has become a powerful and amorphous office," so powerful that the Constitution itself has been weakened. Congress "alone has the [constitutional] power to declare war," but "the President may so conduct foreign affairs that it has no alternative." The presidency, Hamilton went on, has "outgrown its appointed office" and "has not been subdued into a power that can be called constitutional. Ours, in a word, is a crisis Government." But it could become worse. Wartime needs had made "big business" a partner of the unsubdued presidency. The combination could have been explosive. Sounding much like the political scientists of the 1970s and 1980s who have argued that special interest groups have corrupted both the political and policymaking process, Hamilton wrote:

> Even as in days of old the honorable guilds performed offices for the Crown, so today the worshipped companies of steel, copper, aluminum, chemicals do delegated duty for the Government of the United States. They are insiders, not by the election of the people, but by their own choice and pressure. And, as the separation of the state and economy is ended, they bring to public affairs attitudes, objectives, values never registered at the ballot box.[13]

That judgment was agreed with by Republicans and some Democrats in Congress who began to view the struggle against Roosevelt's growing powers as a fight for Congress's survival as a supposedly coequal branch of government. That conflict greatly sharpened during the war. When Isaiah Berlin reported to London from the British embassy in Washington about the passage of Roosevelt's trade bill in mid-1943, Berlin noted that the scorching floor debate had not been over commercial issues but over the "delegation of power to the executive. . . . The deep congressional jealousies and fears of usurpation of its peacemaking powers by the executive by piecemeal encroachment emerged again and again."[14] Republican Senate leader Robert Taft, who held an exceptionally dim view of presidential powers, publicly charged in 1943 that Luce's call for an "American Century" was a call for an "American raj." Taft added that to run the world as some Americans hoped would require "a permanent army a good deal larger than 11,000,000 men" and "the suspension of any renewal of freedom in the United States." When Taft returned home to the usually friendly political districts of Ohio, he was charged with being not only an "isolationist" but also the "Number One opponent of the President." Taft survived the 1944 election with only 50.3 percent of a vote he usually dominated.[15] On the national level that same election, as Berlin reported, demonstrated the hold that FDR's foreign policy had "over the minds and hearts of American people." Even the many anti-Roosevelt newspapers, Berlin observed, recognized the "'clear mandate on foreign policy' now given to the President."[16]

Taft, Walton, and others who hoped to check executive power then received a further jolt. Secretary of State Cordell Hull resigned in the autumn of 1944. Leading Democrat Senate leaders, led by Tom Connally of Texas and Walter George of Georgia, urged Roosevelt to appoint their close friend James Francis Byrnes. The president instead named Edward R. Stettinius, the former business executive who had risen to power under his White House patron, Harry Hopkins. The State Department was now fully under the control of the president and his few close advisers.[17] There were to be no Robert Lansings after the war. (Indeed, the presidents ensured no more Robert Lansings would arise to challenge their control over foreign policy until Alexander Haig appeared at the State Department in 1981. Haig's tenure as "vicar" lasted only until the White House bishops understood the problem and politically excommunicated him.)

The editor of the influential Roman Catholic journal, the *Commonweal*, watched how FDR had come to dominate policy while preventing any systematic cooperation between Congress and the State Department and then commented: "To use a rather brutal analogy, the Government of the United States in its foreign relations resembles some huge corporation in which the sales and credit departments are never allowed to meet—except in the men's room (I refer to Mr. Hull's admirably intentioned policy of off the record talks with groups of senators)." Harry Binsse recommended changing needed votes on treaty ratification from two-thirds to a simple majority so the Senate could move more expeditiously and also giving the Senate the right to dismiss secretaries of state. These ideas dropped stillborn. Not even any letters in the journal's "Communication" column mentioned this essay.[18] As Lippmann indicated, early 1945 was the time to celebrate, not question, presidential power.

Certain senators nevertheless grew more, not less, concerned. In mid-January, Republican Senator Vandenberg recommended plans for Europe that led staunch internationalists to welcome him home as the former prodigal son of isolationism. The speech also led to a warm exchange between Vandenberg and an obviously relieved FDR. But one month later Vandenberg began to understand that the president was making decisions at Yalta about postwar Eastern Europe that were "totally unsatisfactory" but would not require Senate scrutiny. In Vandenberg's view, the only alternatives to accepting the Yalta deals would be war with Russia or hope that the United Nations might correct the decisions. The first was unthinkable and the second improbable. Nevertheless, the senator sent a cable to Roosevelt, who was then en route home from Yalta, and pleaded for a UN review of the decisions. The distinguished senator received a form letter from Stettinius, through Undersecretary Joseph Grew, that said, "Your . . . helpful comments in regard to our recent efforts are deeply appreciated." Vandenberg was left to ask himself plaintively, "What can we do about it?"[19] Roosevelt seemed to be making crucial decisions about the postwar world as if the Senate did not exist.

As Roosevelt well knew, for some Americans with a sense of history it would have been better at times if the Senate had not existed. Congress's performance in foreign affairs between 1919 and 1939 had left bitter memories, evil connotations for the term "isolationist," and the impression that U.S. security was best protected by worldly presidents rather than parochial congressmen. *Time* magazine caught this general impression in a March 1944 cover story on Senator Connally, the popular and powerful Texan. Connally and Vandenberg were seen as the two pivotal figures in the Senate's postwar foreign policy debates. As *Time* phrased it, however, Connally was "hampered by a vast lack of erudition. He has no real foreign policy himself; he has not attempted to think his way through the problem of the Polish frontiers" or other potential problems. Instead "he seems content to take whatever proposals the White House and the State Department send down, amend them to suit the Senate's temper that week, and pass them on." Connally's wife, *Time* reported, noted that the senator "has begun reading himself to sleep for a half hour or so each night," but unfortunately the reading was "almost exclusively" on the Civil War. Connally loudly declared that the 1919-20 "mistake" would not be repeated, but, *Time* added, the senator could be under a "profound misapprehension," because many doubted that Roosevelt was going to give the Senate "a total peace to accept, amend, or reject." Instead, *Time* argued, the Big Three would make peace "piecemeal, by private conferences and agreements." Connally could swear the Senate would not be bypassed, but he and his colleagues "may be presented with other executive agreements in the form of *faits accomplish* which they will have no choice but to accept."[20]

Connally and Vandenberg may have fit a cartoonist's stereotype of how a U.S. senator should look, but they certainly fit the White House preference of how a senator should think. By 1944, especially after FDR's fourth-term victory, few participants in the growing debate over presidential powers assumed those powers were going to be checked by Congress. Perhaps that assumption only intensified the debate. Certainly it helps to explain the involvement of two intellectual heavyweights who entered the debate during the last two years of the war. The first was Charles A. Beard, whom *Life* magazine introduced to its millions of readers as "one of America's great historians and thinkers." *Life* serialized Beard's 1943 book, *The Republic*, a kind of Socratic dialogue, with Beard playing Socrates, on the fundamentals of the American constitutional system for which so many Americans were dying. Beard was widely known, but *The Republic* may have been the most popular of his many books. Its regular sales numbered more than 180,000, and the *Life* editions sold more than 40 million copies. It was read over school intercom systems and then discussed in classes. The circulation would have been much greater, but when the Council on Books in Wartime tried to distribute *The Republic* to soldiers, the U.S. military authorities barred it under a congressional act prohibiting the dissemination of election propaganda among the troops.[21]

The authorities knew what they were doing. *The Republic* invoked history to blast away at Roosevelt's exercise of presidential powers. Beard did not use a blunderbuss, as he would four years later in two controversial books on FDR. He instead used a scalpel and sometimes hid the instrument behind a scholarly analysis of constitutional history. Beard's subtlety misled even some of his followers. Eric Goldman, a perceptive and sympathetic analyst of Beard's thinking, read *The Republic* and *A Basic History of the United States*, by Charles and Mary Beard, that appeared in 1944. He wrote that "old Beardians were breathing normally again." The pre-1941 attacks on FDR's foreign policy and the "economic interpretation" were now muted. Beard, Goldman believed, still had mementoes of despair (he quoted Beard as defining human history as "the story of a tomcat being pulled by its tail to a place it doesn't recognize"). But Goldman nevertheless concluded that the author's next books "will almost certainly mean that another generation of

American liberalism, like its fathers, will build on the Beards."[22] Little could Goldman have imagined just how bitterly the next generation of liberals would reject Beard, especially after the historian's two assaults on Roosevelt's use of presidential powers.

Other liberal reviewers agreed with Goldman's assessment. Lindsay Rogers wrote in the *Saturday Review of Literature* that Beard's earlier work reminded him of David Lloyd George's remark that British Field Marshal Horatio Kitchener resembled a revolving lighthouse that sometimes flashed light far out into the surrounding darkness, but every once in a while turned dark. Rogers obviously saw the Beard of 1934 to 1941 as dark, but *The Republic* was "a lighthouse that always throws gleams and never gets dark. . . . The conversations [constructed by Beard in the book] not only chisel down to the truths, but then they polish the bedrock off." Lindsay was delighted that Beard showed such "faith in our Republic."[23]

Luce no doubt serialized *The Republic* in *Life* magazine because he read it quite differently than did Goldman and Rogers. At first, Luce and Beard seemed perfect to play the political odd couple. When Luce published his famous articles in 1941 arguing for the need for an American century, Beard publicly lumped the publisher with Josiah Strong and Alfred Thayer Mahan, other misguided imperialists whom Beard blistered for their belief that American civilization was civilized enough to be exported around the world. Luce's vision of world trade profits for U.S. merchants was so glittering, Beard wrote caustically, "as to make Marco Polo's lures look like Stygian murk."[24] In Beard's view the British Empire had been bad enough. Why would Luce ever want to replace and refine it with an American empire? Luce, however, doubtless saw highly redeeming features in Beard's ideas by the time *The Republic* appeared. The historian still had severe reservations about the New Deal, although he seemed to be more upbeat about the American future than he had been before the war. Beard even wrote an introduction for a new 1943 edition of Brooks Adams's *The Law of Civilization and Decay* (an edition that received considerable attention in midwar) in which he refused to accept Adams's cyclical theory and his pessimism about American history. Perhaps above all, Luce could see how Beard shared his fear of Roosevelt's use of executive powers. The businessman no doubt set out to use the intellectual.

In reading the excerpts in *Life*, the identities of the user and the used quickly become confused. True, Luce gave little space to Beard's argument that the "supreme object" of U.S. foreign policy must be "to protect and advance American civilization on this continent" rather than try to spread an American century to the world's distant corners. Beard, however, made his point in other ways. With more insight and consistency than Luce possessed, he used *Life*'s pages to damn both presidential power and the idea of U.S. global hegemony. Luce's editorials focused only on the question of the presidency and "Democrats" in Congress who, as Luce's introductory editorial to the Beard series put it, "have delegated so many powers to the executive that Congress can hardly keep track of how much it has given away." When Beard began to argue that domestic and foreign affairs could not be compartmentalized and then suggested that the surest way to suffer from an imperial president at home was to follow an imperial policy abroad, Luce could not or did not want to keep up. Luce wanted a global New Deal, but one without Roosevelt. Beard was not going to fall into that trap. Luce walked into the trap by directly borrowing from Beard in a long editorial: "'Foreign affairs' are so closely intermingled with 'domestic affairs' that any President who took absolute power over foreign affairs would automatically become a complete dictator over domestic affairs." Luce then tried to scramble out by pleading with the president to listen closely to Congress as he conducted the new global foreign policy. Unfortunately for Luce's argument, he had just admitted that Congress had given away too many of its powers to the president. By the publisher's own analysis, Roosevelt did not need to deal systematically, or even constitutionally, with Congress.[25]

Life's editorial writers thought they had finally found a way out of the trap when Roosevelt died. In an editorial on FDR's passing, *Life* quoted the young Texas congressman Lyndon Johnson, who lamented that "plenty of us" remain "to try to block and run interference . . . but the man who carried the ball is gone—gone. . . . He was just like a daddy to me always." The editorial then emphasized that "the best tribute the people can pay to Roosevelt is to show they can get along without him."[26]

Beard was off in quite another direction, asserting that the president had been elected by a minority vote and so had not automatically spoken for all Americans. The argument then moved to the observation (and even quoted Alexander Hamilton to this effect) that Congress had to have a powerful voice because the executive department was too open to "improper foreign influences." Beard then asked in which provision of the Constitution or "our political tradition" was it written that "the President's voice is the voice of the nation which all citizens are bound to accept as such? . . . The answer is, None absolutely None. The constitution does not use the term foreign affairs. It does not declare the President to be the symbol of national unity or his voice to be the voice of the nation." Between these declarations, Beard condemned Woodrow Wilson's belief that a shrewd president is "irresistible" to a country whose "instinct is for united action, and . . . craves a single leader." Beard had one of his characters in *The Republic* comment "with flashing eyes" that Wilson's statement about Americans "craving for a single leadership sounds to me a lot like Hitler's doctrine."[27] The historian offered no way out of the problem unless U.S. foreign policy objectives were scaled back. He noted that the Founding Fathers expected "Congress should be the dominant branch," and if Presidents had gained the upper hand, the problem "lies with Congress, not with the Constitution." But Beard was certainly closer to Edward Corwin than to Luce in believing that Congress could not reclaim its powers amid a crusade for an American century.

The Republic was one shot of a double-barreled Beardian attack. In 1944, Charles and Mary Beard published *A Basic History of the United States*. Sold in a sixty-nine-cent edition through drugstores, the book had a first printing of 150,000 copies, was a Book-of-the-Month Club dividend, and soon ran up sales of 650,000 copies. *Time* again liked the Beards' work, and Henry Steele Commager lauded it as "magisterial." But other former Beardians, led by Lewis Mumford, denounced it. Mumford even asked for a massive analysis of all of Beard's recent writings "to save another generation from Beard's studied misguidance."[28] A number of the authors' points might have alienated Mumford and others, but perhaps one was their assertion that "in its regimenting and disruptive effects," World War II was "so revolutionary that it made [World War I] look like an episode." And nowhere was that revolution more notable than in powers given the president, "power almost without limit," even at home. The New Deal, the Beards charged, had become transformed into a "process of centralization . . . under the 'economic royalists' " once condemned by FDR. The authors then raised Henry Adams's question of 1895: Had Americans entered their last great period of "centralization" before the system headed downhill? The Beards saw no help coming from Congress. They noted the long bitter debate in 1943 between the House and Senate over the terms of the U.S. entry into a postwar organization, then drily commented that "the proceedings were made somewhat academic by the announcement, on November 1, that President Roosevelt, on his own motion, had committed the United States to 'united action' with Russia, Great Britain, and China" after the war.[29]

Charles Beard's work has been open to criticism from many sides. It would be strange if a person who wrote as much as he did, on such sensitive topics, and who fought as many battles as he did, was not an open target. Eugene D. Genovese, a leading Marxist historian, has coherently argued that Beard became inconsistent (changing, for example, from an economic to a political to a military interpretation of history) because he backed off from making a true Marxist class analysis of the American dilemma and instead settled for merely analyzing interest groups.[30] Beard was inconsistent in trying to choose between two competing interpretations of the Constitution. One view holds that the document embodies a higher natural law standard that can be found in the Founders' intentions and especially in the limitations they explicitly imposed on popular majorities, governmental power, and presidential authority. The second view holds that the Constitution is organic and living and that the majority's needs can shape, for example, presidential powers.[31]

Beard's fear of a strong president fit into the first view, but his gut feeling for democracy—a result of his Midwest upbringing and his Fabian Socialist days and a sentiment noted by many reviewers of his 1943 and 1944 books—fit into the second view. He had difficulty reconciling his belief in the American people with his fear of the presidency those people had apotheosized. At least Beard clearly understood that although he might not reconcile that fear with his constitutional theory, he certainly could reconcile his fear of presidential power with his foreign policy. In that he was utterly consistent during the last fifteen years of his life. His writings of 1943 and 1944 were prophecies about those whom we finally scourged but never fully understood, as dangerously imperial presidents in the 1960s and 1970s.

In early 1944, Corwin reviewed *The Republic* and declared it not only "notable" but also "a noble book" that was "a worthy successor to *The Federalist* and comes to this day as opportunely as that greatest product of American political thinking came to its day."[32] The book was apparently one of the few shafts of light the great scholar of the Constitution could find by the end of the war. He believed in 1945 that constitutional law ("the most distinctive feature of the American system of government") seemed "to be undergoing a fundamental revision—even to be in a process of dissolution." Corwin understood the difficulty of trying to apply 1787 writings to a postatomic world. "One is reminded of an old conundrum," he wrote in 1945. "Query: 'Does your brother like cheese?' Answer: 'I have no brother.' Query: 'But if you had a brother, would he like cheese?' "[33] Corwin did not want to get into that kind of game, but on the other hand he, like Beard, took the Founders' intentions seriously and feared that too many of their principles had been subverted by the mid-1940s, especially the restraints they had placed on presidential power.

Corwin pinpointed how these restraints had been loosened. The demands of war certainly contributed, but he thought the roots of the problem went far deeper. He focused repeatedly on the Supreme Court's landmark *Curtiss vs. Wright* decision of 1936. In 1792, Corwin related, the Supreme Court had refused to deal with the argument that the power to wage war did not come from the Constitution but was inherent in the American people as a community. In 1936, however, the Court bought the argument by denying that the power to wage war was merely an enumerated power. The U.S. government, Corwin later warned, had become a government of open-ended plenary powers in the waging of war, not a government of the Founders' enumerated powers.[34] It was precisely the transformation of the Constitution that had alarmed Beard. Both men knew, moreover, that the Court had gone on to declare in 1936 that it was the president who had "the very delicate, plenary and exclusive power . . . as the sole organ of the federal government in the field of international relations." Beard and Corwin bitterly disputed that opinion, but Roosevelt's advisers naturally used it to justify some of the president's wartime actions.[35]

Corwin also had carefully watched Roosevelt pull power into his hands during the crises of 1939-41. The professor did not know about FDR's private query to his attorney general about the 1939 Neutrality Act: "How far do you think I can go in ignoring the existing act even though I did sign it?"[36] But Corwin understood how Roosevelt had deliberately misinterpreted his rights in order to exchange fifty naval vessels for British bases in 1940, and he had insight into FDR's extension of his powers throughout 1941. These actions, Corwin later concluded, gave the president "a truly royal prerogative in the field of foreign relations, and [did] so without indicating any correlative legal or constitutional control to which he is answerable."[37] Finally, Corwin realized that "personality and crisis" had stamped the new presidency. "Presidential power today is dangerously personalized power," he wrote several years after the war, and is so in "two senses." First, presidential leadership is "dependent altogether on the accident of personality, against which our haphazard method of selecting presidents offers no guarantee"; and second, the president is "not bound to consult" any other government body before he makes a decision.[38]

His only major proposal at the close of the war to prevent a breakdown in the constitutional relationship was to change the Senate's two-thirds vote on treaties to a simple majority. Corwin had no great faith in the Senate, "a body," as he liked to note, that had to take "seven years to approve the recession of the Isle of Pines to Cuba." But he hoped that a simple majority rule would no longer allow small minorities to hide behind constitutional provisions and, instead, would make them become more responsible.

He especially hoped that an easier treaty process would help convince presidents to make more treaties and fewer executive agreements,[39] the kind Roosevelt was making secretly at the Big Three conferences. If Congress did not reorganize and exert itself, Corwin warned in 1943, "it seems likely to be gradually reduced to the level of a badly tarnished pageant, and little more. . . . There is always a tendency, even in democracies, for the emergency device to become the norm."[40]

Corwin was proven to be correct. Roosevelt's successor, Harry S. Truman, discovered the emergency device he needed to conduct foreign policy in the Cold War. Truman, as Berlin accurately noted in 1945, had superbly carried out a difficult transition process after FDR's death and had even brought such conservative lions as Westbrook Pegler and Arthur Krock into the president's "era of good feeling."[41] If Truman had faltered, he was surrounded by advisers such as James Forrestal and Dean Acheson who were determined to build executive power. In the instances of Forrestal, Thomas Finletter, and later George Kennan, they even seriously considered the need for an executive-dominated parliamentary system to replace the Founders' checks and balances so foreign policy could be carried out more efficiently.[42] It turned out, however, that parliamentary government was unnecessary. Truman found the secret—the political equivalent of discovering the law of perpetual motion—with his Truman Doctrine in 1947. By declaring that the world was simply divided between the enslaved and the free and then asking Congress (who failed to question Truman's first assumption) which side it was on, the president had discovered how to consult Congress, especially when he needed money, without being bound by Congress. Truman and later presidents could follow Oscar Wilde's advice that "one should always play fairly when one has the winning hand."

In retrospect, however, Truman's discovery did not resolve but rather worsened the problems identified by Corwin, Beard, and other critics of growing presidential power between 1943 and 1945. These critics, with considerable courage as well as foresight, raised fundamental questions about Roosevelt's expansion of presidential powers, even amid a total for survival. Beard, Corwin, and their fellow questioners wondered aloud whether the means—that is, carefully placed constitutional restraints on executive power—were not being needlessly sacrificed to the ends (defeating the Axis and creating an orderly postwar world) with too little debate and excessive enthusiasm. In Beard's case, the attack on presidential power formed an integral part of a wider assault on the whole idea of a postwar American century. Beard and Corwin did not believe that America could act as the world's policeman without ultimately threatening the constitutional rights of the policeman's home-precinct citizens—those whom he was pledged to protect in the first instance. The two men's priorities were clear (constitutionally protected rights at home were more important than the power to project U.S. forces overseas rapidly), and the manner in which they defined those priorities separated them from Lippmann, Luce, and, ultimately, Vandenberg. As the critics defined the problem, the crisis was not merely personal and due, as some believed to Roosevelt's overpowering political presence,[43] but institutional and due to an ambitious foreign policy that had the support of a growing consensus. Defying that consensus, Beard and Corwin warned that the foreign and domestic arenas could not be neatly separated: power used to impose order on the former could be used to impose order on the latter.

Prophets with honor (and book sales) but too little influence in their own time, Beard and Corwin raised the fundamental questions and developed the historical case for the concerns that later Americans finally and tardily rediscovered during the constitutional crises of the 1970s and 1980s. Among other points, by noting FDR's growing power and the growing public support for that power, they undermined the later idea that "power revealed is power reduced"; that is, whenever Americans think their presidency is most powerful is actually the moment when they begin mobilizing countervailing checks on that power.[44] The 1942-1945 debate offered little evidence to support such a comfortable conclusion. Rather, one of the most important roots of the Watergate and Oliver North episodes runs back to the debate waged by Beard and Corwin at the end of World War II. The root lived because the two scholars lost that debate.

NOTES

1. Edward S. Corwin, "The War and the Constitution: President and Congress," in Richard Loss, ed., *Presidential Power and the Constitution. Essays by Edward S. Corwin* (Ithaca, NY, 1976), pp. 114-15.
2. Theodore Lowi, *The Personal President* (Ithaca, NY, 1985), p. 65.
3. Robert J. Samuelson, "The Great Postwar Prosperity," *Newsweek*, 20 May 1985, p. 57.
4. *Time*, 3 January 1944, p. 14.
5. Barry Karl, *The Uneasy State* (Chicago, 1983), pp. 221-22.
6. Oscar Cox to Harry L. Hopkins, 13 February 1943, box 69, Oscar Cox Papers, Franklin D. Roosevelt Library, Hyde Park, New York (hereafter cited as Cox Papers).
7. Walter Lippmann, *U.S. Foreign Policy: Shield of the Republic* (Boston, 1943), pp. 81-82, 108-10.
8. *New York Herald Tribune*, 7 April 1945, p. 13.
9. Walter Lippmann Oral History, Columbia University Library, p. 217.

10. Samuel P. Huntington, *The Common Defense: Strategic Programs in National Politics* (New York, 1961), p. 14.
11. James Grafton Rogers, *World Policing and the Constitution: An Inquiry into the Powers of the President and Congress, Nine Wars and a Hundred Military Operations, 1789-1945* (Boston, 1945), pp. 85-91, 9.
12. John W. Davis et al., "The President and Peace Forces," with the *New York Times* editorial reprinted from 5 November 1944, in *International Conciliation* 156 (December 1944): 795-802.
13. Walton Hamilton, "The Ever-Growing Power of the Presidency," *New York Times Magazine*, 29 August 1943, p. 6.
14. H. G. Nicholas, ed., *Washington Despatches, 1941-1945: Weekly Political Reports from the British Embassy* (Chicago, 1981), p. 201.
15. David Green, "The Shaping of Political Consciousness," manuscript, chap. 5, pp. 54, 56.
16. Nicholas, ed., *Washington Despatches*, p. 458.
17. Ibid., pp. 464-65.
18. Harry Lorin Binsse, "The United States and the World," *Commonweal*, 9 March 1945, p. 511.
19. Arthur H. Vandenberg, *Private Papers of Senator Vandenberg*, Arthur H. Vandenberg, Jr., ed. (Boston, 1952), pp. 148-49.
20. *Time*, 13 March 1944, pp. 15-16.
21. Max Lerner's review of *The Republic* in *American Political Science Review* 38 (August 1944): 783; Thomas C. Kennedy, *Charles A. Beard and American Foreign Policy* (Gainesville, FL, 1975), p. 118.
22. Eric F. Goldman, "A Historian at Seventy," *New Republic*, 27 November 1944, pp. 696-97.
23. Lindsay Rogers, "Twentieth Century Dialogues: A Socratic Approach to Mr. Beard's New Book," *Saturday Review of Literature*, 9 October 1943, p. 5.
24. Kennedy, *Beard*, pp. 108-12.
25. "Beard's *The Republic*," *Life*, 20 March 1944, p. 36.
26. *Life*, 23 April 1945, p. 32.
27. *Life*, 28 February 1944, p. 53.
28. *Time*, 21 August 1944, pp. 98-99; *Weekly Book Review*, 6 August 1944, p. 3; Kennedy, *Beard*, p. 123.
29. Charles A. Beard and Mary Beard, *A Basic History of the United States* (New York, 1944), pp. 472-79, 484.
30. Eugene D. Genovese, "Charles A. Beard and the Economic Interpretation of History," in Depauw University, ed., *Charles A. Beard: An Observance of the Centennial of His Birth* (Greencastle, IN, 1976).
31. Introduction in Loss, ed., *Presidential Power and the Constitution*, p. x.
32. *Columbia Law Review* 44 (March 1944), p. 283.
33. Edward S. Corwin, "The Dissolving Structure of Our Constitutional Law," in Loss, ed., *Presidential Power and the Constitution*, pp. 141, 150.

34. Corwin, "War and the Constitution," p. 112; idem, "The Impact of War on the Constitution. A Lecture Given . . . During the Spring Quarter of 1951," Emory University. Edward S. Corwin Papers, box 17, Princeton University, Princeton, NJ (hereafter cited as Corwin Papers).

35. Cox to Floyd J. Mattice (clerk), Senate Judiciary Committee, 7 December 1942, box 69, Cox Papers.

36. FDR to Frank Murphy, 1 July 1939, in Donald B. Schewe, ed., *Franklin D. Roosevelt and Foreign Affairs*, vol. 10 (New York, 1979), p. 46.

37. Edward S. Corwin, "The President's Power," *New Republic*, 29 January 1951, pp. 15-16. I am indebted to Richard Mandel for the FDR quote of 1939, which is in a letter of 1 July 1939 to Attorney General Frank Murphy.

38. Edward S. Corwin. "The Presidency in Perspective," manuscript box 15, Corwin Papers.

39. Edward S. Corwin to Frank W. Grinnell, 4 December 1944, Corwin Papers; Corwin to editor of the *New York Herald-Tribune*, 28 June 1944, box 17, Corwin Papers.

40. Corwin, "War and the Constitution," p. 120.

41. Nicholas, ed., *Washington Despatches*, p. 550.

42. James Forrestal, *The Forrestal Diaries*, Walter Millis, ed. (New York, 1951), p. 19; Alfred McClung Lee, "Overhauling the Machinery of Democracy," *Saturday Review*, 21 April 1945, p. 12 (a review of Thomas K. Finletter, *Can Representative Government Do the Job?* [New York, 1945]); George F. Kennan, *American Diplomacy, 1900-1950* (New York, 1951), pp. 81-82.

43. Karl, *The Uneasy State*, p. 233.

44. Samuel P. Huntington, *American Politics: The Promise of Disharmony* (Cambridge, MA, 1981), p. 76.

5

The Legacy of World War II for American Conventional Military Strategy: Should We Escape It?

Russell F. Weigley

Since World War II, it became the stated policy of the U.S. Army that the principal responsibility for which the army must prepare was the waging of war in Europe. The army regarded its most difficult challenge and its main consideration in the design of its weapons and force structure as resistance to an invasion of Western Europe by the Soviet Union and its Warsaw Pact military partners.[1] So consistently has the American army focused its strategic, technological, and organizational planning on Europe for the past forty years that the American army has become in its main purposes virtually a European army.

This condition would have been inconceivable before World War II. Neither national policies nor military realities would have permitted the American army before 1939 to focus its peacetime activities on preparation for war in Europe. While it is true that the U.S. Army historically displayed a strong kinship to European armies in its borrowing of organizational patterns, military thought, tactics, weapons, and customs from them—to the detriment, in fact, of its abilities to meet the peculiar problems of warfare against the North American Indians[2]—nevertheless the army's service to the military dimensions of national policy in no way had been skewed by any special army interest in Europe as a likely arena of combat. The latter statement could not be made so confidently about the U.S. Army since World War II. On the contrary, the most important single change effected by the war of 1941-45 upon American military strategy, except for the impact of nuclear weapons, has been the orientation of the army's strategic thought (and with it almost every other aspect of the U.S. Army) so completely toward Europe that the army has become a continental one in the most historic European sense. It has become in both force structure and purpose a European army, and this focus of military thought and preparation may well have skewed the army's contributions to national policy over the generation and more since the end of World War II.

At the close of World War I, the commanding general of the American Expeditionary Forces (the leader of the 1917-18 intervention in Europe), General John J. Pershing, explicitly rejected the proposition that henceforth the American army should be organized and equipped for a possible repetition of conflict in Europe on the model of the war just completed. Instead, Pershing argued, the army's most likely prospective roles would be extensions of its history as a constabulary on the North America Indian frontier and the Mexican border and as a counterinsurrectionary force in the Philippines. It would go on performing police and counterinsurgency tasks in the outposts of American empire and in various areas of the Western Hemisphere. Therefore the army's force structure should be tailored not for the deployment of heavy divisions in European war but for the ready creation of agile long-range expeditionary forces into what today would be called Third World environments.[3] To be sure, Pershing proved mistaken in not foreseeing the renewed European intervention that came with World War II. But his successors in army command, at the close of the latter conflict, chose almost precisely the opposite prescription for the future in deciding to prepare primarily for European wars at the expense of creating lighter, more agile formations for ventures into the Third World, and their reversal of Pershing's judgment has proven at least as much a mistake.

Since 1945 the U.S. Army in force structure and weaponry has been mainly an army designed for European war. The military tasks that the army has been obliged to undertake actively, and in particular the wars in which it has been engaged, have been not those of Europe but those of the Third World.

At least since 1945 the army has consistently devoted serious planning and preparation to the deterrence and conduct of conventional war, and thus to the species of warfare that has actually occurred and is most likely to continue to occur. In doing so the army has made a virtue of necessity, because the apportionment of roles among the armed forces under the National Security Acts of 1947 and 1949 and particularly the creation of an independent U.S. Air Force under the former statute have not permitted the army to contemplate a primary role in the delivery of atomic or nuclear weapons in the most total kind of war, strategic nuclear war. The air force, first with bombers, then with missiles as well as manned bombers, has from its inception naturally regarded itself as the principal deliverer of such weapons, and it has consequently tended toward a preoccupation with nuclear deterrence and nuclear war-waging to its frequent considerable neglect of weapons and doctrine for conventional war.

The Army Air Forces' experience of World War II in Europe with prenuclear, conventional weapons, however, also did much to shape the post-1945 preoccupations of the air force. The new service emerged with the conviction, reasonably well supported by the evidence, that so-called strategic bombing, the use of air power independently of the traditional armed forces to bomb the enemy's economic and urban vital centers, had substantially defeated Germany and Japan in World War II to the extent that by 1945 the invasion of neither enemy country by surface forces was essential toward inducing its surrender, even using "conventional" bombs alone. The apocalyptic closing of World War II in the atomic attacks on Hiroshima and Nagasaki on 6 and 9 August 1945, respectively, could not help but confirm the air force's confidence in the decisiveness of independent air power, but the confidence was already well formed before Hiroshima.[4]

The predecessor organizations of the air force, the air branches of the army that grew into the nearly independent Army Air Forces of World War II, had early developed a preoccupation with strategic bombing similar to that of the postwar air force, a preoccupation that made deficiencies in tactical aerial support of the ground forces during the war. This tendency received predictable reinforcement from the 1947 divorce of the air force from the army, so that when the Korean War broke out in 1950 the air force was even less prepared than the Europe-oriented army to wage war on an Asian peninsula without recourse to atomic weapons. The army was at least geared to fight a ground war, if not for the particular variety of it that erupted on 25 June 1950. There was little interest between 1945 and 1950 in the sort of tactical support of ground combat that the Korean War required. The air force had especially failed to prepare adequately to deal with the almost excessive speed of jet aircraft in trying to cooperate with troops on the ground. The navy's carrier-based airplanes, in contrast, had been obliged to continue regarding at least a certain kind of extension of World War II methods of tactical support for ground forces—air cover for amphibious assaults by the navy's own army, the Marine Corps—as a major mission. At least in the early phases of the fighting in Korea, consequently, the army as well as the marines preferred to receive tactical air support from the blue-painted carrier-based planes rather than from the silver wings of the air force.[5]

While the air force improved in its tactical proficiency as the Korean War dragged on, it also remained unable to restrain itself from shifting its activities toward as close an approximation of strategic bombing as the nature of the conflict permitted. This tendency involved it in a campaign to interdict the flow of enemy supplies southward through the Korean Peninsula, a largely unsuccessful effort because like most strategic bombing strategy, it proceeded from assumptions about the enemy's vulnerability to the delicate intricacies of the economic and communications networks of a modern industrial power such as World War II Germany. Transport systems that were primitive to begin with, and that could rely on human beings lugging A-frames as a transportation pool, proved comparatively impervious to interdiction by aerial bombing.[6]

Nevertheless, the Korean War experience did not change the focus of an air force whose legacy from World War II was a belief mainly in strategic and especially in nuclear war. The air force was not much better prepared to render support to ground forces in the next war, the struggle in Vietnam and the adjacent Indochinese states from the early 1960s until 1972. By the time the Vietnam War developed, however, the army had rebuilt a tactical-support air force of its own in the form of fleets of heavily gunned helicopters. These craft became the principal means of direct tactical assistance from the air as well as a new source of tactical mobility, speedily shifting troops through the skies above a terrain that was often painfully obstructive to movement on the ground.[7] Army aviation embodied in helicopters freed the air force during the Vietnam War largely for missions in the rear of such fighting fronts as existed—that is, for missions against the enemy's logistics that approached the strategic bombing role the air force preferred.

The way in which the previous history of the air service and particularly World War II had skewed the air force to favor strategic bombing over all other forms of aerial warfare was most dramatically displayed in Vietnam by the conspicuous reliance on the most "strategic" of all the available aircraft, the B-52, which had been designed primarily as an intercontinental carrier of nuclear weapons. Denied by policy the possibility of using such weapons in Vietnam, the B-52 could nevertheless drop huge loads of conventional bombs, and until the introduction of powerful Soviet surface-to-air missiles (SAM) late in the war, the B-52 operated at altitudes so high that it was almost immune to enemy defenses. As in the Korean War, however, strategic bombing suitable for crippling the industry and the transport system of a complex and therefore delicate modern economy such as America's enemies had possessed in World War II worked much less effectively against a relatively primitive economy.

In particular, the air force attempted to apply against North Vietnam one of the most salient conclusions about the World War II bomber offensive against Germany: that the most effective attacks were those aimed at the enemy's POL (petrol, oil, lubricants) industry. Against Germany, such attacks, by the spring of 1945, had so fully paralyzed the country that Germany would have been helpless to prolong the war much further even if no Soviet or Anglo-American soldier had set foot on German soil. By analogy, the air force diligently bombed North Vietnam's POL facilities, but with proportionately far less impact upon the transport system of an economy and a war machine much less dependent on the internal combustion engine than Germany's had been.

Late in the Vietnam War the aerial campaign against North Vietnam benefited from the introduction of "smart" bombs—precision-guided munitions (PGM) that could home in on their targets with the aid of miniaturized television cameras and radiation beams. But the use of PGMs to destroy some of the most important bridges in the North Vietnamese transportation net nevertheless failed to produce the crippling effect that was hoped.[8] One of the most technologically sophisticated methods of war, strategic aerial bombardment also demands technologically sophisticated targets if it is to achieve its fullest effect. For this reason the Europe-centered strategic convictions with which the air force, like the army, emerged from World War II proved much less than completely applicable to the strategic problems of the years following 1945.

The legacy of World War II to the navy and the Marine Corps necessarily lacked the Europe-centeredness of the army's and to an only slightly lesser degree the air force's inheritance. The Pacific war against Japan had been essentially the navy's war, and notwithstanding the navy's World War II experience of the difficulties of keeping open the sea-lanes to Europe in the face of hostile submarines, it was long after 1945 before the rise of Soviet naval power caused the navy to shift a due share of its strategic attention to the role it might play in deterring or countering the Soviet threat in Europe. The navy long remained preoccupied with carrier task-force operations in the far Pacific and adjoining waters, reminiscent of the war against Japan. In the wake of the atomic climax of the Pacific war, however, the navy also gave much of its post-1945 thought and energy to securing itself a major role in the delivery of strategic nuclear weapons.

To the latter end, the navy in the immediate post-1945 years cited the limited range of available land-based bomber aircraft to insist that a considerable proportion of the nation's atomic bomb capacity should be carrier-based, thus exploiting the aircraft carriers' capacity for global dispersion as a means of overcoming the range limitations of airplanes. Designing carrier-based airplanes big enough to fly the cumbersome atomic bombs of the early atomic age proved a perplexing but not insurmountable problem, while gaining executive and congressional support to finance aircraft carriers large enough to accommodate the airplanes comfortably was a collateral problem. The funding battles over "supercarriers" fought between the navy and the air force during the Truman administration arose from the navy's effort to assure itself a share of the apparently primary post-World War II mission of the armed forces: the deterrence and waging of strategic nuclear war.[9] Fortunately for the navy, an infinitely more assured share of that mission fell to it through technological progress, with the development in the 1950s and 1960s of nuclear-powered submarines and, more importantly, submarine-launched ballistic missiles carrying nuclear warheads.

The Pacific Ocean orientation of the navy and the Marine Corps provided better preparation for the wars in which the United States actually engaged in the post-1945 era than did the army's focus on Europe. For both the Korean and the Vietnam wars, the navy was ready to maintain control of the adjacent seas and to provide tactical support for the ground forces with both carrier-based aviation and ships' gunnery. We have already noted that carrier-based aviation, on the whole, was better trained for such tactical support than the air force. In both wars, Marine Corps troops were available for early deployment. On the less positive side, the Marine Corps' World War II legacy of focusing upon amphibious assault as the principal mission of the corps had less relevance not only to the actual needs of the Korean and Vietnam wars but also to any likely scenario in an era when beaches may well be defended by tactical nuclear weapons, and the feasibility of such assault because of that and other defensive improvements becomes increasingly doubtful.[10]

Having toured the horizon of the armed forces, however, a consideration of the impact of World War II upon American conventional military strategy must turn again to emphasize the army. It was upon the army that the main burden of the post-1945 wars in Korea and Vietnam fell. It is to the army that the task of deterring further conventional wars must primarily belong. It is the army that faces the most difficult puzzles of force structure and doctrine that must be solved if deterrence of further conventional wars is to succeed, or if upon the failure of deterrence such wars have to be waged. In the most likely as well as the most dangerous conventional war scenarios, the air force and the navy would play largely supporting roles to the army.

The Europe-centeredness of army thought, organization, and war preparations since 1945, with its corollary of equipment-heavy formations to do battle with the Soviet army, has been all the more readily the major theme shaping the U.S. Army because it accords with an image of warfare deeply ingrained in the army long before World War II but thoroughly confirmed by the experiences of that war. From the American Civil War onward through World War II, the United States was a nation so rich in resources mobilizable for war that its army was able to count on superior quantities, and often superior quality, of weapons and equipment with which to overwhelm its enemies. In all the wars of the United States from 1861 to 1945, the U.S. Army was also able to call on more than ample manpower, even if its advantages in numbers of men were not so consistently overwhelming as in economic resources.

In all the major American wars from 1861 to 1945, furthermore, the overwhelming material power of the United States appeared to offer the most expeditious means of securing the objects of the wars. In the American Civil War, the complete surrender of all Confederate states' pretensions to sovereignty sought by the United States seemed to be attainable only through the destruction of the Confederate armies. Because the Confederate military commanders and particularly General Robert E. Lee were too skillful to permit the destruction of their main armies by any means short of a campaign of attrition aimed at their ultimate annihilation, using the superior resources of the North to inflict casualties upon them—and indeed simply to trade casualties with them—until their destruction was almost complete, Lieutenant General Ulysses S. Grant as general in chief of the Union armies ended by waging such a campaign of attrition and carried it to success. Although Grant would have preferred to conduct a more subtle and less costly kind of war—he had shown himself a superb general of maneuver warfare and an economizer of casualties in his Vicksburg campaign of 1863—he subsequently became identified in American military history with a direct, straightforward strategy of crushing enemy armies under the weight of superior U.S. military resources.[11]

The circumstances of World War I by the time of American intervention offered little scope for any military strategy save a repetition of the attrition of Grant's Virginia campaign of 1864-65. The experience of combat on the Western Front in 1918 confirmed the U.S. Army's conviction that the direct application of the economic and manpower resources of the United States to overwhelm an enemy was the only practicable means to victory in modern war.[12] During World War II, with U.S. policy avowedly pursuing the unconditional surrender of the Axis powers, exploiting the superior resources of the United States and its allies to overwhelm the enemy with so complete a destruction of enemy strength that it would produce utter malleability in the face of American and Allied demands, seemed the only fitting strategy as much as it had in the closing years of the Civil War. Therefore, in the war's most notable expression of this American style of direct strategy, the United States continually advocated (against the reluctance of its British ally) a cross-Channel invasion as early as possible to assail German strength in the West where it was greatest, relying on American resources to outmatch even the enemy's main strength and, by bringing down that main strength, to cause the rapid collapse of all the enemy's outposts of power as well.[13]

The American army's preferred strategy of the direct application of superior resources to destroy any enemy's primary strength served it well from the Civil War through World War II, and accordingly this strategic conception emerged from World War II replete with continuing vitality to influence post-1945 strategy. Replete with vitality in the other services and in the nation at large as well as in the army, the preference for a direct strategy of overwhelming power contributed much to the prompt postwar preference for a strategy built upon the atomic bomb and for the persisting strategy of overpowering nuclear deterrence, as atomic and nuclear weapons became the most conspicuous embodiments of American power. In issues involving conventional weapons, however, the post-1945 period soon made it evident that a direct strategy of overwhelming power was no longer so appropriate as it had been in the past. For the army especially, this discovery ushered in a time of strategic puzzlement, and the puzzles are not yet resolved.

Two strategic puzzles are particularly noteworthy. First, the application of overwhelming power in post-1945 has been inappropriate even when possible. In the Korean and Vietnam wars, circumstances that were at least as much political as military prevented the application of an overwhelming margin of force that might have been available. In the Korean War the U.S. government was inclined to believe well into the war that the conflict on a distant Asian peninsula might be merely a communist feint to divert American strength from the European arena. This belief long restrained the armed forces from concentrating the bulk of their power in Korea. Even after the notion of a feint died, it still seemed important to utilize the wartime mobilization to bolster North Atlantic Treaty Organization forces in Europe. In addition, after the entry of the People's Republic of China into the war there was fear that too vigorous an application of power might further widen the conflict. And after truce negotiations began on 8 July 1951, the United States hoped, perhaps wrongly, that restraint might facilitate peacemaking.[14]

During the Vietnam War there were similar fears that too vigorous a prosecution of the war might widen it, particularly by again provoking China. The unconventional nature of much of the war also deprived the American army of obvious targets against which to hurl an overwhelming offensive; even operations on a relatively modest scale tended to be so difficult to conceal during their buildup that when they struck they hit thin air rather than the enemy. And the larger the scale of American military operations in Vietnam, the more they tended to yield the counterproductive effect of further destabilizing an economy and society whose stabilization was a major object of American involvement, while carrying the ground campaigns into North Vietnam was politically unacceptable.[15]

But the second puzzle confronting the American strategic tradition, and particularly the World War II legacy, of applying overwhelming power is a still more intractable one. Even if the United States were to engage in an all-out war against the Soviet Union with policy objectives comparable to the World War II aim of unconditional surrender, in conventional forces and weapons a power sufficient to overwhelm the enemy is no longer available. In atomic and thermonuclear weaponry, the United States managed to retain overwhelming superiority well into the 1960s, which is a major reason why strategic nuclear war so much preoccupied American military thought in the early post-1945 years; in such a war traditional American strategic conceptions might still have applied. In conventional war, however, from the earliest acknowledgment of the Soviet Union as the most important and a very likely potential adversary, American strategic planners had to grapple with the prospect that to overcome the Soviets as the Germans and the Japanese had been overcome in World War II (by means of the superior weight of American and Allied manpower and especially by means of the might of U.S. economic resources) was a solution manifestly not in the cards. Given the persisting uncertainties about the attitudes and commitment of America's post-1945 allies on the one hand and the resources of the Soviet Union on the other, in a war against the Soviets fought with conventional weapons the United States would probably find itself not the superior but the inferior belligerent in quantities of both manpower and material. And the performance of some Soviet weaponry (tanks, for example) in World War II also indicated that no American qualitative superiority to offset quantitative inferiority could be assured.

In the face of Soviet quantitative superiority, American strategic planners in the immediate post-1945 years found their strategic conceptions so lacking in suggestions for making do in spite of inferior conventional strength that they contemplated the early loss of nearly all the outlying military positions of the United States under any major Soviet attack, including Western Europe and probably Great Britain. In early post-1945 contingency planning, the issue was perceived not as how to hold American overseas bases but how to evacuate American personnel with minimum losses. In the early postwar Pincher series of war plans, successive refinements of the planning only emphasized the difficulties of extricating overseas contingents and the necessity to rely on atomic weapons as the only military resource in which the United States could with assurance place its trust.[16]

After the Korean War made possible a partial remobilization of conventional forces, this renewed conventional strength, along with the creation of the North Atlantic Treaty Organization alliance, inspired a measure of new hope that Great Britain and Western Europe at least might be held against a Soviet onslaught, perhaps even with conventional rather than nuclear weapons. Simultaneously, however, smaller, so-called tactical nuclear weapons made their appearance, and ever since that juncture in the early 1950s, periods of hope for a viable defense of Western Europe with conventional weapons have alternated with periods of gloomy resignation to a nuclear defense as expectations for increases in conventional strength have repeatedly found only partial fulfillment. The hopes for a viable conventional defense also have suffered from their repeated collisions with the lingering assumption of American strategists that a successful conventional defense would require the superiority in resources to which the U.S. Army became accustomed before and during World War II. The habit of thinking in terms of superior resources has made it exceedingly difficult for American strategic planners to envisage successful conventional war in the absence of such superiority.

Efforts to find strategic and related operational and tactical methods that might compensate for inferiority of resources in conventional war inevitably lay in the background of all the relevant doctrinal publications and thinking of the U.S. Army from the beginning of its early 1950s' hopes of defending Western Europe rather than merely evacuating Americans in the face of a Soviet invasion. The issue of inferior resources was most explicitly faced, however, at a relatively late date, in the 1 July 1976 edition of the army's basic field manual, FM 100-5, *Operations*. This edition of the manual embodied a major effort to rethink army strategy and doctrine to bring them into accord with the realities of the late-twentieth-century world.

The new version of the field manual stated at the outset that "we must assume the enemy we face will possess weapons generally as effective as our own. And we must calculate that they will have them in greater numbers than we will be able to deploy, at least in the opening stages of a conflict."[17]

While recalling that the United States was accustomed to winning its wars by mobilizing superior forces after the declaration of hostilities, the new manual pointed out that a future war might be decided in the first battle, with no time for American mobilization, thus further undercutting the strategic tradition of World War II. Furthermore, "our Army must expect to fight its battles at the end of a long, expensive, vulnerable, line of communications."[18] The army must therefore expect to fight in conditions of austerity. *"The US Army must prepare its units to fight outnumbered, and to win."*[19]

The bulk of the 1976 version of FM 100-5 failed, however, to follow through with a realistic application of these assertions. As this author reads it, the main text of the manual persistently falls back on the assumption that somehow, in some way, American forces gripped in general battle with the Soviets will contrive to find available the amplitude of resources to which U.S. forces had become addicted since the Civil War. If the resources did not grow to be superior, at least they would be amply sufficient.

To the latter end, the manual counts heavily on the inherent advantages of the defense in contests in which the United States would presumably be fighting defensively. It urges commanders in defensive battle to make skillful use of concentration of resources at the decisive points, but this means mustering sufficient strength to prevent being overpowered by superior enemy strength at the places that count most. "As a rule of thumb," the manual states, *"they* [the American generals] *should seek not to be outweighed more than 3:1 in terms of combat power."*[20] To concentrate at the decisive points admittedly implied accepting risks elsewhere.[21] But would a superior enemy permit this sort of concentration in certain sectors of the front without taking advantage of the weakening of other sectors to break through there, if at perhaps less sensitive places still with enough strength to make the ruptures disastrous? During the Civil War President Abraham Lincoln had consistently recognized that if the superior Union forces took the offensive almost simultaneously along the entire periphery of the confederacy, then the weaker Confederate forces could not defend effectively everywhere, and their periphery would begin to cave in.[22] When Lincoln found in Grant a general in chief who accepted the same principle and applied it, the predicted defensive crumbling occurred. Would not a Soviet high command accustomed to broad-front offensives during World War II recognize and apply the same principle that the militarily unschooled Lincoln had perceived, thus rendering the risks of concentration prohibitively high?

The reader of the 1976 FM 100-5 suspects that at bottom the manual's writers feared that the Soviet command would do so, for those writers proceeded to demand at least qualitative superiority if they could not expect a quantitative advantage, in spite of their own initial observation that the Americans had to expect to face enemy weapons generally as effective as their own. "Obviously, an outnumbered force must be more effective man-for-man, weapon-for-weapon, and unit-for-unit than the opposition," they assert.[23] But such qualitative superiority could hardly be much better assured than the old quantitative superiority. In terms of man-for-man and unit-for-unit effectiveness, the Soviet and Warsaw Pact forces have found it easier for political and social reasons to maintain individual and unit readiness through tough, realistic training in peacetime than have the American and NATO forces. As for weaponry, Soviet equipment, already often comparable in quality to American during World War II, remained at least as formidable as it had been then, if not always matching American technological sophistication then nevertheless compensating in durability and ease of use.

The nearest approach to realistic appraisals of American versus Soviet power to be found in the 1976 FM 100-5 concern defensive war, flawed though even those perceptions are. Yet the U.S. Army had consistently taught its officers that wars are won not on the defensive but on the offensive, that to prevent an aggressor enemy from gaining substantial advantages he must be punished by counteroffensives, that merely to halt him defensively might still leave him in possession of prizes that the United States could not afford to lose. But how, according to their own terms of reference, could the writers of the manual envisage a successful American counteroffensive? "The General," they say, "uses the available resources . . . to strive for a combat power ratio of at least 1 to 3 in the defense, or 6 to 1 in the offense."[24] Yet they offer no persuasive suggestion for the means of attaining the latter advantageous margin over the Soviets.

Thus its initial realism notwithstanding, the 1976 FM 100-5 ultimately calls for the kinds of ratios of strength to which past wars and particularly World War II had accustomed the American military. The World War II legacy had not been shaken off, but it no longer permitted the American military to plan with cogency.

The deficiencies of the 1976 version of FM 100-5 became obvious enough soon enough that the army felt obliged to prepare yet another new version at an early juncture, dated 20 August 1982. The writers of this edition clearly made a more earnest and self-conscious effort than their predecessors to acknowledge the unlikelihood that a major war against the Soviets could be fought as the United States had fought World War II and to contemplate with consistency the problems of fighting with inferior resources quantitatively and no certainty of qualitative superiority.

The recourse of the 1982 FM 100-5 lies in attempted application of an interest in maneuver warfare that had sprung up among a circle of American military men and military critics as they tried to confront the implications of losing assured quantitative and qualitative superiority. The new manual sought to make skillfully executed maneuvers a substitute for superior weight of resources. It continued the preceding version's interest in the virtues of concentration of resources but pushed much further the call for the mobility that would make rapid redistribution and concentration of force possible. Mobility was now to permit not only concentration at decisive points but also maneuvers so swift and skillful that they might turn the very weight of the enemy's strength to his disadvantage, as an able practitioner of the Oriental martial arts does against a clumsy opponent.

More specifically, the manual sought a renewed integration of ground forces with revitalized tactical air power that would make battle an "AirLand Battle."[25] The AirLand Battle would be a deep battle, a battle ranging over an exceedingly extensive area, waged against the enemy's rear echelons and rear areas as well as his cutting edge:

> By extending the battlefield and integrating conventional, nuclear, chemical, and electronic means, forces can exploit enemy vulnerabilities anywhere. The battle extends from the point of close combat to the forces approaching from deep in the enemy rear. Fighting this way, the US Army can quickly begin offensive action by air and land forces to conclude the battle on its terms.[26]

Thus the new version of FM 100-5 sought also to escape the 1976 preoccupation with the defense and to restore the offensive capabilities that had customarily seemed essential to military victory. The deep AirLand Battle was to be a battle of maneuver in which the ground forces would exploit mobility to find their way into the enemy's rear lines and join the air forces in wreaking havoc with its lines of communications, supply depots, and centers of command and control, all more vulnerable than its hardened front lines. The disruption of the enemy's sensitive logistical and communications systems in its rear lines would destroy its military power as surely as would the breaking of its frontal assaults in a more direct and costly confrontation, yet the logistical and communications systems would be much easier to disrupt if they could be reached. Maneuver war would reach them and would permit the American army to win despite the loss of superior material power. The concept of maneuver war would at last free the American army from the habits of thought inherited from World War II and earlier wars but now outmoded.

No doubt the emphasis on maneuver war has been a healthy corrective to certain stultifying aspects of the military legacy of World War II in America. Unfortunately, however, the fashionable ideas about maneuver war are by no means new—in large part they echo the familiar precepts of the British military critic Sir Basil Liddell Hart[27]—and in fact the ideas have often been tested in war and demonstrated to be more seductive than applicable. Reaching the enemy's sensitive rear lines is a notion of readily apparent persuasiveness but one that military history suggests is not so easy to realize in practice.

After all, the historic American reliance on superior weight of resources had not been simply an expression of the availability of the resources. It was a pragmatic response to recalcitrant problems of modern war. General Grant did not resort to overwhelming the Confederate armies with superior force because he was too unimaginative a general to employ maneuver war, although before 1864 he was a conspicuously successful practitioner of maneuvering his way into the enemy's sensitive rear lines and rendering its position untenable. Resorting to battles of attrition that relied on superior numbers to wear down and ultimately to destroy the enemy was only Grant's second-best solution, but the one upon which he had to fall back because Lee proved too skillful an opponent to be outmaneuvered into allowing union forces to rampage in his rear lines.

While Lee's skills were no doubt exceptional, most modern military commanders reasonably well schooled in their profession have similarly proved able enough to prevent enemy armies from running free in their vulnerable rear lines. It is much easier to contemplate the damage that one might inflict upon those areas than to get there.

The larger relevant truth, moreover, is that in the Civil War and both world wars the United States and then its allies also resorted to the warfare of overwhelming force rather than of subtle maneuver because modern great powers guarded by massive armed forces of their own, and possessing their own deep reserves of economic strength drawn from land masses continental in extent, are altogether unlikely to be defeated in war by maneuver unaccompanied by at least a strength virtually matching theirs, however much subtle maneuver may temporarily disrupt their sensitive communication. They are unlikely to accept defeat until their armed forces are substantially destroyed, and attaining that result requires not only skillful maneuver but also sustained combat in which superior resources, if they are not indispensable, are most certainly invaluable. Behind current ideas of maneuver warfare as behind the older ideas of Liddell Hart (conditioned as the latter ideas were by the decline of British military resources) lies the notion that there must be some relatively inexpensive way for the relatively impoverished power to win wars. The experience of World War II, however, rightly suggests that there is not. In that sense the military legacy of World War II should not be, indeed cannot be, rejected.

In that sense, then, the post-World War II military problems of confronting the Soviet Union remained intractable. There is no readily apparent escape from the military dilemmas posed by the loss of superior resources. Perhaps in time new military developments, or perhaps new technologies such as further development of precision-guided munitions, may ease the dilemmas. But the escape is not apparent yet.

If the prospects of a World War III centered in Europe and developing on the model of the European campaigns of World War II writ large remain at best doubtful for the United States and its allies, with the issue all too likely to turn, like that of World War II, on superior resources, it is some consolation that for a complex of reasons both political and military such a war is among the least likely to occur. This observation suggests, however, that another part of the American inheritance from World War II might in fact be escaped: the Europe-centeredness of the American army. World War II fixed the army's focus on Europe, and the focus has scarcely wavered despite two major post-1945 American wars and innumerable rumors of war elsewhere, and despite the much higher continuing prospects of military involvement outside Europe. World War II made the American army essentially a European army. Breaking free from that part of the impact of the great war of 1939-45 is long overdue. And outside Europe, away form the prospect of direct military confrontation between the superpowers, there might actually exist an arena suitable for applying the 1982 FM 100-5's concepts of maneuver to war.

POSTSCRIPT 1992

World War II in Europe writ large—the new Great War for which the U.S. Army planned so long under the influence of the 1939-45 war—has never occurred. With the demise of the Soviet Union during 1991, that war almost certainly will never occur. Instead, the same momentous year that ended with the resignation on 25 December of Mikhail Sergeievich Gorbachev as presumably the last Soviet president had begun with the United States fighting an apparently very different kind of war in the Middle East. In the Gulf conflict, the United States triumphed in short order with a skillful flanking maneuver that might be interpreted to mean the American armed forces had escaped their historic fixation on a strategy of direct confrontation supported by overwhelming power. Yet in spite of that climactic maneuver, the war against Iraq was in truth the kind of war the U.S. military could best fight in keeping with its strategic inheritance from World War II. The Gulf War permitted the deployment of the armor- and technology-heavy divisions and the kindred aerial squadrons and warships designed for a conflict against the Soviet Union without the perplexing problem of an enemy who could match or exceed American quality and quantity.

When Operation Desert Shield of 6 August 1990 to 16 January 1991, preventing Iraq from advancing beyond its 2 August conquest of Kuwait, gave way on 16 January to Operation Desert Storm, there followed until 24 February an exercise in the overwhelming of an enemy by sheer superior force that was as unalloyed as is ever likely to occur. With no effective resistance in the sky and little from antiaircraft artillery on the ground, the U.S. Air Force, with allied assistance, pummeled not only Iraqi military targets but also the Iraqi power, communications, and transport infrastructure into a wreckage utterly incapable of supporting modern warfare. With the way thus prepared, on 24 February the U.S. Army Central Command unleashed against the battered Iraqi army over 300,000 American and allied troops with 12,000 tracked combat vehicles and over 100,000 wheeled vehicles. The abrupt termination of the ground war just four days later, with Iraqi acquiescence in a temporary cease-fire that became permanent on 3 March, indicates how little capacity to resist Iraq retained after forty days of the aerial bombardment that preceded the ground campaign. The Iraqi army may still have deployed a half million men on 24 February—although an estimate of 300,000 may be more realistic—and 7,000 tanks, but the tanks had been largely immobilized by digging them into the sand as virtual pillboxes. Supplies could no longer reach the soldiers, and morale was near zero. Superior power had simply overwhelmed the Iraqi enemy in the classic American tradition.

It is true, on the other hand, that the superbly planned and executed enveloping maneuver around the enemy's right flank and into its rear lines, accompanied by equally admirable deception and secondary attacks that diverted his attention from the main blow until too late, suggests that the American armed forces and particularly the army had profited after all from their post-1945 wrestle with the dilemma of how to apply a strategic tradition of reliance on overwhelming power against a Soviet enemy whose power had seemed too great to be overwhelmed. The Americans had learned something about maneuver warfare. Desert Storm's climactic left hook will stand as a textbook example of the successful employment of maneuver. Still, this theme should not be pressed too far. The Desert Storm victory remains the application of irresistibly superior power.

The enveloping maneuver would not have been likely to succeed so well against an enemy less far down the road to ruin and with his wits less dulled before the maneuver began. Beyond the pounding that the Iraqi army had already suffered in the aerial phase of Desert Storm, especially in its logistics and communications, the Iraqis must have been close to the limit of their ability to absorb punishment even when they began their invasion of Kuwait. Too many Iraqi soldiers had already endured too much warfare during the long war with Iran from 1980 to mid-1988. Through most of that eight year period, the Iraqis suffered the demoralizing effects of continual defeat, even though they finally gained a stalemate with a brief series of winning battles in the final months. When the Iranian war ended, however, the soldiers who had expected to go home mostly found themselves held in uniform because the Iraqi economy offered no jobs for them after the strains of the war. For the internal stability of Iraq, it was better to retain men in the army than to consign them to mass unemployment. Nevertheless, that decision, following upon nearly a decade of war, meant that Iraq entered the Persian Gulf conflict with an army already on the thin edge of exhaustion and disintegration.

So the circumstances of Desert Shield/Desert Storm were fortunate for the United States in a variety of ways, and it would be dangerous to count on a repetition of such good fortune in any future conflicts. The whole pattern of modern warfare suggests that prolonged and indecisive wars are the rule and that short conflicts such as the Gulf War are the aberrations. With the decline of ideological warfare as a corollary of the death of the Soviet Union, wars in the foreseeable future are likely to be wars of nationalism, and opponents inspired by nationalism tend to be especially patient and resolute, particularly if one has to confront them without the good luck of a nine-year Iran-Iraq War in their immediate past. Rarely will even the geography of conflict serve the United States so well as in the Gulf, where unchallenged sea power so much facilitated the logistics of deployment, and the open desert—so different from the arena of the Vietnam War—so exposed the targets of the devastating aerial offensive.

Nor, with the military cutbacks following the close of both the Cold War and the Gulf War, are the American armed forces likely ever again in the foreseeable future to enjoy the wealth of material resources available to them in Desert Shield/Desert Storm with which to continue the World War II tradition of exerting overwhelming power. More than ever, the key to successful future military operations must lie in lean, agile, easily maneuvered, lightly supported forces. Less than ever should a military be bound by a World War II legacy of dependence on sheer weight of resources. The Gulf War does not assure us that the American military transition from World War II to less massive varieties of warfare has gone much beyond a beginning.

NOTES

1. Headquarters Department of the Army, FM 100-5, *Operations* (Washington, D.C., 1 July 1976), p. 1-2 states categorically that "the US Army is structured primarily for that contingency," that is, "Battle in central Europe against forces of the Warsaw Pact." FM 100-5, *Operations* (Washington, D.C., 20 August 1982) takes greater cognizance of a possible variety of missions, envisaging combat in either of two environments, a sophisticated battle field primarily in Europe or an unsophisticated battlefield primarily in Southwest or Northeast Asia (p. 1-1).

2. On the injuries to the army's ability to deal effectively with North American Indians caused by its historic European orientation, see especially Robert M. Utley, "The Contribution of the Frontier to the American Military Tradition," in James P. Tate, ed., *The American Military on the Frontier: The Proceedings of the 7th Military History Symposium, United States Air Force Academy, 30 September-1 October 1976* (Washington, D.C., 1978), pp. 3-13. Also published as Robert M. Utley, *The Contribution of the Frontier to the American Military Tradition: The Harmon Memorial Lectures in Military History, Number Nineteen* (Colorado Springs, CO, 1977).

3. Wrapper endorsement (forwarding of Report of American Expeditionary Forces Superior Board on Organization and Tactics) to Secretary of War Newton D. Baker, 16 June 1920, esp. pp. 1-3, Record Group 120, Records of the American Expeditionary Forces, 1917-1923, National Archives, Washington, D.C.

4. The most judicious discussion of the successes as well as the limitations of American strategic bombing in World War II is Bernard Brodie, the RAND Corporation, *Strategy in the Missile Age* (Princeton, NJ, 1959), chap. 4, "Strategic Bombing in World War II," pp. 107-44. For a recent highly critical assessment, see Ronald Schaffer, *Wings of Judgment: American Bombing in World War II* (New York, 1985).

5. On the latter point see Malcolm W. Cagle and Frank A. Manson, *The Sea War In Korea* (Annapolis, MD, 1957), pp. 49-67. See also Robert Frank Futrell, *The United States Air Force in Korea, 1950-1953*, rev. ed. (Washington, D.C., 1983).

6. See Futrell, *The United States Air Force in Korea*, chap. 6, "The Strategic Bombing Campaign," pp. 183-98; chap. 10, "Target Logistics," pp. 313-40; chap. 14, "Ten Months of Comprehensive Railway Interdiction," pp. 433-74; chap. 15, "Toward an Air-Pressure Strategy," pp. 475-504; and chap. 20, "Air Mission Accomplished," pp. 689-711. But for a succinctly stated

critical view, see David Rees, *Korea: The Limited War* (New York, 1964), pp. 374-83.
7. John J. Tolson, *Airmobility, 1961-1971* (Washington, D.C., 1973); John J. Hay, Jr., *Tactical and Material Innovations* (Washington, D.C., 1974); Ray L. Bowers, *Tactical Airlift (The United States Air Force in Southeast Asia)* (Washington, D.C., 1983). For the background on the development of post-World War II army aviation, see Frederick A. Bergerson, *The Army Gets an Air Force: Tactics of Insurgent Bureaucratic Politics* (Baltimore, 1980).
8. For the bombing of North Vietnamese POL resources, see David Halberstam, *The Best and the Brightest* (New York, 1972), pp. 630-31. For the attacks against Germany's POL, see Brodie, *Strategy in the Missile Age*, pp. 110-13, 119; and Walt W. Rostow, *Pre-Invasion Bombing Strategy: General Eisenhower's Decision of March 25, 1944* (Austin, TX, 1981). A succinct introduction to the use of precision-guided munitions in Vietnam can be found in Drew Middleton, *Crossroads of Modern Warfare* (Garden City, NY, 1983), pp. 255, 260-65.
9. One of the best introductions to the defense funding battles of the Truman administration and of the strategic issues behind them remains Samuel P. Huntington, *The Common Defense: Strategic Programs in National Politics* (New York, 1961), pp. 39-47. For a much more detailed account, see Richard F. Haynes, *The Awesome Power: Harry S. Truman As Commander in Chief* (Baton Rouge, 1973), and particularly pp. 124-27 for the battle over the supercarriers. For the World War II background, see Michael S. Sherry, *Preparing for the Next War: American Plans for Postwar Defense, 1941-45* (New Haven, 1977).
10. The first critical history of the Marine Corps is especially good on post-World War II issues: Allan R. Millett, *Semper Fidelis: The History of the United States Marine Corps* (Louis Morton, gen. ed., *The Macmillan Wars of the United States*, New York, 1980), Part Four, "Force in Readiness, 1945-1970s," pp. 445-626.
11. On the influence of Grant on American strategic thought after the Civil War, see Russell F. Weigley, "To the Crossing of the Rhine: American Strategic Thought to World War II," *Armed Forces and Society: An Interdisciplinary Journal* 5 (Winter 1979): 302-20. But that essay places too much emphasis on the Grant most often emphasized by later strategists and not enough on the Grant of maneuver strategy, who would have preferred to capture Lee's army; see Ulysses S. Grant, *Personal Memoirs of U.S. Grant*.
12. Weigley, "To the Crossing of the Rhine," pp. 306-14.
13. This interpretation of American strategy dominates the highly detailed accounts in Maurice Matloff and Edwin M. Snell, *Strategic Planning for Coalition Warfare, 1941-1942* (*United States Army in World War II: The War Department*, Washington, D.C., 1953) and Maurice Matloff, *Strategic Planning for Coalition Warfare, 1943-1944* (*United States Army in World War II: The War Department*, Washington, D.C., 1959). For interpretations minimizing the differences between American and British strategy in World

War II, see Richard M. Leighton, "OVERLORD Revisited: An Interpretation of American Strategy in the European War," *The American Historical Review* 68 (July 1963): 919-937, and Kent Roberts Greenfield, *American Strategy in World War II: A Reconsideration* (Baltimore, 1963), II, "American and British Strategy: How Much Did They Differ?" pp. 24-48.

14. For the idea that the North Korean attack was a communist feint, see Joseph Lawton Collins, *War in Peacetime: The History and Lessons of Korea* (Boston, 1969), esp. pp. 78-81 (General Collins was Chief of Staff of the Army during the Truman administration's conduct of the Korean War). On fears after the entry of China, see Collins, especially pp. 248-51, 189-293, and Walter G. Hermes, *Truce Tent and Fighting Front (United States Army in the Korean War)* (Washington, D.C., 1966), pp. 13-14. On the truce negotiations see Hermes, esp. p. 73.

15. The best accounts of the military operations and quandaries of the Vietnam War are Dave Richard Palmer, *Summons of the Trumpet: U.S.-Vietnam in Perspective* (San Rafael, CA, 1978) and Shelby L. Stanton, *The Rise and Fall of an American Army: U.S. Ground Forces, 1965-1973* (Novato, CA, 1985). For the larger political, economic, and other issues, see George C. Herring, *America's Longest War: The United States and Vietnam, 1950-1975* (Robert A. Divine, ed., *America in Crisis: A Series of Books on American Diplomatic History*, 2d ed. (New York, 1986).

16. For discussion and representative documents of early post-1945 contingency planning, see Thomas H. Etzold and John Lewis Gaddis, eds., *Containment: Documents on American Policy and Strategy, 1945-1950* (New York, 1978), pp. 30-48, and chap. 6, "Implementation: Military Planning, 1947-50," pp. 277-381. For more detail, David Alan Rosenberg, "Planning for a Pincher War: Policy Objectives and Military Strategy in American Planning for War with the Soviet Union, 1945-1948," paper prepared for the session "Cold War Origins: Another View," fourth national meeting of the Society for Historians of American Foreign Relations, 4 August 1978.

17. FM 100-5, *Operations* (1 July 1976), p. 1-1.

18. Ibid., p. 1-2.

19. Ibid.

20. Ibid., p. 5-3.

21. Ibid.

22. For Lincoln's strategy, see Thomas Harry Williams, *Lincoln and His Generals* (New York, 1952), esp. pp. 305-08.

23. FM 100-5, *Operations* (1 July 1976), p. 12-1.

24. Ibid., p. 12-2.

25. FM 100-5, *Operations* (20 August 1982), p. 1-5.

26. Ibid. The foregoing analysis does not need to be modified in light of a new edition of the basic field manual that appeared after the preparation of this paper; FM 100-5, *Operations* (Washington, D.C., 5 May 1986). This latest edition displays the same difficulties as its predecessors—it seeks to over-

come operational difficulties particularly by prescribing seizing the initiative: "Initiative means setting or changing the terms of battle by action. It implies an offensive spirit in the conduct of all operations" (p. 15).

27. For Liddell Hart's thinking, see especially B. H. Liddell Hart, *Strategy* (2d rev. ed., New York, 1967). For an introduction to recent thinking about maneuver warfare beyond the official manual cited, see Charles W. Specht, "Is There *Really* a Better Way to Win a War in Europe?" *Air University Review* 31, no. 1 (November-December 1979): 74-77, with "A Response" by William S. Lind, pp. 77-79, by Russell F. Weigley, pp. 79-80, and by Lieutenant General Raymond B. Furlong, USAF (Ret), pp. 80-81.

6

America and Wartime Changes in Intelligence

Bradley F. Smith

World War II cut a wide swath through the center of the twentieth century, destroying property, killing millions of people, and reshaping institutions and attitudes in every corner of the world. Although the intensity and scope of the war's impact varied greatly from country to country, laying waste some nations including China, the USSR, and Poland while merely lapping gently against the shores of Latin America and sub-Saharan Africa, the whole globe was fundamentally affected by the second, and greater, world war.

In many ways the United States of America fell near the midpoint in the spectrum of the war's effects, for though not devastated like many Asian and European nations, American institutions, public values, and international activities were profoundly, if comparatively gently, transformed by World War II. The relative subtlety with which the war changed the government and way of life of the American people has made it difficult for historians, and the general public, to grasp the revolutionary importance of the years from 1941 to 1945 for the history of the United States.

The gossamer film of gentle wartime change has also contributed to the difficulty which Americans have had in recognizing the scale and importance of the transformation that the war brought to the most shadowy of businesses, the intelligence system of the United States. That in turn has made it hard for the American people to accept that those changes inevitably became a watershed in their political life. In addition to the inherently unobtrusive nature of intelligence activity, which is supposed to develop in ways other than the obvious, the traditional American dislike of secret intelligence and secret police systems has led people then and since to ignore or deny that this war inevitably moved their country into the ranks of the "normal" great powers who use such instruments as secret intelligence and covert operations to get what they want in international relations.

Not all the responsibility for the slow and reluctant manner in which Americans have faced up to the reality of the war's intelligence transformation can be attributed to traditionalism, or the mild way in which wartime change moved through the United States, however. In fact, the war's innovations in intelligence systems were both uneven in their impact and relatively slow in developing, not only the in American system, but in that of all belligerents. While conceding the innovative wonders of Magic and Ultra, as well as acknowledging that many clever pieces of espionage equipment and secret radio devices were produced during the war, it is sobering to reflect on the fact that between 1940 and 1945, the total number of British Special Operations Executive (SOE), Special Intelligence Service (SIS), and Political Warfare Executive (PWE) agents parachuted into Europe by the Royal Air Force (RAF) did not equal 10 percent of the British carrier pigeons that were dropped there.[1] Furthermore, despite much talk in Britain early in the war about making subversive warfare into an important instrument with which to overthrow Nazism, even SIS and SOE took a long time to develop appropriate operational methods and effective means of placing agents into Europe. Between October 1940 and March 1942, SIS was only able to air lift a grand total of fifty-seven intelligence agents into Europe,[2] and as late as June 1943 the sum of RAF aircraft assigned to intelligence and subversive operations for the whole area of Europe, the Middle East, and the Mediterranean theater was a minuscule fifty-four.[3]

Many of the obstacles that slowed British intelligence and special operations efforts early in the war also delayed the Americans when they made similar attempts following the attack on Pearl Harbor. Along with technical problems, diplomats on both sides of the Atlantic were nervous about indiscreet intelligence activities or covert operations which might produce political problems. Most military leaders were also suspicious of subversive warfare and intelligence activities which clashed with what the generals and admirals saw as their code of honor. Even an Eastern six-bloc general, who had fought in western Europe during the war, recently confided to me during a French conference on the D Day invasion, "I am a professional soldier and therefore never cared much for this resistance business."

The doubts and reservations of governmental traditionalists often restricted the scope of subversive and intelligence operations. All governments were cautious about the intelligence activities which they carried out on neutral territory. Despite much subsequent published humbug, the British actually executed no significant clandestine operations against what they perceived as Axis activities in Latin America prior to the U.S. entry into the war. Even after Pearl Harbor, Washington put the Good Neighbor policy first and sharply restricted its own, as well as British, operations south of the Rio Grande.[4] In North America, too, the British were initially cautious; the first SOE training school in Canada did not actually begin to come into being until October 1941, on the eve of Pearl Harbor.[5]

The pressures of military conventionality also played a part in exacerbating the rivalries and struggles that existed within subversive warfare and secret intelligence organizations. In both Britain and the United States, the military nearly always favored intelligence collection above covert operations, since generals are somewhat disapproving of subversive activity.[6] As the British Chiefs of Staff put it in early 1943 during a controversy about commando operations, whenever "the proposed activities of S.O.E. and S.I.S. and minor raids clashed in any area, S.I.S. would ordinarily be given priority."[7]

When all these bureaucratic and professional rivalries were reinforced by the technical difficulties mentioned above (such as those of finding suitable means of delivery and communications), it is little wonder that the development of effective intelligence and covert operations was a slow and halting process. But even this was not the end of the general troubles, for within the Allied camp effective intelligence and covert operations not only depended on genuine Anglo-American cooperation—which was often difficult to secure—but also frequently required direct help from the numerous governments in exile and, on occasion, those of the USSR and China as well. The complexities of the boundless liaison which this entailed further slowed the march toward a modern subversive warfare and intelligence system.[8]

All these general obstacles stood in the way of an effective subversion and intelligence system for the Allies, one that could be applied with special force to the "shadow warfare" efforts of the United States. It is a truism that the American government was ludicrously unprepared to wage a total war in the late 1930s and that in no regard was it more backward than in the realm of intelligence and special operations. With the solitary, but vitally important, exception of the Magic system for deciphering some Japanese codes, the United States had nothing approximating a modern intelligence system. There was no secret intelligence service, no intelligence centralization or system of coordination existed, and only the haziest notion prevailed of the diverse ways vital information could be gathered and collated and subversive operations actually carried out. Despite what retrospectively appears to have been Britain's own intelligence weaknesses in the early war period, Admiralty officials were in liaison with the U.S. Navy and understood that the Office of Naval Intelligence (ONI) really did not have any intelligence centers outside the United States, and that if operational intelligence cooperation was going to occur it would have to take place at British bases, or at sea, on board the flagships of the various American naval commanders.[9]

This initial backwardness inevitably exerted great influence on the form and operation of the American wartime intelligence machinery. Despite the fact that a number of new agencies appeared that dealt with intelligence in one way or another, and that a series of restructurings occurred in the course of the war, none of the traditional intelligence-related agencies (U.S. Army Intelligence [G-2], ONI, U.S. Air Intelligence [A-2], FBI, and the State Department) was totally barred from the intelligence field. Full centralization of the intelligence effort therefore never came close to realization, and no effective system of pooling information was established during the wartime period.

Rough lines of jurisdiction were ultimately drawn. The FBI was confined to Latin America and the United States; the Committee on Intelligence-Office of Strategic Services (COI-OSS) had at least a theoretical monopoly on secret intelligence operations elsewhere in the world; air, naval, and army intelligence staffs were each supposed to cover their own beats. But numerous incidents of organizations poaching on each other's territories occurred and no American intelligence official ever came close to acquiring the prestige or exercising the influence that Brigadier Menzies ("C") enjoyed within the British government. Despite many liaison arrangements, such as the creation of a top secret intelligence "map room" in the White House and the formal establishment of a Joint Intelligence Committee ostensibly analogous to the British JIC, American wartime intelligence arrangements never took on the shape of a triangle with a distinct crowning point.

How little centralization was actually achieved in the United States during the war was graphically illustrated in September 1944 (just eight months prior to VE Day and eleven months before VJ Day), when London proposed sending its JIC to Washington to consult with the American JIC on coordinating intelligence for the final stage of the Far Eastern matters in individual talks between the United States and British directors *for each service*, since the Americans were not prepared for a combined three-service discussion on the matter. What was perceived as the essential intelligence function of each service and agency in the United States had basically remained its own business to such a degree that serious Anglo-American JIC to JIC coordination activity was not possible even in late 1944. Therefore, after the war, the central files of the American JIC were routinely destroyed by the Joint Chiefs of Staff (JCS) because it held—quite understandably in light of the wartime system—that the important JIC conclusions had been integrated into JCS papers, while the materials related to JIC deliberations had been retained by the representatives of each of the services and departments (Navy, War, Army Air Corps, and State), and had been filed, ignored, or destroyed as each individual service had thought appropriate.[10]

Given this local autonomy in intelligence matters in the United States, it has not been possible to produce an American series comparable to those written by British official historians, nor would it be desirable for such a series to be attempted, because that would suggest a unity and symmetry in American wartime intelligence which simply did not exist.[11] The American way actually consisted of separate authorities who pooled the fruits of their labors for specific purposes, especially the determination of strategic policy and the conduct of specific military operations. Therefore, to grasp where we now stand in our knowledge of U.S. intelligence in World War II it would seem that we primarily need to see how much of the history and achievement of the separate intelligence organizations has been investigated, how much we know about specific intelligence methods (decoding, photo reconnaissance, special operations), and whether or not significant conclusions have been drawn about the success, failure, and relative impact of the various organizations and intelligence methods on decision making and the waging of major campaigns.

The most casual consideration of these three topics—organizations, methods and impact—suggests that the history of U.S. intelligence in World War II is still in its infancy. Aside from the overriding fact that an enormous and unprecedented volume of intelligence information was produced by American wartime intelligence organizations, the history of only a few of them, especially OSS and to some degree ONI, have been studied in fair detail. But even here, the net for catching documentary sources has not been cast very wide, and the floodgates of declassification that are periodically opened and closed can quickly turn all the work which is currently in print (including my own) into rough approximations of what happened between 1941 and 1945. The situation in regard to G-2 and the JIC is worse, with little or nothing in print beyond in-house chronological surveys. Serious research into the intelligence work of the State Department, A-2, the Treasury, and the FBI is virtually nonexistent, nor have we done more than lift the corner on the wartime intelligence exchanges which the United States made with

Britain, the Allied governments in exile, the United Nations Relief and Rehabilitation Administration (UNRRA), Nationalist China, and Russia.[12]

In the realm of specific intelligence techniques there has been rather more systematic research, and some aspects have been quite clearly delineated. American covert operations of the SOE type have received much attention, although the study of black propaganda activities has not advanced very far and counterintelligence is still a virtual blank.[13] Both Ultra and Magic have been swamped with memoirs, and good beginnings have been made in examining high-level decoding methods, the allocation of special intelligence data, and the effects of such data on operations and planning decisions. American "Y" service intelligence, which mainly acquired information from the flow of enemy radio traffic, has not been so well served, nor has enough attention been given to the American team at Bletchley Park led by Telford Taylor, although this wartime U.S. cooperation with the British Ultra team surely had important effects on American decoding activities and capabilities. There are also great holes in our picture of the activities of American secret wartime agents—despite an even larger flood of memoirs—because of the nature of the subject as well as the screen of security regulations put up by all governments, offering few prospects of serious espionage studies emerging in this century.[14]

Two highly important World War II intelligence methods which could have been studied more effectively—prisoner-of-war (POW) interrogation and photo reconnaissance—have by and large not been well treated by historians. A recent bibliography of books on World War II published in English during the last decade contains no entries on POW interrogation and only one general book on photo reconnaissance covering all belligerent countries.[15] In addition, at least to my knowledge, little or no research has been done on the evaluative methods of American wartime intelligence organizations, or on considerations of what changes the war produced in the ways various organizations made sense out of the ever-increasing flood of information that they had available to them.

So much needs to be done, therefore, to explore what the various United States wartime intelligence organizations did, as well as the techniques that they employed to gather and evaluate data, that these areas may be considered nearly virgin research territory. But there is an even bigger deficiency in our knowledge regarding the effect and importance of the various organizations, and the varied kinds of intelligence they gathered, in shaping the significant wartime decisions of the United States government and its constituent departments. Fortunately, at least some aspects of the broad intelligence impact question are not as constrained by secrecy regulations as many other matters connected with the history of American wartime intelligence. The decimal filing systems used by the State Department and the American military often permit a researcher to follow a specific issue or campaign such as the Torch landings in North Africa or the Operation Husky invasion of Sicily backward from the JCS to the Operations Division of the War Department and then to G-2, as well as forward to the theater commander and then to various other operational commands. Ronald Spector's recent article "Allied Intelligence and Indochina 1943-1945" is a near perfect example of the light which a close study of local and theater military unit records can throw on broader questions of intelligence gathering and its impact.[16]

The threads of intelligence connection which extend up and down through American naval, and especially Army Air Corps, records offer equally inviting prospects. How promising these are is suggested by the parallel British records in which Admiralty, and especially RAF, documents frequently offer more comprehensive insights into intelligence policy, operations, and impact than do those of the War Office.[17] The British connection offers an additional rich source of information for judging the impact of intelligence on American decision making, for wherever Anglo-American joint commands existed, and especially where the theater commanders were British as was the case with Southeast Asia Command (SEAC) and Air Force Headquarters (AFHQ) Mediterranean during 1944-45, the bulk of the theater records are already available in one coherent group in the Public Record Office in Kew, England. Furthermore, under the postwar agreements made between Britain and the United States, when the records of such joint commands were deposited in one country, microfilm copies went to the other. Significant pieces have therefore inevitably fallen through the cracks of the screening process because two groups of declassifiers have worked on two different sets of the same records. Comparisons of the AFHQ originals at the Public Records Office (WO 204) with the microfilms at the National Archives repository at Suitland, Maryland (RG 331) show that the British omitted some materials from the microfilm project (notes reading "do not film for the Americans" are still clipped on some files), and more frequently than one might suppose, an item which is closed in London is open in Suitland, and vice versa.

Surely, delineating the intelligence components of many high-level wartime political policy decisions is much more difficult than doing the same thing for military operations, in part because of Franklin Roosevelt's nimbleness in avoiding written records detailing decision making, but also because of the indirect ways that intelligence data frequently moved in and out of the State Department and White House administrative machinery. But one can find cases in which specific items of intelligence do seem to have played significant roles in policy formulation. For example, a late 1944 OSS Research and Analysis Department study of the Soviet economy apparently did help to stiffen State Department resistance to the granting of a postwar American recovery loan to the Soviet Union. Therefore, if all researchers were sensitive to the importance of such incidents, sufficient data might gradually be built up to allow scholars to advance tentative hypotheses regarding the which, when, how, and why of the impact of intelligence on basic wartime policy making.[18]

Self-evidently, energetic research in the area of American wartime intelligence organizations, carried out with an eye to both methods and impact, would greatly extend our general knowledge of World War II and how, as well as to some degree why, many things happened the way that they did. But there would also be a further bonus provided by such research because of the light which it could throw on the general development of the postwar intelligence system of the United States. As things now stand, except for a few memoir references and two histories of the evolution of American wartime and postwar intelligence which are currently in print or in preparation (both written by Britons),[19] we have little except straight-ahead, chronological, administrative accounts of the creation of such organizations as the CIA. Yet a broader perspective of study is called for, because what seems to have happened between 1941 and 1950 was a two step development. A diverse and loosely coordinated intelligence system took shape during the war, and after much initial postwar tugging and pulling, it evolved into a permanent, better coordinated but hardly centralized postwar intelligence system pivoting on the CIA, the NSA, and a Department of Defense intelligence empire, a maze of subkingdoms and nearly independent satrapies.

Quite obviously, no matter how diligently one examines the course of the government committees which nominally created this postwar system, administrative history cannot possibly tell us how and why the postwar domestic and foreign political situation played an important part, as did the shifting views of President Truman and other leaders. But it also must be emphasized that by 1945 (for the first time in American history), thousands of people in Washington had extensive direct intelligence experience, and many thousands more had grown accustomed to making policy judgments on the basis of an extraordinarily rich harvest of intelligence data drawn from Magic, Ultra, foreign intelligence services, and dozens of other sources available during World War II. Surely neither the producers of intelligence nor those who had become its consumers were eager to abandon such large-scale harvesting operations, and in this sense the volume and form of World War II's intelligence operations directly shaped what happened in the postwar period.

Furthermore, the years between 1941 and 1945 changed many of the feelings and attitudes not only of the people directly involved with intelligence matters but also of the general population of the United States as well. A respected historical commentator recently asserted that a major cause of the undulations in American postwar intelligence policies was the perpetuation of Americans' traditional opposition to secret intelligence activities.[20] But from the first phase of the postwar period public opinion on national security was changing, and polls show clearly that the overwhelming majority of respondents favored creation of a worldwide American secret intelligence system. This strongly suggests that after 1945 many new winds were blowing in public as well as governmental attitudes toward intelligence.[21]

Yet even the expanded range of experience in intelligence activity, and the shift of the various opinions about the need for it that were produced in the United States between 1941 and 1945, may not have been the war's greatest long-run intelligence legacies to America. The war brought at least as great changes in the range of what could properly be comprised within the intelligence rubric, for it now contained covert activities and black propaganda. Furthermore, when intelligence activities were pushed into the heart of military and political processes, the lines between information and action became badly blurred, and the basis was laid for more serious ethical questions regarding intelligence activism.

The wartime changes in intelligence did far more to alter the moral climate that surrounded this activity than merely shelving Secretary of War Henry Stimson's doubts about the propriety of gentlemen raiding each other's mail. Once intelligence came to embrace large-scale covert or subversive operations, the nature of the great game fundamentally changed, especially because such operations were carried out in an environment where the basic rules were laid down by that most ruthless and immoral of systems, Hitlerian Germany. To wage covert warfare against Nazism took a very strong stomach; rough methods were required, and the civilian populations of Nazi-occupied Europe inevitably paid the highest price. Just how tough policymakers had to be when dealing with this matter emerged very clearly in a British Cabinet Defense Committee meeting in August 1943 when Prime Minister Winston Churchill pushed hard in support of strong measures to stimulate "resistance amongst the people of Europe." In his defense of this course Churchill showed that he had not the slightest doubt about the human and moral costs involved, for he declared flatly that he "recognized that acts of rebellion against the Germans frequently resulted in bloody reprisals, but 'the blood of the martyrs was the seed of the Church,' and the result of these incidents had been to make the Germans hated as no other race had ever been hated. There[fore] nothing must be done which would result in the falling off of this most valuable means of harassing the enemy."[22]

The point at issue is not whether such a hard line policy was indispensable, or on balance desirable, in the war against Hitler. What is relevant to a discussion of the impact of the war on American intelligence history is the undeniable fact that the execution of such policies involving enormous immediate suffering by "friendly" peoples had become for the first time an "intelligence" activity. It is safe to say that a decade earlier no intelligence official or cabinet minister in any western country would have believed for a minute that such things belonged within the pale of "intelligence" operations.

A further, less sensational but in the long run perhaps even more important bundle of emotional, political, and perhaps moral side effects of the extension of intelligence activity in World War II arose from the changes which Magic and Ultra brought in their train. The possession and development of these great secrets imposed an enormous burden of responsibility on those intelligence people who became the keepers of the flame, not only for the specific operations for which Ultra and Magic provided the vital intelligence data, but because the maintenance and care of the great secrets were, or seemed to be, the vital elements in achieving victory, protecting the nation, and saving civilization. Surely no group of intelligence people in earlier periods of history had been gripped so justifiably with the sense that they were really the most important people standing guard at the gates of the city.

Aside from exacting a great tool in psychological strain among those in the Bletchley (Ultra) and Magic teams, this sense of absolute indispensability basically changed and enhanced the importance attached to all intelligence activity in Britain and America. At the same time, since the maintenance of the great Ultra and Magic secrets was deemed more important than the success or failure of any particular military operation (except possibly Overlord), special intelligence officers continuously intervened in the actual conduct of operations as no intelligence personnel had ever done in the past. Examples of intervention on the battlefield abound in such works as Lewin's *Ultra Goes to War* and are even more prominent in the in-house studies made by the Admiralty and other British authorities soon after hostilities terminated. In North Africa, Ultra liaison officers even dictated how many Axis supply vessels might be sunk and how the sinkings were to be arranged in the great battles of 1942-43, because any misstep might alert the enemy, make him change his codes, and thus at least temporarily nullify the Ultra asset which was thought more important to the Anglo-American cause than any single operation success in that theater.[23]

This picture of Allied air and submarine crews not being allowed to fire at enemy craft that were in their sights—because intelligence men had decided that they shouldn't—may stand as an appropriate symbol of the degree to which World War II transformed the nature and significance of intelligence for America and the rest of the world. Such intelligence macrochanges were so obviously important, and micro-changes of the details of American wartime intelligence history are so inviting, that historians should rush forward during the next decade to fill in our share of what British historians Christopher Andrew and David Dilks have called the "missing dimension" in modern history. Surely, if we can secure a broad and deep understanding of the history of American intelligence in World War II, we will catch hold of many clues to that age, and perhaps to our own age as well.

NOTES

1. See reports in AIR 20/8450 and 8496 and then pursue the details through the files indicated in AIR 20, shelf 55, Public Record Office, Kew, Surrey, England (hereafter cited as PRO).
2. "Operations Carried Out by the R.A.F. on Behalf of S.I.S.,"14/42, AIR 8/1750, PRO.
3. "S.O.E. Requirements for Air Transport," AIR 8/1749, PRO.
4. J.P. (42) 570, 3 June 1942, "Axis Activities in Latin America," in AIR 20/7964, plus additional material and communication with the Joint Staff Mission Washington, WO 193/634, PRO.
5. Report of October 1941, WO 193/535A, PRO.
6. See Bradley F. Smith, *Shadow Warriors: OSS and the Origins of CIA* (London, 1983), chaps. 3 and 4. A delightful British example of the same attitude is the RAF Coastal Command's reaction to a proposed SOE operation in August 1942; AIR 15/494 (PRO).
7. Chiefs of Staff minutes (43) 3rd (0), 4 January 1943 in WO 193/535A, PRO.
8. *Shadow Warriors,* chaps. 3-7. A large number of items related to the British Mission 30 intelligence liaison with the USSR are now showing up in the PRO. See for example: AIR 46/23ff; WO 193/641ff; ADM 116/5719; ADM 1/16836.
9. Memorandum, "United States Naval Co-operation," 16 October 1940, CAB 122/159, PRO.
10. "Visit by the Directors of Intelligence," 28 September 1944, CAB 122/1417, PRO (author's emphasis). Information on the destruction of the

American JIC records came from a private communication by an American archivist.

11. F. H. Hinsley, Michael Howard, et al., *British Intelligence in the Second World War*, 5 vols. (Cambridge, 1979-90).

12. Dr. Sally Marks has a study of wartime State Department intelligence in preparation.

13. Not until the Barbie affair splashed into public attention was any serious regard given to the army's Counter Intelligence Corps, but there are mountains of this organization's records in the Federal Record Center, Suitland, Maryland.

14. A start has been made by Thomas Parrish, *The Ultra Americans: The U.S. Role in Breaking the Nazi Codes* (New York, 1985).

15. Arthur L. Funk, *The Second World War: A Select Bibliography* of Books in English Since 1975 (Claremont, CA, 1985).

16. Ronald Spector, "Allied Intelligence and Indochina, 1943-1945," *Pacific Historical Review* 41, no. 1 (February 1982), pp. 23-50.

17. On occasion, British records turn up gems on American intelligence history in unlikely places, just as Christopher Andrew has shown repeatedly that they do for British intelligence history; see his *Secret Service: The Making of the British Intelligence Community* (London, 1985). For example, although the record of Colonel William Donovan's June 1942 meeting with the British Chiefs of Staff Committee has been removed from the main series (CAB 79), a copy of it is nestled into WO 193/324, PRO.

18. Smith, *Shadow Warriors*, pp. 381-82.

19. The two Britons are Rhodri Jeffreys-Jones, *American Espionage: From Secret Service to CIA* (New York, 1977), and *The CIA and American Democracy* (New Haven, 1989); and John Ranelagh, *The Agency: Rise and Decline of the C.I.A.* (New York, 1987).

20. Walter Laqueur, at a British study group meeting in London during the autumn of 1985.

21. In a March 1946 poll question: "Should the United States have a secret agent network around the world?" 77 percent responded Yes; 6 percent had no opinion. *Public Opinion Quarterly* 10, no. 1 (Spring 1946). See also Bradley F. Smith, "An Idiosyncratic View of Where We Stand on the History of American Intelligence in the Early Post-World War II Era," *Intelligence and National Security* 3, no. 3 (October 1988).

22. "S.O.E. Requirements of Aircraft." D.O. (43) 7th Meeting, 2 August 1943. AIR 8/1749, PRO.

23. See especially Admiral G. E. Colpey's 379-page report, "Admiralty Use of Special Intelligence in Naval Operations," ADM 223/8, and Group Captain Humphry's 18-page report of October 1945 on the use of Ultra in the Mediterranean and North African theaters, AIR 40/2323, PRO.

7

Soviet Espionage and the Office of Strategic Services

Hayden B. Peake

For thirty-three centuries, wrote Richard Rowan in 1937, spies have "exerted more influence on history than on historians."[1] Today, the circumstances are qualitatively different. Some historians are careful to point out the role played by spies. Others, including those with espionage experience, have written about the history of intelligence itself. They, together with their journalist colleagues, have begun a process of critically assessing the contribution of intelligence to domestic and world affairs. Following this precedent this chapter looks at the origins, reality, and consequences of Soviet espionage against the Office of Strategic Services (OSS) during World War II.[2]

The perspective adopted is that of a counterintelligence (CI) analyst whose task is to develop, evaluate, and report details about suspected spies. Like a scholar, the analyst seeks to extract probable reality from a web of conflicting meanings and often fragmented relationships, while carefully separating fact and judgment, estimates and speculation. Finally, the evidence developed need only be sufficient for reasonable people to decide whether espionage has been committed and to justify appropriate countermeasures.[3]

EMERGENCE OF THE SOVIET INTELLIGENCE SERVICES

The security and intelligence organs of the Soviet Union, both military and political, were created shortly after the Bolsheviks took power in 1917. The political service, called the Cheka, was putatively an administrative organ with only an investigative function, but under its founder Felix Dzerzhinsky it rapidly evolved into an all-purpose political police whose primary objective was Communist party security.[4]

The Cheka got off to a fast start because Dzerzhinsky's men captured the files and co-opted the informants of its czarist predecessor, the Ochrana. Having thereby effectively penetrated many of the monarchist and émigré counterrevolutionary movements, the Cheka proceeded to eliminate them in a variety of deception operations that served as the embryo for the successful "front organizations" years later. The most effective operation of this kind, known as the Trust, lured leaders of European émigré groups into the Soviet Union to assist clandestine "anti-Bolshevik" organizations actually manned by the Cheka. Once there, they were imprisoned and often executed. The Trust provided a training ground for the espionage skills required for international operations encouraged by Lenin. By 1924, Dzerzhinsky had established "a network of information [and] intelligence agencies in all large centers of Europe and North America."[5]

The first contact with American espionage came early in the revolution when State Department secret agent Xenophon Kalamatiano was arrested with Sidney Reilly as part of the Lockhart, or "envoys," plot to overthrow the Bolsheviks.[6] Although Kalamatiano, a U.S. citizen of Greek-Russian birth, held an official "confidential" position in the State Department's Russian bureau, no effective action was taken on his behalf, even after he was sentenced to death in December 1918. Only his value in exchange for food saved him, and he was finally sent home in August 1921. The Kalamatiano case is indicative of Soviet espionage policy at the time; namely that the United States

> is weakest and . . . most vulnerable in . . . counterespionage because its intelligence officials are (a) unable effectively to exploit those who have deserted the Soviet services, and (b) incapable, unwilling, or fearful of acting on the basis of information acquired by their own agents. This mistrust . . . must be encouraged.[7]

Kalamatiano's own report of his experience was ignored by a State Department that had no intelligence element.

The Cheka was not the only Soviet intelligence organ operating internationally. By the late 1920s the GRU (chief directorate of intelligence of the general staff) had developed its own foreign espionage capability to collect military and scientific data. This task was not too difficult, said a former member, because "nobody took very seriously the efforts of the Soviet Union in the military sphere, and few countries went to great pains to hide secrets from it. Moreover, by then [the 1930s] Communists the world over were obsessed by the idea of helping Soviet intelligence." As will be seen the GRU played a major role in espionage operations in America.[8]

The final player in prewar Soviet foreign intelligence, the Communist International (Comintern), cooperated with both the OGPU (successor to the Cheka) and the GRU, executing its intelligence tasks in conjunction with local Communist parties. Although not primarily an intelligence organization, the Comintern was a source of highly motivated and dedicated recruits, couriers, agents, and agents of influence.[9]

By the late 1920s each of these Soviet espionage organs, led by the OGPU, was operating (without diplomatic immunity) in the United States often under cover of a legitimate Soviet business such as the Amtorg Trading Corporation of New York. In the early 1930s several cases of Amtorg espionage surfaced due to defectors and one because the agent was caught smuggling by customs. These were exceptions; most of the "Communist spies seem to have had little trouble eluding the counterintelligence agencies." When in 1934 the People's Commissariat for Internal Affairs (NKVD) succeeded the OGPU, it was the world's largest, most powerful, centralized, and formidable intelligence service.[10]

AMERICA'S RESPONSE TO PREWAR SOVIET ESPIONAGE

After World War I the United States, unlike the Soviet Union, dismantled or reduced its wartime intelligence organizations. Although some code breaking continued, it focused more on economic and diplomatic issues than on domestic subversion or espionage.[11] While military attaches and diplomats reported on the policies and activities of Soviet intelligence, stringent economies limited analysis, and in the late 1920s the State Department was "unable to evaluate and disseminate" the reports "in an appropriate manner" due to cutbacks in personnel.[12] Likewise, military and naval intelligence concerns about the Amtorg agents and the growing subversive problem went unheeded, a tight budget precluding effective response. The financial constraints were so tight that the army limited "collection of information by G-2 regarding the radical situation in the United States to that which appears in the public press."[13]

The espionage issue gained some Congressional attention during hearings in 1919 and the early 1920s, but its focus was on Bolshevik political subversion and propaganda and contributed to Justice Department raids (working with local authorities) on secret communist meetings between 1920 and 1924. Predictably they only drove the communists further underground, making detection more difficult without stopping their activities. The next congressional hearings (1930) followed a similar path.[14] This political problem was further complicated by the Great Depression. President Herbert Hoover attempted to deal with the subversion by denying diplomatic recognition. He noted later that "we were aware that the communists were carrying on underground organization [sic] and propaganda for the overthrow of our government by violence. But denial of recognition kept their potency from being serious."[15]

Espionage, on the other hand, was handled as a criminal matter and not viewed as a pervasive threat. Thus, for a variety of complex interlocking reasons, there was no coordinated CI program in the government to deal with Soviet espionage in the late 1920s and early 1930s. As David Dallin points out, "the large number of . . . espionage incidents which pointed to Amtorg, failed . . . to make a serious or lasting impression on public opinion in the United States. Incredulous and skeptical, the press and intellectual circles were inclined to overlook the organic ties between the various events."[16] It will, therefore, come as no surprise that when in 1933 the new president decided on diplomatic recognition of the Soviet Union, and two cases of Soviet espionage against the United States were almost simultaneously exposed, they had no effect on the negotiations.[17]

The Soviet Union, on the other hand, not wanting to risk disturbing the status quo during the initial period of formal relations, ordered the GRU and its Comintern surrogates to "lie low and freeze its spy apparatus for the time being. . . . The Soviet military intelligence agency in the United States became for a time [1933-34] a dormant apparat." In fact, so tight were the constraints that Whittaker Chambers was unable to pass on very sensitive documents acquired from his contacts in the U.S. government to his GRU control.[18]

No such limits, however, were placed on the political intelligence operations of NKVD, which expanded its efforts to penetrate the government itself.[19] It was during this period in the early to mid-1930s that NKVD officers such as Jacob Golos, J. Perers (NKVD liaison with the Comintern), and Max Bedacht, among others, recruited America's ideological spies such as Chambers, Alger Hiss, Harry Dexter White, Louis Budenz, and Elizabeth Bentley, plus the Silvermaster and Perlo networks.[20]

Although in 1934 Roosevelt ordered the Federal Bureau of Investigation and the Secret Service to "undertake a general investigation of fascist and Nazi groups," it was not until August 1936, and then in part because of naval intelligence warnings, that he "directed J. Edgar Hoover . . . to broaden the investigation to include Communist groups."[21] As a result the bureau expanded its efforts and at the request of the State Department, placed undercover FBI agents in U.S. embassies overseas, including Moscow.[22] What it did not do was develop any counterintelligence program for identifying spies within the government. Thus, unless a penetration agent made an error or was defected, detection was not likely. A good example is Chambers, who served the GRU by collecting confidential information from members of the government (including Hiss and White) from 1932 to 1938.

The pervasive high-level disinterest or disbelief in charges of communist espionage in the government is best illustrated by Chambers's attempts to reveal it. On 2 September 1939, he met with Assistant Secretary of State Adolf Berle, Roosevelt's international security adviser, at his home. He identified more than thirty communist agents and Soviet spies, including several State Department officers, such as Alger and Donald Hiss, and gave examples of military espionage. For reasons he never explained satisfactorily, Berle did not notify the State Department, the FBI, or the War Department, each of whom had its own CI interests. Apparently Berle did notify the president, but Roosevelt "scoffed at the charges of Soviet espionage rings within the government," notwithstanding that the Soviet Union was a German ally at the time. Despite further allegations that Chambers was a communist, the FBI took no further action until 1945.[23]

Berle, however, did not completely ignore the problem. On 10 July 1941, the day before the creation of America's first national intelligence entity, the Coordinator of Information (COI), and just after the Soviets became a Western ally, Berle wrote to FBI Director Hoover expressing his concerns about future Soviet behavior, "I think it useful at this point to crystallize the attitude of the department with regard to the activities which the FBI has been carrying on with respect to Russian agents with which may also be included the Communist agencies in the United States and in the Western Hemisphere." Noting Soviet "espionage and propaganda have completely changed direction," he warned that "the Russians will attempt to take advantage of this situation to establish their agents . . . in advantageous positions wherever possible." For these reasons, he continued, "the Department feels that it would be unwise to abandon surveillance over the activities of the Russian and Communist agencies in the United States and in the Western hemisphere; and it would be unwise to permit agents of these groups to establish themselves in strategic or influential positions."[24] Berle's accurate foresight is puzzling considering he had chosen not to act on Chambers's allegations which described the very situation about which he was warning the FBI.

In this atmosphere, it is easy to see how, by late 1941, the Soviet intelligence services could have penetrated most of the departments of the government, especially since communists in general and their agents in particular were encouraged to find positions with current or anticipated access to government data and secrets. They were expected to work hard and advance. Those already in government were required to help place new agents and to keep themselves in sensitive positions.[25] According to former NKVD agent Louis Budenz, by the summer of 1941, and especially the period after Pearl Harbor, "Communists planted themselves everywhere . . . in the publicity services of the armed forces, the Office of War Information (OWI), the Office of Strategic Services (OSS), the Board of Economic Warfare (BEW), and strengthened their channels into the State Department."[26]

These, then, were the operating conditions relating to CI when the president considered a recommendation from war hero, dynamic world traveler, and former Assistant Attorney General Colonel William J. Donovan to form a national level intelligence agency.

THE OFFICE OF STRATEGIC SERVICES

The organization that became OSS was formed at the president's request despite strong opposition from the military intelligence chiefs, Hoover at the FBI, and the State Department. Donovan was appointed COI on 11 July 1941, with a mission to provide America with a coordinated, if not truly centralized, strategic intelligence system.[27]

At the outset, executive authority was a long way from executive operations. Unlike Dzerzhinsky and the Cheka, Donovan started the COI with no experienced staff, line officers or agents, no files, and less than willing cooperation from other agencies. But one thing was clear from the start: hiring loyal personnel was "one of COI's prime concerns," and personnel security grew more thorough and sophisticated as the office expanded, although in the beginning personal recommendation by a staff member was sufficient for employment, a policy never entirely abandoned. After the attack on Pearl Harbor, the FBI was given the responsibility for security checks, but by 1942, just before COI had become OSS (13 June 1942), the burden was too great and an independent Office of Security was created. Specific attention was given to preventing "employment of persons of dubious allegiance or affiliated with anti-American elements." There were, in fact, rejections of personnel with Nazi sympathies and with "doubtful loyalty through past activities with the Communist Party . . . or possibly subversive organizations."[28]

By August 1942, as OSS expanded overseas operations, it had become clear that personnel security was only part of the problem; operational security against espionage was at least as important and OSS lacked a CI/CE (counterespionage) section. Until then the British had been supplying OSS this kind of intelligence from their sources, and they suggested that OSS establish a CE program to protect overseas operations. After several months of planning the CE Division, designated X-2, was officially formed on 1 March 1943, with headquarters in Washington, nearly two years after the creation of COI/OSS.[29]

It would seem, then, that after a slow start, for mostly understandable reasons, OSS took the necessary CI/CE security precautions to prevent penetration by foreign intelligence services. But by then more than twenty OSS officers and potential moles were already in place.

SOVIET ESPIONAGE AND THE OSS

Because space will not permit a discussion of each of the cases of Soviet penetration, several examples will be represented that reflect the methods of recruitment, the types of personnel involved, the kinds of the material acquired, and the nature of the operations conducted. As to just how the NKVD first learned of the new American intelligence agency there is no specific evidence, but the information most likely came from one or all of several sources in the government such as Hiss at State, White at Treasury, or concurrently indirectly from penetrations of the British intelligence service.

The British Contribution

One of the first NKVD sources on the COI was from a Soviet agent placed in the British Security Coordination (BSC) station (Intrepid) in New York, then headed by William Stephenson. He and members of his staff had worked closely with Donovan prior to establishing COI and were fully apprised of the details; this relationship continued throughout the war.[30]

The initial BSC complement included Cedric Henning Belfrage, a Cambridge University graduate and communist who came to the United States in April 1926 to work nominally as a journalist in Hollywood and New York. At the BSC, Belfrage first supervised "British black propaganda," later became head of the Political Warfare Division, and performed liaison work with OSS.[31] In November 1945, NKVD agent Elizabeth Bentley told the FBI that "toward the latter part of 1942 or in early 1943 I learned that one Cedric Belfrage [code name Benjamin] was contacting [Jacob] Golos [her NKVD boss] and turning over to him certain information. I learned through Golos that Belfrage was connected with British intelligence in the United States and operated out of a 'cover' office in Rockefeller Center."[32]

In the Belfrage case, his service with BSC, his Communist party membership, the existence of the documents Bentley described and which were passed to Golos by Belfrage were all supported after the war through testimony of others and decoded NKVD intercepts. One of the documents mentioned by Bentley contained a detailed account of British clandestine tradecraft, personnel requirements and techniques "apparently emanating from Scotland Yard." Belfrage served the NKVD for most of the war and there is every reason to believe he passed along whatever OSS material came his way. In 1954 Belfrage admitted to the FBI and the British consul in New York that he had passed documents concerning Scotland Yard surveillance and other topics to Valintin Sorokin, an NKVD officer, but only as part of a "double game" as a BSC officer. His explanation was rejected, and he was deported on "grounds of Communist Party Membership," which he had not mentioned on his visa application.[33]

Belfrage was not the only member or associate of the BSC staff of about one thousand who supported Soviet intelligence. Nigel West notes that another BSC officer and suspected mole was discovered long after the fact, in this case in 1953:

> A routine telephone tap on the Russian Embassy in London caught two Soviet intelligence officers boasting about a London based publishing house which, they claimed, had been financed by a "soft" loan from Moscow. The person concerned . . . although he admitted having been a Communist Party of Great Britain member, denied passing secrets to any Soviet contacts in America. His denials were not accepted.[34]

A third suspected spy was Stephenson's deputy, Colonel Charles "Dick" Howard Ellis. Throughout most of the war and especially during the formative days of the OSS, Ellis, an experienced MI6 officer, was the liaison between BSC and OSS. In 1966 when Ellis came under suspicion in Britain, he confessed to spying for the Germans prior to the war but denied any links to the Soviets. The evidence suggests otherwise. First it was established that one of his prewar "German agents," who happened to be his brother-in-law, also worked for the Soviets and that Ellis knew it. Second, there is evidence that Kim Philby shelved Ellis's file during the war to protect him. Third, postwar decrypts of NKVD messages backed up these charges. Hence, the question is: Did the NKVD use its knowledge of Ellis's spying for the Germans to blackmail him into serving the NKVD while at the BSC? That appears likely.[35]

In summary, one can conclude that there was indirect penetration of OSS through the BSC and that joint operations, personnel names, cover assignments, training techniques, and plans were made known to Soviet intelligence. The complete OSS picture could only come, however, from moles inside OSS and agents in related government agencies, and to these issues we now turn.

Soviet Moles in OSS Washington

In March of 1941, just about four months before the COI was established, Bentley was asked by Golos, her NKVD case officer, to make contact with Mary Watkins Price, who was then secretary to columnist Walter Lippmann. Price had previously been turned down for a job in OSS because of her communist associations. The initial meeting went well and arrangements were made for Price to communicate information she collected from the many communists she knew in the government to Bentley using a letter drop in New York City. Price also made frequent trips to New York where she met directly with Bentley and Golos. On one of these trips she asked Golos if he would be interested in a young man who was a friend of her sister (also a communist) and who was going to Washington to work in the OSS. Naturally Golos was enthusiastic and thus began a relationship among Price, Bentley, and one Duncan Chaplin Lee that was not exposed until after the war.

Born in China, Lee was a proud descendant of the Civil War general. He was a graduate of Yale and a Rhodes scholar at Oxford, where he studied law and married his English sweetheart, Isabelle. After returning and attending Yale Law School, he joined the law firm of William J. Donovan in New York City. When OSS was formed, Donovan brought Lee to Washington as a confidential assistant; it was then that he made contact with Mary Price. Bentley noted that Lee initially provided information through Price, but that she was soon meeting him directly.[36]

The Lee case is both typical and unusual in several respects. First, Bentley testified that she obtained some very sensitive information about the OSS from him:

He began to supply me with OSS information of a varied nature. These data were always given by him orally. . . . His information included facts on various phases of anti-Soviet work by OSS, its activities in various European countries with respect to uncovering Russian activities, the location of OSS personnel in foreign countries, and the nature of their activities. Golos attached great significance to such information inasmuch as it appeared to concern most directly activities of the United States Government as they concerned Russia.[37]

In the latter part of 1944, Lee told Bentley that OSS had "complied a list of Reds in OSS" that had three categories: (1) known Soviet agents; (2) known Communist party members, one of whom, Donald Wheeler, was one of her agents; and (3) known communist sympathizers, including Maurice Halperin (chief of the Latin American Division of the Research and Analysis Branch, OSS), another of her agents. Her relationship with Lee continued for most of the war.[38]

The second unusual feature of the case is that with the exception of two topics, Lee's own congressional testimony agreed with Bentley's testimony concerning him. He admitted that he and his wife knew Bentley and met frequently with her. He also acknowledged knowing Price and dining with Golos in New York. He explained the relationships as friendships gone sour. Lee's exceptions came only when he challenged Bentley on every point involving Communist party membership and being a Soviet agent. Under oath, he denied it all but could not account for details such as dining in uniform with Golos, a known communist. What he attributed to her neuroses, she explained as espionage. Recalling that Lee was an experienced intelligence officer who rose to the rank of lieutenant colonel, his explanations are unconvincing.[39]

The third unusual aspect of the Lee case is his apparent change of heart during the latter part of the war and Bentley's formal recognition of the fact in her statement and testimony. She had been aware that he was apprehensive about being under FBI surveillance (although the FBI files available do not indicate that he ever was while in the OSS) and about becoming a pawn in the bureaucratic battle for "control of all United States intelligence activities. . . . The FBI would very much like to place OSS personnel in an embarrassing position." In this context she described an incident in which Lee told her that Donovan was planning to exchange "agents" with the NKVD (which he was indeed proposing to the president; the Soviets already had agreed, but Hoover convinced the president not to do it), and he was concerned lest the NKVD reveal his association with their service.[40] It was under these circumstances then, during the final stage of their association which ended about December 1944 that she said Lee

> mentioned many times that he did not like the work he was engaged in, that is, the collection of information for me, and he appeared to me to be troubled with a severe conflict of ideas. I subsequently learned . . . that Duncan Lee had indicated to the person who took him over after I ceased my activities that he did not desire to continue his contacts with the Russian espionage setup any further.[41]

OSS records indicate that Lee completed his service without event as chief of the Chinese section of OSS Secret Intelligence. There was no action taken by either side after the congressional hearings. There was too much evidence for Lee to risk a lawsuit and not enough for the government to prosecute. The case was kept open for a while and although the FBI files contain reports on him as late as 1954, nothing more appears to have been done.[42]

The charge, mentioned above, that Halperin was a Soviet agent did not surprise his peers when it became public shortly after the war. One former colleague, Arthur Schlesinger, Jr., had tried to deal with the problem during the war.

> The reports from our Latin American section, in my view, showed a clear communist slant. In order to document my suspicions, I began to follow LA affairs myself and soon was rejecting the party line reports in favor of my own notes. . . . The Chief of the section protested; and I was instructed . . . to use the reports from the LA desk or nothing. . . . I had the eventual satisfaction of knowing that Maurice Halperin, the Chief of the Latin American section, was indeed a member of the Communist Party and sought refuge behind the Iron Curtain.[43]

Other analysts recalled that when the door to the Latin American section was locked to outsiders, they joked that Halperin was holding a "cell meeting."[44]

Halperin joined COI/OSS in September 1941 from a teaching post at the University of Oklahoma. A Harvard graduate with a doctorate in economics from the Sorbonne, Bentley said he contacted Golos through the local Communist party and was introduced to the Washington apparatus by Mary Price. Subsequently, according to Bentley, he began supplying reports and "excerpts from State Department cables" on a regular basis, first through Price and then through Bentley, although he also met from time to time directly with Golos. Bentley's last meeting with Halperin was in December 1944, although she reported hearing in 1945 from the NKVD case officer who took over for him that Halperin had been "accused by General William Donovan of being a Soviet agent and that after this accusation had been leveled at him . . . Halperin failed to appear two or three times to meet his contact."[45]

A case where the mole in OSS headquarters operated in a support position is that of Carl Aldo Marzani. Born in Rome, Italy, a Phi Beta Kappa Williams graduate, he also studied at Oxford after service with the Republicans in the Spanish civil war. Marzani joined COI/OSS in 1942, eventually becoming deputy chief of the Presentation Branch. His work permitted him to see very sensitive material prepared for general officer briefings and reports. According to Budenz, he was a member of an OSS espionage ring, but no direct evidence was found as to what, if anything, he supplied the Soviets. After the war Marzani transferred to the State Department where the new, more stringent postwar security procedure revealed his Communist membership. He was dismissed from the civil service, tried, and sent to prison because he had lied about being an active Party member since before the war.[46]

A final example involves Helen Tenney, a young woman instructed by Golos in 1943 to apply for a position with OSS. In her case it was not difficult, despite her well-known communist activities in support of the Spanish civil war; she had previously worked for a firm set up by OSS to recruit men for the clandestine service. She served as a secretary and then as an editorial analyst in the Spanish and the Balkin divisions. Tenney worked through Bentley, providing "highly confidential material" for most of the war, remaining with the Strategic Service Unit/Central Intelligence Group (SSU/CIG) well into 1946 with access to "Russian espionage" and "CE work." At her last official meeting with Bentley, she thought she was under suspicion because the family "chauffeur told her the FBI had been asking questions"; she was subsequently dismissed for security reasons. After some time in a mental institution she testified before Congress, taking the Fifth Amendment on all questions.[47] No charges of espionage were brought against these NKVD moles, no doubt for lack of the kind of hard evidence that Chambers produced in the Hiss case.

NKVD and GRU Agents with Access to OSS

There were a large number of Soviet agents in other organizations, government and civilian, collecting intelligence about OSS who had direct access to OSS personnel and documents. In the civilian category the Institute of Pacific Relations (IPR), based in New York and one of the first think tanks on Far Eastern affairs, was preeminent. The IPR operational concept was simple: prestigious staff and publications, many legitimate scholars mixed in with secret Communist party members, agents of influence, and fellow travelers. Soviet financial support was hidden, but its influence was not. R. Harris Smith notes correctly that IPR was "a prime target of the McCarthy era demagogues." But that does not change the facts: before and during the war IPR was "a vehicle used by the Communists to orient American Far Eastern policies toward Communist objectives." By 1929 IPR was strongly influenced, if not controlled, by well known communists led by Frederick Vanderbilt Field and Edward C. Carter. During the war the IPR "helped the OSS Research and Analysis Branch recruit . . . Far East experts" while supporting Soviet agents in other organizations with access to OSS.[48]

One IPR member and Soviet agent was Joseph Fels Barnes, a former foreign editor for the *New York Herald Tribune* once stationed in Moscow, who served as secretary of the American Council of the IPR from 1931 to 1934 and later joined COI. He was publicly identified as a GRU agent (along with Owen Lattimore) after Soviet defector Alexander Barmine testified he was told about Barnes in Moscow by the head of the GRU, General Jan Berzin. This incident occurred in about 1935 during a discussion of GRU penetration and use of IPR as a cover for intelligence operations. The situation was later confirmed in a 1938 conversation in Paris with former GRU/NKVD officer Walter Krivitsky (head of NKVD western European operations) shortly after the latter defected.[49]

Other direct and indirect OSS links with IPR included Duncan Lee, who was connected with IPR while in New York, and Mary Price's sister Mildred, who introduced Mary and Lee and who recommended Michael Greenberg to Golos. Greenberg, an Englishman, joined the Communist party in the 1930s at Cambridge University where he met Karl Wittfogel, who would later testify to these events. Greenberg joined IPR and succeeded Lattimore as editor of the IPR journal *Pacific Affairs*. In 1942 he became assistant to Lauchlin Currie, another IPR member with OSS access then serving in the White House as a presidential assistant for Far Eastern affairs. Both men maintained contact with IPR during the war. Wittfogel said he told a security officer about his contacts with Greenberg, but nothing was done. Greenberg allegedly passed items received from Currie to Mary Price, who gave them to Bentley for transmission to Golos.[50]

In 1944 the magazine *Amerasia* published an article taken almost verbatim from a classified OSS report. *Amerasia* made so few changes that the security breach came to the attention of the OSS Office of Security. This provoked a raid on *Amerasia*'s offices, in which there were found hundreds of classified documents from the State and War departments, OSS, and other government agencies, many bearing the warning that "illegal possession is a violation of the Espionage Act." More documents were found in the home of *Amerasia* publisher Philip Jaffe, who pleaded guilty to unlawful possession of classified documents and paid a fine. As Dallin later wrote, "There is no doubt that the amazing collection of secret documents in the hands of the magazine and its ability to procure confidential material from government agencies must have been alluring for the zealous and ubiquitous Soviet intelligence operators."[51]

In sum this sample of domestic OSS penetrations by the Soviet intelligence services indicated considerable breadth and depth, yet none of those involved was suspected of espionage, with the possible exception of Halperin. Before assessing the damage caused, it is necessary to examine the situation overseas.

Soviet Penetration of USS Overseas

In July 1941, when Donovan began to build a COI staff, the White House provided five names for consideration as general counsel. Heading the list was Alger Hiss, described thereon as the " 'perfect lawyer,' if such there be in government"; he was not selected. That he did not view this devastating rejection with lasting resentment, at least toward the OSS product, is suggested by Hiss's later request prior to the Yalta Conference in 1944 for copies of all confidential studies prepared by the OSS Research and Analysis Branch (R & A) on America's wartime allies. This attempt to do his "homework" failed, not because security denied access, but because such an "extensive request for highly classified intelligence data, which vacuumed the R & A inventory" was not submitted in time to be filled before the conference.[52]

This is the same Hiss who before the war competed with, and lost to, NKVD agent Hede Massing for the espionage services of another State Department officer, Noel Field. Despite early education in Europe and attending college at Harvard, Field had genuine reasons for modesty. He left State in 1936, and went to Switzerland where he worked overtly with the League of Nations. Still an ideological communist, he joined the Swiss Communist party and became an GRU agent under Walter Krivitsky, with whom he served for two years.[53] During the war, Field worked "nominally as an official of the Unitarian war relief organization" and also "made himself useful, for a short period, to the OSS office in Berne. He knew many Communist and left-wing exiles with whom the allies at that time had common cause against the Nazis."[54] Some of Field's work with OSS involved the Free Germany Movement (FGM) founded by Moscow to help form the postwar political infrastructure in various European countries. In 1944 Field proposed to Allen Dulles, OSS station chief, that he (Field) select some of his FGM émigré comrades for training and eventual infiltration into Germany to make contact with and support the anti-Nazi movement. Dulles saw some merit in the proposal and sent Field to Paris with a letter of introduction. Field reached Paris in January 1945 and went to OSS headquarters where he presented his scheme to twenty-seven-year-old political analyst Arthur Schlesinger and his colleague, Bert Jolis. "I was immediately suspicious," said Schlesinger, "the plan was of obvious dubious value and the man was preposterous, no sensible person would have been taken in by him, he wore his Communism openly." Schlesinger suggested that Dulles's support of Field was related to the fact that Field's father had worked for Dulles in his World War I intelligence operation in Switzerland. Another likely reason was that Dulles, a practical man, had said he would work with the devil himself if it would help win the war for the Allies. The proposal was rejected.[55]

While continuing his own espionage, Field "helped" OSS in other ways, such as helping his foster daughter to get a job with the Berne OSS station as a secretary-interpreter; she later worked for the Frankfurt office in the same capacity where she continued after the war. She, too, was a Soviet agent all the while and later admitted providing the communists, as her father had done, with whatever she could.[56]

The use of the FGM as a source of Allied agents to insert behind German lines was a program conceived in London under William Casey and approved by Donovan. Other attempts to recruit qualified Germans had failed. Those on the political right were unacceptable to all; qualified, motivated middle of the roaders were an endangered species, thus the decision to go with left-socialist émigrés or escapees. The details of the operation are well covered elsewhere. Of particular concern here are the intelligence aspects.[57]

To begin with, agent recruitment was assigned to Lieutenant Joseph Gould, a former movie publicist, from the labor division of OSS. He had no prior intelligence experience or training, but he was a resourceful New Yorker and sought help at a leftist London bookstore. He was given the name and address of a potential contact, Jurgen Kuczynski, with links to the FGM. Deciding on the bold approach and not knowing the FGM was Soviet sponsored and controlled, Gould went directly to Kuczynski's flat and explained his need for a highly motivated native German anti-Nazi to undertake a dangerous intelligence-related mission. Kuczynski was nominally a German émigré economics professor who told Gould he "was the first allied intelligence officer to contact him." Kuczynski said he was ready to help but would have to talk with some "colleagues" first. After they quickly approved, a plan was agreed upon; men were selected, trained, and dropped into Germany, with mixed results. When asked after the war whether he had been concerned that the pro-communist Germans might actually work for postwar Soviet interests and help negate the goals the Allies had fought for, Gould replied, somewhat testily, that "politics was not the issue; we were fighting a war, and these men were dedicated well qualified agents who did their patriotic duty well, some being lost in the process."[58]

What Gould clearly did not know at the time and found hard to believe over thirty years later was that Kuczynski himself was a GRU agent. Moreover, when Kuczynski had sought approval of his colleagues, he had worked through another longtime GRU agent in Britain, his sister Sonja. Both worked with atom bomb spy Klaus Fuchs.[59]

Gould's attitude, then and now, is understandable. He was not in the CI business, and his actions were consistent with OSS policy. Of course he knew the Americans and British were aware of the potential problems should members of the FGM become involved in communist politics in Britain or the occupied countries. To minimize the risk they had placed a condition on the use of FGM members: no mixing in local politics, to which the FGM agreed and subsequently ignored.

Gould took standard security precautions to keep the operation secret. He concluded years later that "there seemed to be no leaks at all." He was apparently correct insofar as the Germans were concerned, but the Soviets were kept fully informed through the Kuczynskis.[60] The seven agents selected for Gould's operations, which got started only in March 1945, participated in five missions. Whatever their contribution to the Allied war effort, Sonja commented that they "returned to their country of origin to play their part in the establishment of a communist dictatorship and Soviet client state—the German Democratic Republic."[61]

As in the States, indirect penetration of the OSS stations overseas was also a problem. One example from the London station is instructive. After the creation of the OSS CI/CE element (X-2) in London, whose primary mission was to handle the Ultra product for American forces, contacts with the British CI increased. James Murphy, former head of X-2, recalled that contacts with the British went well, in part

> because we had an OSS man in their Section V (counterintelligence) office on Ryder Street and we coordinated all joint matters. One of their key officers of course, was Kim Philby, with whom I occasionally dealt, but only on a profes-

sional basis. He was very competent and had full access to our operations, including the ULTRA material. He and Jim Angleton spent a good deal of time together, especially after Philby became head of the new M16 Section Nine, looking at soviet intelligence services. I was very surprised when Philby defected to the Russians.[62]

Kim Philby makes clear in his book that he took advantage of the arrangement by passing everything to the NKVD and also that he did what he could to create bureaucratic friction between MI6 and OSS.[63]

While Soviet intelligence monitored and influenced OSS operations overseas through political organizations such as the FGM, they also attempted to place moles on the staff of OSS field stations. In the case of Jane Foster Zlatovski, they were successful. Foster, like many of her OSS comrades, was a well-educated (Mills College), affluent American. She acquired her communism while traveling in the Far East, joining the Party with her husband prior to the war. After working on the Board of Economic Warfare she was recruited by OSS because of her experience in Indonesia. Foster "penetrated the OSS, the early CIA, and US Army CI in Salzburg (through her husband) and was obviously a valuable source . . . [she] was indicted for espionage [committed after the war] in 1957 but never returned to the United States to face the charges."[64]

Another example of penetration in the field occurred in Italy and involved several OSS officers who were communists and veterans of the Abraham Lincoln Battalion. In the autumn of 1943, following the same general policy he applied to the FGM in Britain, Donovan approved a plan for the station in Italy to negotiate an agreement with Italian communists operating in the resistance behind German lines. The arrangement was that the Italian communists would provide intelligence, agents, and safe houses for OSS personnel operating in the German-occupied north. The OSS, in return, would provide supplies and allow the communists to use OSS communications, wireless and pouch, provided the message content did not involve communist politics. To be sure of the latter, all communist traffic was reviewed prior to transmission, a condition to which the communists agreed.[65]

By April 1945 several teams were functioning well. Lieutenant Irving Goff was named OSS liaison officer with the communists. Vincent Lossowski, Irving Fajans, and Milton Wolff were assigned to assist him. All four were known by the OSS to have "leftist sympathies"; each was identified after the war as a Communist party member. Gradually apparent success was marred when it was discovered that the communists were skimming supplies and, according to some, violating the agreement not to use the communications links for their own political purposes. The communists, however, denied the charge, saying that the army misinterpreted the message content and no evidence of improper conduct by Goff was produced.[66]

At this point a series of complicating events occurred. The House Military Affairs Subcommittee began investigating fourteen soldiers known to be communists; Goff, Wolff, and Fajans were among them. In Italy, the army CIC placed a mail watch on Goff, Wolff, Lossowski, and Fajans that revealed they had been receiving communist literature; CIC requested X-2 to evacuate the men promptly. Then someone brought up a War Department directive stating that Communist party membership "will not affect the status of Army personnel if it is established that their loyalty to this country is greater than any other loyalty." It did not say how this was to be done.[67]

Back in the States, Donovan, unaware of the results of the mail watch, made his own investigation and eventually came to their defense publicly, describing the men as loyal, brave, efficient Americans, whom "I've been in the trenches with. I've been in the muck with, and I'd measure them up against any other men." As to being communists, Donovan said, "I find that they were not." Then, when informed the men were very likely communists and had been receiving communist literature through the mail, he ordered another investigation. The results showed that OSS headquarters had approved all actions concerning the project, the men had all performed well, and the intelligence return had been of high value. It concluded:

> OSS had certain intelligence and operational objectives to obtain, among which was political intelligence, regardless of the color of the intelligence. The Communist Party is among the stronger in North Italy. To leave out contacts with it would seem disastrous for a balanced picture. . . . The price has been cheap for the results obtained.[68]

What the report did not comment on was the short-term payoff to the communists regarding their awareness of OSS personnel, plans, and operations, or the long-term benefit of the supplies and the opportunity to establish a political base. Whatever the communists achieved, the OSS teams had followed the policy of higher headquarters. In the end, compromise prevailed. Goff and the others returned to the United States, were promoted, and were honorably discharged; Goff received a Legion of Merit, the fifth highest award in the army. After the war Goff returned to a position within the Communist party in New York and became a leader of the National Veterans Committee of the Abraham Lincoln Battalion, a thinly disguised front of the Communist party.[69]

WARTIME IMPACT OF SOVIET PENETRATION

We have seen that the NKVD and GRU penetrated all levels of the OSS where they attempted to acquire secret information and influence policy and operations. Clearly, they learned the secret details of OSS tradecraft, training, personnel, operations, organization, estimates, and analytical reports, and they used OSS operations and materials to assist them in their postwar political struggles. Even worse, the moles were not exposed until after the war (then only by defectors) when OSS had been abolished. For any intelligence service this would normally be considered a disaster, but in this case it was mitigated because the Soviets were allies. The questions for CI analysts and historians alike are why did penetration remain undetected, and what was the impact on the services of both countries?

Looking at the last question first, the evidence suggests the wartime negative impact on OSS was minimal, but mainly because the Soviets chose that policy. Certainly they did not want to jeopardize their agents whom they hoped would continue in place after the war when they might be needed even more. Furthermore, the OSS penetrations helped the Soviets evaluate intelligence collected clandestinely from their many agents elsewhere in the government as well as the intelligence voluntarily provided by their American and British allies. Similarly, the intelligence collected gave them a check on whether they were receiving all the information from their allies that they considered vital to their interests and, of course, they were not—the atom bomb spies are a case in point. All this input was used to guide agent tasking and to appraise the political leadership. In terms of particular OSS operations, the penetrations revealed just about everything, including Ultra and, perhaps equally important, that OSS was not running operations against the Soviets. Thus, in terms of their own self-interest, the Soviets were careful not to let the knowledge gained from the penetrations reveal the source or interfere with OSS operations, although they used it to help their own. In short, the penetrations probably did not damage the OSS contribution to the war, but rather kept the NKVD informed and helped to reassure Stalin.[70]

As to how and why the penetrations occurred and persisted, there are two principal and not independent reasons. The first concerns personnel security measures that obviously did not work well enough, again for two reasons. First, some key penetrations occurred at the beginning, before detailed screening procedures were implemented; Lee is a good example. Second, there was a conscious policy to hire or retain communists in certain circumstances; J. Kuczynski, Irving Goff, and the FGM members are examples. While it is true that some OSS elements avoided communists, as with

Schlesinger in Paris and Goldberg in London, in general there was a tolerant attitude toward the political left so long as the primary allegiance was outwardly to the Allies and anti-Fascist. As Donovan stated, "I'd put Stalin on the OSS payroll if I thought it would help us defeat Hitler."[71] For these reasons penetration for the Soviets was not difficult.

The second and professionally most important reason that helps to explain why most of the Soviet moles and agents were not caught is that there was no formal effort within OSS to find them once they were employed. To understand why this was so, it is necessary to examine the wartime division of CI/CE responsibility—that is, who was supposed to prevent, discover, eliminate, or counter penetrations? On paper the assignments were clear. In Washington the FBI, Army, Navy, and the State Department each looked after its own agency. At some point when espionage was suspected, the FBI was also responsible for the rest of the Western Hemisphere; the OSS for everywhere else.[72] The X-2 Branch had the responsibility

> (1) To institute such measures as may be necessary to protect the operational security of OSS, and to prevent the penetration of our espionage and other secret activities. (2) To cooperate with counter-intelligence agencies of the United States and *our Allies*, and afford them timely information of *enemy attempts at penetration* or subversive action from areas in which X-2 is authorized to operate.[73]

A strict interpretation of the first item suggests that X-2 was to be concerned with penetration by any source, but in the context of the second item, the enemy was Germany (in the Far East theater of operations (FETO), Japan), and not the communists. To a large extent this is initially what happened. From the latter part of 1944 on, however, studies in the OSS flies indicate an increasing concern with worldwide Soviet espionage, penetration, and Communist violations of agreements. In Italy, James Angleton, the premier student of ambiguity, began examining his bulging files, giving increased attention to Russian related questions. Additional attention was given to the problem of monitoring communist activities, including the spies being infiltrated from Russia into Italy, Greece, Romania, and other Balkin countries. There is no indication, however, of CE missions conducted against the Soviets. Furthermore, so far as can be determined, X-2 did not employ CI techniques to assess whether OSS in general or X-2 in particular was penetrated by their Soviet counterparts.[74]

It should be emphasized that this lack of CI effort against the Soviets was consistent with wartime policy and priorities, both British and American.[75]

Certainly, Soviet agents and moles themselves did not give OSS or other U.S. intelligence services much reason to change. But in the immediate postwar period the situation changed.

SOVIET MOLES AND THE OSS LEGACY

President Truman abolished the OSS on 20 September 1945 (effective 1 October 1945) but not its resources; the analysts were transferred to State, and the clandestine service was redesignated the Strategic Service Unit (SSU) and given to the War Department. To show that he was not rejecting, in principle, the need for a centralized national intelligence organization, Truman instructed the secretary of state to develop a "comprehensive and coordinated foreign intelligence program for all government agencies concerned."[76] These decisions created an unprecedented bureaucratic battle in Washington for the national intelligence mission and resources. Meanwhile, unknown to the president, a series of events already had begun that, together with the bureaucratic competition and his own desire for foreign intelligence, would force him to take action before the State Department could offer a solution.

In October 1945 Canadian authorities informed the United States that GRU Lieutenant Igor Gouzenko had defected on 5 September 1945 and provided evidence implicating Hiss as a Soviet agent. Then on 8 November 1945, Bentley, still an active NKVD agent, went to the FBI in New York and began revelations that took one month to complete. She told of her nearly ten years as an agent and named over eighty persons connected with Soviet espionage including Duncan Lee and Alger Hiss.[77] On 10 November 1945, Prime Minister Mackenzie King of Canada, visited President Truman to inform him that the Gouzenko revelations indicated that the Soviets had penetrated the Manhattan Project. Later that same month, Hoover notified Truman that there were indeed indications that Hiss was a "Russian operative"; an investigation had finally begun.[78]

In early 1946 former NKVD agent and *Daily Worker* editor Louis Budenz, who had left the Party in October of the previous year, told the FBI about his role in Soviet espionage that included moles in OSS. Throughout this period the State Department worked to create some form of intelligence entity but without success. Thus on 22 January 1946, Truman seized the initiative and created an interim organization, the Central Intelligence Group (CIG), the immediate predecessor of the CIA.[79]

The consequences of these events, in conjunction with the wartime intelligence experiences, were profound. The defector revelations left no doubt as to the seriousness of the problem, and the FBI acted, albeit deliberately, domestically. The situation with regard to foreign intelligence and CI was more complicated and confused because the different agencies continued to compete for the mission and resources even after CIG was formed. Nevertheless, exposure of the Soviet moles and agents linked to OSS gave the CIG/CIA the justification required for the more comprehensive Soviet-oriented security and CI program that was begun. By the time CIA was created (26 July 1947), new personnel selection and security procedures had been implemented. As one former OSS officer who was there wrote, "Many of the communists who had worked in the OSS were well known and left government service of their own accord, or were quickly screened out by the intensive postwar investigations."[80] As to overseas operations, the SSU CI (formerly X-2) was also progressing. Angleton in Italy and Dulles in Germany already had begun adapting the basic CI practices developed during the war to cases and databases on communist espionage and subversion. They did not need revised procedures so much as a solid organizational foundation and data on which to operate. This the CIG and then the CIA began providing.

The demise of OSS had an unforeseen benefit that could not have happened had the organization remained intact: CIG/CIA was forced to start almost from scratch. From a strength of more than nine thousand at the end of the war, by early 1946 the SSU had nine hundred officers who were absorbed by CIG. The R & A analysts transferred to State had suffered a similar contraction, and those remaining also went to CIG. Instead of reducing, reshuffling, and reinvestigating an existing staff, CIG/CIA selectively brought back those who really wanted to come. Overseas, those who had stayed on had to a large extent already been filtered but were able to add personnel on the same basis.

In the end the Soviet penetrations of OSS had a paradoxical yet decisive impact on U.S. intelligence. While they existed they did little damage to the war effort despite rendering OSS an open book. They were eliminated not by good CI work but by Truman's abolishing the OSS, and the knowledge gained from their exposure, coupled with the X-2 experience and Soviet defector inputs, provided the impetus and foundation for building the counterintelligence capability within the CIA. Spies had influenced history.

NOTES

1. Richard W. Rowan, *The Story of Secret Service* (New York, 1938), p. 1. An example is John Buchan's, *A History of the Great War*, 8 vols. (Boston, 1922). Buchan, an intelligence officer during the war and author of espionage fiction, makes only occasional mention of espionage and none at all to intelligence.

2. For works by historians see Robert A. Asprey, *Frederick the Great: The Magnificent Enigma* (New York, 1986); David J. Dallin, *Soviet Espionage* (New Haven, 1955); Bradley F. Smith, *The Shadow Warriors: OSS and the Origins of the CIA* (New York, 1983); Wesley K. Wark, *The Ultimate Enemy: British Intelligence and Nazi Germany, 1933-1939* (Ithaca, NY, 1985); Ernest R. May, ed., *Knowing One's Enemies: Intelligence Assessment Before the Two World Wars* (Princeton, NJ, 1984); Christopher Andrew, *Secret Service: The Making of the British Intelligence Community* (London, 1986); and Anthony Cave Brown and Charles B. MacDonald, *On a Field of Red: The Communist International and the Coming of World War II* (New York, 1981). For intelligence history by former intelligence officers see F. H. Hinsley et al., *British Intelligence in the Second World War*, 4 vols. (London, 1979, 1981, 1984, 1988); Thomas F. Troy, *Donovan and the CIA: A History of the Establishment of the Central Intelligence Agency* (Frederick, MD, 1981); and Richard Dunlap, *Donovan: America's Master Spy* (New York, 1982). For works by journalists see Nigel West, *The Circus: MI5 Operations 1945-1972* (Briarcliff Manor, NY, 1983); Chapman Pincher, *Too Silent Too Long* (New York, 1984); and Anthony Cave Brown, *Wild Bill Donovan: The Last Hero* (New York, 1982).

3. Counterintelligence (CI) involves the planned collection, analysis, and use of information about foreign intelligence and security services to prevent or neutralize their operations against the national service concerned. Counterespionage (CE), a branch of CI, involves penetrating foreign intelligence services (with moles) to acquire information and manipulate the service.

4. The Cheka was created on 7 December 1917 as the All-Russian Extraordinary Commission for Combatting Counterrevolution and Sabotage, from which the acronym was taken. It subsequently underwent many name changes and is currently called the KGB. Cheka, OGPU, and NKVD will be used synonymously herein. For a complete chronological list of the other names see Robert Conquest, *Inside Stalin's Secret Police: NKVD Politics 1936-1939* (Stanford, CA, 1985), p. 1-2. Party security meant elimination of anti-Bolsheviks and the Red Terror (1918-1921) conducted by the Cheka served to institutionalize arbitrary arrest and execution as a "deliberate calculated instrument of Bolshevik domestic policy," for sustaining Party rule. George Leggett, *The CHEKA: Lenin's Political Police* (Oxford, 1981), pp. 17-29, 30-31.

5. In 1920 Lenin expressed regret that his splendidly organized Cheka did not yet extend to the United States of America. See Lennard Gerson, *Secret Police in Lenin's Russia* (Philadelphia, 1976), pp. 236-37. For more on the Trust see Geoffrey Bailey, *The Conspirators* (New York, 1960). The term tradecraft includes agent spotting, recruiting, handling, passport forging, secret writing, ciphers, concealment, and surveillance detection as well as avoidance, communication, and related techniques. See Alexander Orlov, *Handbook of Intelligence* (Ann Arbor, MI, 1965).

6. The so-called Lockhart plot to overthrow the Bolsheviks is discussed in Leggett, *The CHEKA*, pp. 280-84.

7. For the Kalamatiano story see William R. Corson and Robert T. Crowley, *The New KGB: Engine of Soviet Power*, updated ed. (New York, 1985), pp. 47-64 (quote from p. 64).

8. Victor Suvorov, *Soviet Military Intelligence* (London, 1984), pp. 4, 8, 17-18.

9. Dallin, *Soviet Espionage*, pp. 15-17. Agents of influence need not commit espionage or be Party members in order to contribute positively. Usually, no obvious link between the Party and the individual concerned is desired or permitted. An individual's value lies in his or her willingness to use position and personal relationships to the Party's ends.

10. Gerson, *Secret Police*, pp. 236-37; Dallin, *Soviet Espionage*, pp. 392, 396, 401. In 1930 a former Amtorg vice president disclosed Soviet spying on the army and the navy. Later that same year, another Amtorg officer was caught smuggling Swiss watch movements and U.S. birth certificates for false passports; he turned out to be the OGPU resident in Newark, New Jersey. Still another Amtorg official told of attempts to acquire industrial secrets.

11. Herbert O. Yardley, *The American Black Chamber* (Indianapolis, 1931), pp. 239-83.

12. Bruce W. Bidwell, U.S. colonel (ret.), *History of the Military Intelligence Division: 1775-1941* (Frederick, MD, 1986), pp. 257, 265. Typical attache reports are *Establishment of the Intelligence Department of the Red Army Staff*, from MA, Riga, Latvia, 17 December 1923, National Archives (NA) file no. 4-1 9944-D-5; and *G.P.U. Troops and Counter-Espionage Work*, from G-2 Riga, Latvia, 3 January 1924, NA file no. 4-1 9944-D-29.

13. Bidwell, *History of the MID*, pp. 281; see also ibid., pp. 275-88.

14. U.S. Congress, Senate Subcommittee on the Judiciary, *Hearings on Brewing and Liquor Interests and German and Bolshevik Propaganda*, 66th Cong., 1st sess., vol. 3, 1919. R. M. Whitney, *Reds In America* (New York, 1924); report of the Bridgman raids in Michigan, H. Rep. 2290, *Investigation of Communist Propaganda*, 71st Cong., 3d sess., 17 January 1931.

15. Herbert Hoover, *Memoirs: 1930-33* (New York, 1952), p. 182.

16. Dallin, *Soviet Espionage*, pp. 396-402.

17. The first case involved a plan to exchange counterfeit dollars in Latin America and the United States. The second concerned an American army enlisted man arrested and convicted as a Soviet spy in Panama. See Dallin, *Soviet Espionage*, pp. 398-99. Roosevelt did express concern about the

political threat from the Soviet Union and insisted on a firm pledge that the Comintern would cease to direct the activities of the American Communist party. No pledge was in the final agreement and the United States ignored the omission. Brown and Macdonald, *Field of Red*, p. 335.

18. Dallin, *Soviet Espionage* p. 403-4.

19. Ibid., p. 404.

20. Golos recruited Vassar (1930) and Columbia (1935) graduate Elizabeth Bentley who handled several moles in OSS. In the United States, as in the United Kingdom, the NKVD recruited from universities where Party contacts and organizations were well developed. The Ivy League schools, Stanford, and the University of California were big targets, and City College of New York also provided recruits, for example, Rosenberg. The Party line attraction was "anti-fascism." For descriptions of other networks see Dallin, *Soviet Espionage*, pp. 403-7, 441. While British spies have had more attention, more were recruited in America. Peter Hennesy and Alasdair Palmer, "Good Year for a Mole Mania Revival," *Times* (London), 15 February 1983.

21. Arthur Schlesinger, Jr., *The Politics of Upheaval* (Boston, 1960), p. 206. Jeffrey M. Dorwart, *Conflict of Duty: The U.S. Navy's Intelligence Dilemma*, 1919-1945 (Annapolis, MD, 1983), pp. 82-85, notes ONI (Office of Naval Intelligence) efforts to combat communists were brought to Roosevelt's attention, and he allowed them to continue despite ACLU complaints.

22. J. Edgar Hoover to Edwin M. Watson (secretary to the president), 13 December 1940 , with report "Subject: Memorandum," same date, from Special Agent Beck. FBI agents, unknown to embassy staff and ambassador, had observed U.S. embassy personnel since the summer of 1940 at the request of the State Department. The report describes serious security problems uncovered in the embassy and the corrective action. No counter-espionage operations are mentioned or indicated.

23. Allen Weinstein, *Perjury: The Hiss-Chamber Case* (New York, 1978), pp. 64-5, 329-30, 340-1. Berle did not mention the meeting in his diary, but writer Isaac Don Levine claims that Berle told the president.

24. Department of State Records, Adolf Berle to J. Edgar Hoover, 10 July 1941, 861.20211/137A, National Archives, Washington, DC.

25. Orlov, *Handbook Of Intelligence*, pp. 14-38.

26. Louis F. Budenz, *Techniques of Communism* (Chicago, 1954), p. 164. For additional authoritative details see Orlov, *Handbook of Intelligence*, pp. 108-9.

27. Troy, *Donovan and the CIA*, provides the definitive account. Donovan, at the request of the president, demonstrated the need for centralized strategic intelligence during two missions overseas to make "strategic appreciations" of Europe and the Mediterranean areas. Upon his return from the second trip in March 1941, Donovan sent the president a letter on 26 April 1941 outlining the functions and authority issues involved, thereby leading to his appointment as COI.

28. Kermit Roosevelt, *War Report of the O.S.S. (Office of Strategic Services)* (New York, 1976), pp. 87-8, 134-5. In December 1941, COI and FBI foiled an attempted penetration. But the problem persisted at high levels where personal judgment sometimes overruled other factors. For example, Ernest Cuneo, former White House liaison between OSS and BSC told the author on 11 March 1986 that he was informed (in 1942 or 1943) by the British Security Coordination in New York that there was a Soviet mole high in the American government. Cuneo said he told OSS and the President Roosevelt. When the president indicated that he was not concerned, since the man named was a close friend, the matter was dropped.

29. Roosevelt, *OSS War Report*, p. 190; *OSS, X-2 Handbook*, Memo #11 beginning of X-2 Branch, two pages.

30. Thomas F. Troy, "COI and British Intelligence," unpublished manuscript, 1970; H. Montgomery Hyde, *Room 3603: The Story of The British Intelligence Center in New York During World War II* (New York, 1963). In *Unreliable Witness: Espionage Myths of the Second World War* (London, 1984), Nigel West shows that Sir William Stephenson was #48100, not Intrepid, which was the BSC cable address. Author William Stevenson's book, *A Man Called INTREPID* molded the facts to enhance the story.

31. Testimony of Cedric Henning Belfrage, HUAC, *Communist Activities in The New York Area*, 1953, p. 1271; West, *MI6*, p. 210; West, *Thread of Deceit*, p. 130; David Stafford, *Camp X: Canada's School for Secret Agents 1941-45*, (Toronto, 1986), p. 195.

32. Statement to FBI from Elizabeth Terrill Bentley, dated 30 November 1945, New York, FBI file #65-56604, Serial #220, pp. 43-44; (hereafter called Bentley Statement). Bentley was born 1 January 1908 in New Milford, Connecticut, was a 1930 Vassar College graduate, a schoolteacher in Middleburg, Virginia, an exchange student in Italy (1933-34), and obtained her master's degree from Columbia in 1935. Bentley's veracity has been impugned by those against whom she made allegations, but no one successfully challenged her regarding the espionage facts at issue; see David Caute, *The Great Fear* (New York, 1978), p. 56-58; Hayden B. Peake, Afterword to Elizabeth Bentley, *Out of Bondage*, (New York, 1988), pp. 217-307.

33. British PRO, cable, FO3695057 93937, dated 21 September 1954; British Consul NYC to FO, KG1451/130. Belfrage later claimed he was deported because his "politics were wrong 17 years ago"; see Exhibit 515, p. 1901, part 23, and p. 2190, part 27, Senate hearings on *Interlocking Subversion*, 13 December 1954. Bentley did not claim Belfrage was a communist; she said "As far as I was able to determine from Golos, Belfrage was not a member of the Communist Party." *Bentley statement*, p. 43-44.

34. West, *MI5* (Briarcliff Manor, NY., 1982) p. 242; see also West, *Molehunt* (London,1987), p. 157. The second agent was thought to be James MacGibbon. He was on a list of suspected former Soviet spies in an article by Barry Penrose and Simon Freeman, *Sunday Times* (London), "MI5 Reveals Spy Suspects," 22 July 1984, p. 1. He served in the British embassy in Washington during the war and had contact with the BSC. He admitted

only being a CP member in the 1930s. Later his firm, MacGibbon & Kee, negotiated the rights to Philby's book, *My Silent War.*

35. Nigel West, *The Friends* (London, 1988); Pincher, *Too Secret Too Long*, pp. 440-56. For more on the Venona decrypts see Robert Lamphere and Tom Shachtman, *The FBI-KGB War* (New York, 1986), pp. 82-98 and Peter Wright, *Spycatcher* (New York, 1987), pp. 179-88, passim. Ironically, the decrypts came from Soviet codebooks captured by the Finns and given to Donovan. Reluctant to irritate the Soviets, the State Department succeeded in persuading the president to order Donovan to return them to the Soviets without making copies. Donovan gave them back, but copied them first. After the war they helped solve the Fuchs, Rosenberg, and Ellis cases, among others. See Smith, *Shadow Warriors*, pp. 353-55.

36. Bentley Statement, p. 34. Smith, *OSS* pp. 276-77, notes that "FBI informant Elizabeth Bentley made the absurd charge that Lee was a Soviet spy who passed OSS information to the Russians. Lee denied the accusations under oath and no legal charges were ever brought against him." Smith does not mention the evidence or note that Lee did not bring libel charges against Bentley. He subsequently left the country and settled in Toronto, Canada where he died on 15 April 1988.

37. Bentley Statement, pp. 34-35.

38. IPR Hearings, part 2, p. 413; Bentley says of Lee, "I think he was our most valuable source in the OSS."

39. HCUA, *Hiss-Chamber Hearings*, 10 August 1948, pp. 715-59.

40. Ibid.; Lee, HCUA Testimony; see also Bentley, *Out of Bondage*, p. 259-60.

41. Bentley Statement, p. 35-36.

42. FBI, *Out of Bondage Analysis*, p. 18. In a 28 March 1986 conversation with the author, Donovan biographer and former OSS officer in Burma Richard Dunlop, said that although Lee had Donovan's complete trust initially, at some point toward the end of the war, "Donovan knew all about Lee and his communist affiliations, but didn't think it would be a problem; Lee was given nonsensitive jobs thereafter." Dunlop explained that the Soviets had been given a great deal in intelligence already, much of it by Donovan. And while the operational data Lee revealed were important in the short term, in the long term it would make little difference at least as far as the outcome of the war was concerned. Furthermore, it was "characteristic of Donovan to be very tolerant of a colleague who has erred and even try to help him; Donovan probably felt it was in some way his fault for not taking better care of the lad." He said after the war Donovan, "being a practical man," did not ask Lee to return to his law firm. But Dunlop met Lee there from time to time, and Dunlop thinks Donovan was trying to help Lee even then. A different view was related to the author on 29 March 1986 by another Donovan friend, Walter L. Pforzheimer, first legislative counsel for the CIA. While agreeing with Dunlop as to Donovan's characteristic tolerance, Pforzheimer said that Donovan mentioned the Lee case on several occasions and never even hinted he was aware of any espionage on Lee's part.

43. Schlesinger, Jr., *A Thousand Days*, p. 171. In a March 1986 interview with the author, historian and former OSS analyst Ray S. Cline, related another incident involving Halperin when Cline was editor of a weekly OSS intelligence report. In about 1943, Halperin submitted an article which concluded a certain Latin American country was an advocate of communism and the Soviet Union. It was objected to by many analysts and withdrawn. Cline said that it was one of the few times the communism issue surfaced officially since the "focus was on the Nazis."

44. R. Harris Smith, *OSS*, p. 14.

45. Bentley Statement, p. 31-33. Hearings of the 82d Congress, Senate Committee on the Judiciary, Subcommittee to Investigate the Administration of the Internal Security Act and Other Internal Security laws (hereafter called ISS), *Subversive Influence in the Education Process*, Testimony of Maurice Halperin, part 6, pp. 663- 675; see also Senate hearings on the *Scope of Soviet Activity in the United States*, part 89, 29 November 1957, pp. 4937, 5057-5059; Caute, *The Great Fear*, pp. 417, 553, 586. The OSS files examined to date make no mention of Donovan's accusation. Halperin left OSS in 1945 and joined the State Department as head of Latin American Research and Analysis. Sometime in 1946 he became chairman of the Latin American Department at Boston University. In March 1953, Halperin refused to answer Senate questions (based on other sworn testimony before the committee), relating to his communist links and espionage activities. He was discharged from Boston University in 1954 and subsequently worked in Mexico (1957), Moscow, and Cuba (1967).

46. Budenz, *Men Without Faces*, p. 252. See also HCUA, Hearings,Paunch testimony, 13 November 1956, pp. 6248-49; J. Anthony Paunch, "*The Marzani Case*," in Issac Don Levine, ed., *Plain Talk* (New Rochelle, NY, 1976), p. 172. When confronted by State, Marzani said he had been cleared by a civil service board after questions arose during his OSS service in 1943. Investigation showed this to be true, but the board heard no witnesses. The State Department located three witnesses who positively identified Marzani as an active CP member in New York before the war. One was in the Party undercover for the NYPD when he knew Marzani as a Party member. Marzani was found guilty and sent to prison for lying about his communist affiliations on official documents. One of Marzani's cellmates was the former head of the HUAC, J. Parnell Thomas.

47. Bentley, *Out of Bondage*, pp. 772-86. FBI Report, file #65-56402-939, SAC NY, Subject: *GREGORY* (Bentley's codename), 12 April 1946, *ESPIONAGE-R* pp. 50-54. Tenney was nervous but not dumb; when she learned about the 1945 Canadian GRU spy cases, she disposed of all material, even gifts from Communist party friends, that could link her to the Party. Despite family affluence, Tenney was often in need of money and was one of the few moles who eventually accepted an NKVD salary ($50.00).

48. Smith, *OSS*, p. 268; IPR, Hearings, part 1, pp. 1-5, 1951.

49. ISS, part 3, p. 857. Barnes was with COI in 1942; see also *IPR Hearings*, part 1, pp. 202-05, 208-10. Barmine's discussion with Berzin included two

senior GRU staff officers and concerned GRU plans for infiltrating IPR. Barnes was described as "ours," meaning successful recruitment. Barmine explained IPR provided good GRU cover for west coast operations which until then were nil. He said:

> that is the idea, undercover work when you can have legal reasons and innocent reasons to travel to do specifically military research and reconnoitering work and gathering of information materials, because military intelligence is comprised of the gathering of printed material, classified and unclassified, of every kind. You have reason to keep the foreign members of the military network on the job...

Krivitsky, who served first in the GRU and then NKVD, told Barmine the IPR operation was "flourishing," with good high level contacts; he knew of "Barnes and Lattimore" in connection with IPR and they "were still our men." After he joined OSS as a translator and Soviet analyst, Barmine told the FBI his story; he doesn't know what was done. Barmine then went public in an unapproved 1944 *Reader's Digest* article and was discharged. He died in 1988.

50. National Archive Document #6281-005-01, Foreign Economic Administration (FEA), Foreign Assignment Statement #207, dated 6 September 1944, for Assignee Michael Greenberg, POB Manchester, England, DOB 28 November 1914; Education: Cambridge University England B.A. & M.A. 1933-1939 (Trinity College); Harvard University Graduate School, PhD, 1939-41. Wittfogel identified Greenberg as a communist at Cambridge in 1934; IPR Hearing, part 1, pp. 280-81, Bentley Statement, p. 44.

51. Ralph de Toledano, *Spies, Dupes, and Diplomats* (New York, 1952), p. 140. After the war Donovan's former executive officer, Otto Doering, released a press statement (Friday, 9 June 1950) reaffirming that OSS personnel were not involved with the improper transmission of confidential documents. Dallin, *Soviet Espionage*, p. 446-48. More recently, Harvey Klehr and Ronald Radosh revealed in the 21 April 1986 issue of *The New Republic*, pp. 18-21, that former foreign service officer John Stewart Service did not testify truthfully in Congress when questioned on matters relating to *Amerasia*, and that he characterized himself as Lauchlin Currie's designated leader.

52. Troy, *Donovan and The CIA*, p. 80; Weinstein, *Perjury*, p. 360-61, 202. See also Verne W. Newton, *The Cambridge Spies* (Lanham, NY, 1991).

53. Hede Massing testimony, *IRP Hearings*, part 1, p. 234. He had been interviewed and rejected as an agent by an NKVD officer in Europe, Ignace Reiss, who was later assassinated by the NKVD.

54. Allen Dulles, ed., *Great True Spy Stories* (New York, 1968), p. 240.

55. Author conversation with Arthur Schlesinger, Jr., 27 February 1986. Arthur Schlesinger, Jr., "Left Field," *The New York Review of Books*, 11 February 1965 review of Flora Lewis's book on Noel Field, *Red Pawn* (New York, 1965). Leonard Mosley, *Dulles* (New York, 1978).

56. Lewis, *Red Pawn*, p. 184-189, 240. After the war Field went to Prague and was imprisoned in Hungary because, some said, of a CIA planted rumor he was a CIA double agent. His wife, brother and foster daughter went in search of him and were also imprisoned without any public comment for several years. A Polish defector revealed they were alive, and all were released. Field and his wife chose to stay in Hungary and died there in 1979.

57. Author conversation with Arthur Schlesinger, Jr., 27 February 1986. Schlesinger said Bill Casey, who was in charge of the overall program in London, was for going ahead in general, but in this particular case, the risks didn't warrant it. When necessary they tried to use communists who could be "trusted to carry out their mission," especially where they were likely to have to deal with other communists in the resistance. Schlesinger said they recognized a certain risk but also a certain common goal which took priority. See National Archives, Modern Military History, Entry #91, Box 13, OSS-SI London War Diary (LWD), Labor Division, vol. 6, Book II, passim. See also Joseph Persico, *Piercing The Reich* (New York, 1979), pp. 166-183; Chapman Pincher, *Too Silent Too Long*, 97-102. In a conversation with the author on 3 March 1986, Justice Arthur Goldberg, former head of OSS Labor Branch in London, said he recruited German POW's who were social Democrats because "Hitler was kind enough to have their identification cards stamped 'not politically reliable' and they were still anticommunist for the most part." Goldberg also noted that it was his policy not to use communists as agents, although he knew exceptions had been made late in the war in Europe.

58. Author conversation with Joseph Gould on 27 February 1986 in Washington, D.C. For additional details see Pincher, *Too Silent Too Long*, p. 97-102. The OSS records show that "Lieutenant Gould . . . personally felt strongly that the men were of much higher quality than other agents recruited by OSS and were more secure and more dependable because of their strong political motivation." *OSS-SI, London War Diary*, National Archives, Modern Military History, Entry #91, Box 13, Labor Division, vol. 6, Book II, pp. 290-94.

59. Kuczynski's father, Dr. Rene Kuczynski (a professor at Oxford), was also an active communist. Sonja (now called Ruth Werner) had been a prewar GRU agent in China, Switzerland and other parts of Europe before coming to Britain to continue her espionage. It was Jurgen Kuczynski who had made Fuchs's initial GRU contacts in England in 1942, and he helped Fuchs reestablish contact with the Soviets in England after the war. Ruth Werner, *Sonja's Rapport* (East Berlin, 1977), p. 156-7. See also Pincher, *Too Silent Too Long*, p. 100. There is some dispute over these details of Kuczynski's postwar service. West, *The Circus*, p. 33, states Kuczynski was hired first by the OSS and sent to America as an economic assistant to George Ball. In a 25 February 1986 conversation with the author, Ball stated that he did not recall seeing Kuczynski in the States at any time, and that Kuczynski was certainly not his assistant. In a discussion with the author on 28 February 1986, John Kenneth Galbraith told the author that to the best of

his knowledge Kuczynski worked for the Bombing Survey only in Germany during 1946. Professor Kuczynski, now retired in East Berlin, confirmed this in a telephone conversation with the author on 14 March 1986. Sonja also stated her brother was awarded a Bronze Star. In an 11 April 1986 letter to the author Professor Kuczynski wrote he had been proposed for the Bronze Star but did not receive it. Kuczynski was no stranger to American ways. He attended the Brookings Graduate School in Washington D.C. in 1927 and is a distant relative of Louis Brandeis. *Memoriren: Die Erziehung des J.K. zum Kommunisten und Wissenschaftler* [Memoirs: The Education of J.K. as Communist and Scientist] (Berlin, 1983); Kuczynski, *Abraham Lincoln* (Berlin, 1985), pp. 7-9.

60. Author conversation with Justice Arthur Goldberg, 3 March 1986. As for leaks, Goldberg recalled two incidents concerning teams that were parachuted into Eastern Europe and promptly captured by the Germans, where a leak was suspected at OSS headquarters. The speculation was that the Soviets had been notified and in turn told the Germans, thus keeping the United States out of that area, but as far as he knows the "source was not pinpointed."

61. Werner, *Sonja's Rapport;* letter from FBI Director Hoover to Souers, special consultant to the president, dated 16 July 1950; FBI file number 65-58805, folder #36, p. 3. West, *The Circus*, p. 32.

62. James Murphy, conversation with the author, 16 March 1986. Murphy added, "Philby was smooth and friendly, though formal and did not get close to Americans. Everyone liked him, but he stayed out of the American social life as far as I could tell."

63. Kim Philby, *My Silent War* (New York, 1968), pp. 77-108.

64. Jane Foster, *An Un-American Lady* (London, 1980), p. 102-103. For details of indictment see U.S. Senate, *Scope Of Soviet Activities In The United States*, part 72, 11 July 1957.

65. Brown, *Last Hero*, p. 707.

66. Ibid., pp. 708-09. Aside from congressional questions about their communism, they were so identified in a book on OSS by Stewart Alsop and Thomas Braden, *Sub Rosa: The OSS and American Espionage* (New York, 1946), p. 25-6. Alsop and Braden pointed out, as others had done, their high-quality dangerous service in the army.

67. Brown, *Last Hero*, p. 708-9. CIC stands for Counterintelligence Corps.

68. Ibid., p. 116. All this came at a time when he was trying to make the case for a peacetime extension of the OSS. Faced with having to reverse himself and then defend against the charge that OSS had been penetrated by communist agents, he sent the men home honorably.

69. John Roy Carlson, *The Plotters* (New York, 1946), pp. 211-214.

70. John R. Deane, *The Strange Alliance* (New York, 1947), pp. 49-50. Deane, military attaché in Moscow during the war, said Donovan's organization maintained a constant flow of R & A studies and intelligence gained by operatives in the field, including "documentary proof that the Germans had succeeded in breaking certain Russian codes."

71. Robert Alcorn, *No Bugles For Spies: Tales of the OSS* (New York, 1962), p. 134.
72. Troy, *Donovan and the CIA*, pp. 424-30; Sanford Unger, *FBI* (Boston, 1976), pp. 103-07.
73. OSS GO # 13, 19 June 1943, *London War Diary* 7, p. 18.
74. The 13 October 1944 inventory of 109 reports published by the X-2 Special Studies Office in Washington includes *Communist Penetration of Norwegian I.S.*, *Soviet Intelligence in Scandinavia*, *Communist Active In Europe—USSR*, *Russian Influence in World Politics*, *Communists in Italy*, and *USSR—Espionage Systems*. National Archives, file # 883099, RG 226, Box 80. For more on OSS X-2 and Angleton in Italy see Robin Winks, *Cloak and Gown* (New York, 1987), pp. 356-9, 370-1. For more on OSS in Rumania see Robert Bishop and E.S. Crayfield, *Russia Astride the Balkans* (New York, 1948).
75. Anthony Cave Brown, *"C": The Life of Sir Stewart Menzies* (New York, 1987), p. 350.
76. Harry S. Truman, *Memoirs. Vol. II: Years of Trial and Hope 1946-1953* (New York, 1956), pp. 53-55. Troy, *Donovan and the CIA*, pp. 301, 463. Truman wrote, and his overall actions supported, that he always wanted good intelligence from a single agency. Some think his reasons for abolishing OSS so abruptly centered on a dislike for Donovan. Troy concludes his motivation "is not evident." In a letter dated 20 September 1945, the president instructed State to head an interdepartmental group to plan "the foreign intelligence field and in assigning and controlling operations."
77. FBI file of Elizabeth Bentley, #65-56604, undated report, *Introduction*, p. 1, 6. Several authors have written that Bentley contacted the FBI office in New Haven in August 1945 to make her confession (see for example Burnham, *Web of Deception*, p. 2; and Dallin, *Soviet Espionage*, p. 412). FBI documents show that she did visit the New Haven office on 23 August 1945, but did not mention her Soviet espionage activities. She went to the New York office twice, first on 16 October 1945, but she did not speak of espionage. During her third visit, on 8 November 1945, she began revealing her long-kept secret.
78. Weinstein, *Perjury*, p. 357. Hiss was finally placed under technical and personal surveillance on 20 November 1945.
79. See Troy, *Donovan and the CIA*, p. 464, for copy of Truman's directive establishing CIG.
80. Harry Rositzke, *The CIA's Secret Operations* (New York, 1977), p. 12. The British did not, for whatever reasons, adopt similar procedures and consequently the CIA's indirect penetration problems from this source persisted.

8

U. S. Economic Strategy in World War II: Wartime Goals, Peacetime Plans[1]

Warren F. Kimball

"The defeat in World War II of such a shark as was German imperialism, the defeat of militaristic Japan, the weakening of the once powerful British and French competitors put American imperialism in the position of the leader of the capitalist world by all major indices, economic, financial and military. What seemed to promote the claims of the ruling class of the United States to world hegemony was also the fact that it actually found itself to be the only big country that had waxed fabulously rich on the war."[2] That statement, made by Soviet leader Mikhail Gorbachev on the fortieth anniversary of the end of the European phase of World War II, colorfully, almost luridly, depicted the economic position of the United States following that struggle. To indiscriminately lump Nazi Germany and the United States under the single label "imperialism" is ahistorical and polemical. But no one can quarrel with the statement that the United States was, at war's end, the world's greatest economic and financial power. What Gorbachev's speech also failed to address, except by implication, was whether that postwar prosperity was, to a significant degree, a result of American wartime economic strategy, or just an accident of events and the inevitable result of the vast strength of the American economy.

On the same page of the *New York Times* where the Gorbachev statement appeared was a short news item announcing that the Soviet Union had awarded W. Averell Harriman the Order of the Patriotic War, First Degree, for his " 'great personal contributions to the improvement and strengthening of Soviet-American cooperation.' " Harriman was a key player in American wartime economic strategies. During his tenure as "defense expediter" in England and then as ambassador to the Soviet Union, much of Harriman's efforts focused on fulfilling Franklin Roosevelt's promise of the United States being the "arsenal of democracy."

The juxtaposition of those two Soviet comments suggests the way American economic strategy was divided during World War II. There were two distinct yet related American economic schemes. The first was the strategy designed to win the war. That approach came in two phases. Initially, winning meant bolstering America's allies so as to avoid full participation. But once the United States entered the war, its definition of "winning" became more expansive. Victory meant "unconditional surrender"—a degree of military success that permitted, even encouraged, American leaders to think in terms of opportunities to implement the second economic strategy. As the war progressed and victory became more certain, the United States, like each of its allies, began to emphasize strategies for the postwar world that included economics. It is no insight to point out that war aims always change and evolve as the military situation develops; what is, perhaps, sometimes forgotten is that those war aims can be affected just as strongly by wartime economic developments.[3]

Those two distinct, yet inextricably intertwined aspects of wartime economic strategy need to be studied with the understanding that the word "strategy" frequently implies too much in the way of planning and too little about policy as a reaction to situations, particularly in the case of Franklin Roosevelt, who avoided structured thinking like the plague.[4]

American economic strategy during the early stages of the war developed logically from that combination of frustration and domestic politics that generated the famous—and misleadingly named—neutrality legislation. Secretary of State Cordell Hull's fixation on reciprocal trade agreements reflected a more general concern among New Dealers about the growth of international cartels and a trend toward autarky—just the sort of thing Wilsonians thought created tension between states.[5] Politically, Americans in general believed that World War I had been unnecessary and that the European powers were too selfish and stubborn to accept the leadership of the United States. Europe's petty, though bloody, battles, whether over trade or frontiers, were something to avoid.[6] Perhaps Charles Beard expressed the political part of that American belief more perceptively than anyone else. Arguing for a new economic and foreign policy, Beard contemptuously rejected the assumption "that outward thrusts of national power too strong to be controlled at home can be subdued at international conferences of diplomats representing governments incapable of conquering at home the very forces whose impacts abroad they seek to master through treaties, agreements, and conversations."[7] America followed Beard's prescription for avoiding war insofar as it relied on abstention, rather than so-called peacekeeping. But that most definitely did not include abstention from commercial coercion, despite Beard's diagnosis. After all, economic pressure had been the preferred American way of dealing with external problems since the pre-Revolution boycotts of the 1760s and Thomas Jefferson's use of an embargo during the Napoleonic Wars.[8]

As the European political situation deteriorated in the 1930s, President Franklin Roosevelt and his advisors looked to economic strategy as a means of supporting Hitler's opponents, particularly France and Great Britain. Economic sanctions on the part of the West proved ineffective, even farcical, during the Italo-Ethiopian War and the Spanish Civil War, but that was not for lack of cooperation on the part of the United States. Roosevelt would not join any formal organization that smacked of intervention, but his administration did issue regulations that paralleled the sanctions adopted by Britain and France and enforced them more vigorously. That was a far cry from the kind of aggressive leadership role that the British and French would have liked, but the Americans were remarkably faithful to whatever measures the western Europeans were willing to adopt.[9] An even more striking example came in September 1936 with the Tripartite Monetary Agreement between Britain, France, and the United States. That agreement constituted a public announcement that the United States had abandoned the economic nationalism—or "intranationalism" as one scholar calls it—of the London Economic Conference.[10] But, as the discussions surrounding the agreement make clear, it was German and Italian actions that created the atmosphere needed in the United States to make such international monetary cooperation possible. Time and again, Roosevelt and his advisors, especially Treasury Secretary Henry Morgenthau, Jr., alluded to the political as well to as the economic stabilization the pact would promote.[11]

Despite widespread conviction among Americans that the growing crisis in Europe did not threaten them, the Roosevelt administration continued to follow the same economic strategy. Britain, France, and the United States were, as Morgenthau put it, "the only three liberal governments left." Military intervention in Europe to aid those ideological allies was, in the mid-1930s, unthinkable. After all, even so rabid an opponent of Hitler as Morgenthau referred to the Europeans as "these perfectly mad people." But political/military involvement would not be necessary, even if it were possible, if the United States could provide the kind of economic support that would strengthen and stabilize Britain and France to the point that they could control Germany and Italy.[12]

Viable or not, productive or counterproductive, that broad economic strategy of bolstering those opposed to Hitler remained central to American foreign policy from the mid-1930s until well after the outbreak of war in September 1939—and for a good deal longer. Roosevelt's October 1937 speech calling for a quarantine of the lawless, long pictured as either an aberration or obfuscation, fits in neatly with the president's economic strategy. To his cabinet, Roosevelt equated quarantines with economic sanctions, and he told the British ambassador that blockades did not mean war. Even though that discussion was followed in January 1938 by secret Anglo-American naval discussions that presaged military collaboration, American economic strategy remained the same. Historian David Reynolds has described "F.D.R.'s limited conception of America's world role in 1938-39. The U.S. would act as democracy's arsenal, but she would not be pushed into a position of international leadership or dragged into another war."[13] The unexpected collapse of France in the spring of 1940 forced Roosevelt to consider some type of military intervention, but even then he spoke repeatedly of limiting that intervention to the air and sea war—all the while assuming the use of economic coercion. Whether or not the President actually held to that wishful hope right through to the Pearl Harbor attack is arguable,[14] but it is clear that his economic strategy did not change. Granted, a part of that strategy included expanding the American arms industry, particularly with European capital, thus improving America's defense posture. But even though such capital investments by Britain and France were important, the total amounts involved were relatively small. More important, those investments, as well as a high proportion of American spending, were for the aircraft and shipbuilding industries, which neatly dovetailed with FDR's thinking about limited intervention.[15]

The steady progress by the United States toward deeper and deeper economic involvement—too slow for the British, too fast for Americans—makes sense only when placed in the context of this prewar, and pre-Pearl Harbor economic strategy. The cash-and-carry provisions of the 1937 Neutrality Act stripped that legislation of its original purpose, which seems in retrospect to have been to keep the United States out of World War I.[16] Instead, it became something that quickly drained France and Britain of much of their liquid capital. There is no evidence that Roosevelt's economic strategy aimed at exploiting the European crisis that way, although Treasury official Harry Dexter White commented in 1938 that Britain would have to accept various economic terms set by the United States "since she 'needs our good will much more than we need hers at the present time.' " Either way, the economic benefits to the United States were part of the political strategy for gaining public and congressional support.[17]

As war descended over Europe, Roosevelt stuck to his economic strategy. In fact, with the failure of his occasional attempts at peacemaking (the Welles mission early in 1940, for example), his economic strategy became his only strategy, at least in Europe. The revision of the neutrality laws in November 1939 permitted cash-and-carry sale of arms to belligerents, again combining shrewd business with the economic strategy of building up France and Britain. But that businesslike approach—what historian David Reynolds aptly calls "competitive cooperation"—began to waver as German victories mounted. Britain faced Nazi Germany alone for a full year (from June 1940 until Hitler dropped the other shoe and attacked the Soviet Union in the east), and the American stake in Britain's survival was very large. The collapse of Great Britain would put Hitler only an ocean away from the United States, and that ocean looked like a mere lake if German forces occupied Dakar in West Africa, just a thousand miles from the bulge of Brazil.[18] Still, Roosevelt backed away from political commitments and stepped up the pace of his economic strategy. The informal aid program, which had begun even before the war, had become inadequate. Roosevelt called for America to become the "arsenal of democracy" and then moved to implement his slogan, stepping up the defense production that had begun in earnest after the French surrender six months earlier.[19] Britain's lack of cash ("ready money" as Churchill called it) gave Roosevelt the excuse he needed to propose to Congress an all-out program of financial and military aid: lend-lease. The title of that legislation—an act "to Promote the Defense of the United States"—has often been described as a smokescreen to hide intervention, but Roosevelt's actions throughout much of 1941 suggest that is not the case. There is no evidence that FDR became reconciled to the unrestricted use of American military forces in Europe until after the Pearl Harbor attack, although he spoke more and more of naval and air involvement.[20] Nor is there any evidence that the lend-lease act was drafted with selfish postwar purposes in mind. The aphorism of A.J.P. Taylor—"of all the great men at the top, Roosevelt was the only one who knew what he was doing: he made the United States the greatest power in the world at virtually no cost"—gives Roosevelt too much credit or blame for Machiavellian planning. Taylor referred in large measure to the conditions of lend-lease aid, but those conditions were developed after the program had been conceived and legislated, and by the State Department, not by the Treasury.[21] The only clear postwar purpose in drafting the lend-lease legislation was to deal with the immediate political situation in early 1941 and to avoid a new war-debts controversy, and in those regards it succeeded very well.

The outbreak of war between the Soviet Union and Germany did not alter Roosevelt's reliance on his economic strategy. During the congressional debate over the lend-lease act, the President had successfully opposed amendments forbidding lend-lease to Russia, in part because of growing evidence of German plans to attack in the east. Conservative fears of bolshevism and the competing demands of the American and British military for the limited supplies available delayed an extension of lend-lease to the Soviet Union, but not for long. When presidential advisor Harry Hopkins returned from his trip to Moscow, confident that the Russians were not about to give up, Roosevelt quietly but deliberately moved toward an extension of lend-lease to Russia. It was a courageous decision, given the domestic political climate, but it was consistent with the President's economic strategy for the war. In this case, the things Stalin wanted the most—aluminum and airplanes—were in short supply and little actual assistance could be sent immediately, but the future commitment to aid and alliance was clear.[22]

Pearl Harbor ended America's nonbelligerent status, but not Roosevelt's broad economic strategy. Although military operations immediately became integral to the nation's wartime strategy, Roosevelt continued to operate from the assumption that American economic strength would be decisive in Europe. Americans accepted, even insisted, that their forces take the war to the Japanese, but there was no similar public demand for military action against Germany. Granted, attempts to mobilize economic strength were late, disorganized, and hampered by domestic political considerations, despite the President's only occasionally successful ploy of routinely doubling and tripling the production estimates of his subordinates. Nonetheless, events proved Roosevelt's faith in American economic strength correct.[23]

Entry into the war did, of course, change a fundamental political assumption, a change that was reflected in the scope and techniques of American economic strategy. Prior to Pearl Harbor, when a British and Soviet collapse seemed all too possible, Roosevelt appeared willing though not hopeful for some sort of negotiated peace in Europe, albeit one that effectively quarantined Hitler.[24] But that quickly changed in December 1941. From that point, the President's unwavering goal was the complete and utter defeat of the enemy—what became in February 1943 the "Unconditional Surrender" proclamation. Once into the war, Roosevelt, like his mentor Woodrow Wilson, saw the war as an opportunity to do much more than merely protect American interests. It became an opportunity for reform, a chance to extend the New Deal to Europe and Asia. Moreover, with many of Roosevelt's military planners predicting a Germany victory on the Russian front, full military participation by American ground forces became recognized, slowly but surely, as a necessity.[25] With this redefinition of victory, and the reevaluation of the means necessary, American economic strategy called for overwhelming economic/production superiority in order to achieve overwhelming military/political success. Economic strategy had replaced political strategy in the pre-Pearl Harbor years. Afterwards, with American military forces not able to launch an offensive across nearly 4,000 miles of ocean, economic strategy offered the only effective way to confront Germany, at least until the opening of a major front in Italy in 1943.[26]

This raises the important question of wartime logistics, which needs careful consideration in any study of economic strategy. Stalin advised the British in September 1941 to build up their armies and stop depending on sea power, or they would be defeated. Even though that comment probably related to Stalin's demands for a Second Front (as he defined it), it still ignored the manpower as well as the geopolitical problems faced by Britain, particularly in Asia, and by the United States in both Europe and the Pacific.[27] American planning had to assume long, extended, often vulnerable lines of communication. The Soviets, on the other hand, had shorter (interior) lines of communication even while they fought for survival in 1941 and 1942. As the American shipbuilding program illustrated, planners had to work out the delivery of supplies (and personnel) before they could worry about producing the goods. In other words, a nation's economic strategy for war had to reflect the kind of war it was capable of fighting. For the United States, that meant a long-distance war that emphasized naval and air forces, as Roosevelt had done in the neutrality period. It meant providing supplies to those who were doing the fighting, at least until America was ready to fight its kind of war.

That oft-alluded to story of economic mobilization and planning, that attempt to balance the competing demands of the American, British, and Soviet military are illuminated by what might be called the mobilization of economics. Two examples will explain my meaning. The American War Bond program is one.

Roosevelt and Treasury Secretary Morgenthau decided early in 1942 to establish a voluntary war bonds program. Increased revenue and savings to lessen inflationary pressures were important motives, but far from the only goals of the campaign. A voluntary program would require a huge publicity campaign that could, they agreed, "make the country war-minded." In other words, selling the war, particularly the war in Europe, was a problem for the

American government, and the war bonds program helped to do just that. Radio programs, advertising, voluntary payroll deductions—even Donald Duck—were all mobilized to promote buying the bonds. Morgenthau, with the morals of an upper class reformer, not those of a Madison Avenue ad executive, preferred billboards featuring "a girl from Amalgamated Clothiers Union swathed in overalls" to "a Hollywood actress swathed in mink," but regardless, the program was a psychological and occasionally an economic success. In one remarkable month, December 1942, the Victory Loan program raised nearly $13 billion, although individual subscriptions rarely met stated goals.[28]

A second example where economic mobilization served more than just supply and treasury needs was rationing. Things designated as strategic materials, like wolfram or aluminum, could be easily controlled by allocation regulations, but consumer items like gasoline and rubber, which were in short supply, were another matter. Rationing books soon appeared, although the list of rationed items was short compared to British restrictions. What is interesting is the way in which the rationing campaign was used to "get Americans involved" in the war. Ration stamps featured pictures of tanks, planes, ships, and guns, and public campaigns stressed the idea that each stamp helped provide something needed by the boys at the front. The goal was more than just the rationing of scarce supplies. Roosevelt and his advisers also realized that sacrifices, even small ones, would give the American public a sense of personal involvement in the war.[29] Like the President's decision in 1942 to invade North Africa, which was, in large measure, designed to get the entire nation into the fight, so rationing—including such curious programs as meatless Tuesdays—had the same goal.[30]

American economic strategy for the Pacific war was essentially the same as that for Europe: to crush the enemy and reshape Japan's existing social and political structure. But again the politics of alliance warfare affected economic strategy. Fearing massive casualties, American strategists sought to avoid a major land war on the Asian continent (although the alternative was not apparent until after the Battle of Midway and the success of the Navy's island-hopping campaign). That required keeping China in the war without sending American forces to that theater. In the words of historian Lloyd Gardner, "It was cheaper to buy off China than to fight." In retrospect, it appears that lend-lease, loans, and the allocation of war materials were all governed by the underlying philosophy of giving just enough to make it worth China's while to stay in the war. Taken in this light, the political corruption and venality so often cited as reasons for not increasing aid to China begin to look like excuses, or at least rationalizations.[31]

The overriding goal of defeating the enemy with the lowest possible casualties shaped American economic and political strategies from start to finish.[32] It is fashionable today, and valid, to emphasize the postwar ambitions and plans of the United States. But we must keep that in perspective. Aid to the Soviet Union continued apace long after its armies had taken the offensive against Germany. If postwar greed, ambition, and calculated schemes motivated American policy, why continue wartime aid to Russia? In part, bureaucratic inertia may be the answer. In part, Roosevelt's desire to promote postwar cooperation explains the action. But in part, lend-lease military aid continued because the Red Army was fighting Germany and would help fight Japan—and defeating those two enemies was, after all, the reason for the war. Shipments to the USSR in late 1943 and 1944 exceeded commitments by thirty percent, and continued in that way until the end of the war in Europe. As the war's end approached, lend-lease was seen by some as a tool for the protection and expansion of American postwar interests (see below), but military priorities continued to determine actual lend-lease shipments.[33]

There are other examples of this continued emphasis on winning the war, even after victory seemed certain. Some are military-political and not economic strategies, but they illustrate the prevailing atmosphere. Eisenhower's decision to stay with a broad front approach in western Europe and not to enter into a "race" for Berlin comes to mind. More important, the Pacific war, expected to last one to two years past VE Day, forced a postponement of any shift from a wartime to a peacetime economy.

Still, as victory became more and more certain, Americans did develop strategies designed to implement their visions of the postwar world. Arguments within the United States over these postwar goals were extensive, but a broad pattern did emerge. Perhaps the most immediate American postwar concern was to guarantee that Germany could not and would not cause another war. After forty-five years of preoccupation with the Cold War, Americans of that generation often underestimated the intensity of that fear. Roosevelt firmly believed that the Germans had been "Prussianized," and that their moral character had to be rebuilt. Until that happened, Germany posed a threat to world peace.[34] What is intriguing, perhaps typically American, is that economics formed the basic strategy for achieving a political and social end. The Morgenthau plan for Germany, all too facilely dismissed as a crackpot revenge scheme, was designed to reform the German character by reshaping the Germany economy. For Morgenthau, the example was Denmark, where, he said to FDR, "the people, through small-scale farming, were in intimate association with the land and were peace-loving and without aggressive designs upon others."[35] That may be naive, but it is also an attempt to put economics to the service of politics. It is worth noting that Churchill and Stalin, during their meeting in Moscow in October 1944, both firmly supported the dismemberment and the deindustrialization of Germany.[36]

The number of ways and places that Americans focused on the postwar world are legion, and many, if not most, touch on economics. In fact, what is difficult is to separate ideology, politics, and economics in postwar planning. American thinking on world affairs includes an economic strategy, hardly surprising for a nation that grew out of a group of colonies conceived in the mercantilist trading world of the 17th century. Moreover, the United States began its independent existence at a time when that world of closed empires seemed to threaten the new nation's economic survival. The ideology of the American Revolution included anticolonialism, but so did the economic strategy of Revolutionary leaders. It is a long journey from 1776 to World War II, but American anticolonialism survived intact, if somewhat altered. American pressure for the decolonization of the British and other European empires was in part political (Roosevelt believed that colonial empires posed a threat to world peace), in part military (Roosevelt and his military chiefs wanted to move European outposts further away from the Western Hemisphere and to extend American military strength), and in part economic (closed economic spheres ran counter to traditional thinking that labelled restrictions on American trade as unfair, unwise, and even vaguely immoral).[37]

Perhaps the best example of this kind of thinking is found in the constant Anglo-American talks about the postwar economic relationship of Britain to its empire. Those discussions began in earnest with the attempt in 1941 by the United States to use the lend-lease master agreement as a lever to eliminate special trading arrangements between Britain and her commonwealth and empire. They continued through the Atlantic Conference and Charter of August 1941, and then became institutionalized in the disagreements over to just what the two parties had agreed. As late as 10 February 1945, in the midst of the Yalta Conference, Roosevelt prodded Churchill to open serious official talks on the matter. Churchill responded with a vague statement about the usefulness of current informal talks and suggested that the entire question be postponed. Perhaps the chapter title given that group of the documents in the official collection, *Foreign Relations of the United States*, best sums up American thinking: "negotiations relating to the extension of credit to the United Kingdom, the liberalization of world trade, and the settlement of Lend Lease."[38] Roosevelt may have assured Churchill in February 1942 that the United States had no intention of asking Britain "to trade the principle of imperial preference as a consideration for lend-lease," but that was belied by the facts. By November 1944, the link between lend-lease and British economic concessions was on the table. The specific issue was access to commercial air routes within the British Empire, but the broad principle was the same—the liberalization of world trade. As the president put it to the prime minister: "We are doing our best to meet your lend-lease needs. We will face Congress on that subject in a few weeks and it will not be in a generous mood if it and the people feel that the United Kingdom has not agreed to a beneficial air agreement." Churchill responded with sarcasm, but could only appeal to the American sense of fair play. The British never signed that civil aviation agreement, and the United States eventually resorted to bilateral negotiations, but that is not the point. What is important is to appreciate that the Americans came into the war with certain assumptions about international economics and then, during the war, developed specific strategies designed to put those assumptions into practice.[39]

It is worth noting here that most American leaders, and particularly Franklin Roosevelt, looked not to the Soviet Union for opposition to the "liberalization" of international trade, but expected Great Britain to throw up roadblocks. That, and Britain's long standing role as a major commercial empire, prompted Roosevelt and his cohorts to concentrate on bringing the English around to the American point of view.[40]

Nothing better illustrates this American combination of old ideas, war-time opportunities, and the need to bring Britain around to "our" way of thinking better than the Bretton Woods agreements on an international financial and monetary system. Just six months after the United States had entered the war, Roosevelt and his Treasury officials, using Harry Dexter White as draftsman, had developed a broad economic strategy designed to implement what a Treasury Department memorandum labelled "a New Deal in international economics."[41] In keeping with New Deal thinking, the postwar system would rely on government expertise and planning, although that was later modified in favor of private financial institutions for reasons of both domestic and international politics. Anglo-American distrust, suspicion, and bargaining (the "competitive cooperation" theme again) distracted negotiators for much of 1942 and 1943, but as Morgenthau had pointed out back in the mid-1930s, the two nations (plus France) were the only large liberal countries left in the world. Aware of American financial power and eager to retain some share in world economic leadership, the British compromised and the Bretton Woods system was born.

Yet the notion of a worldwide, comprehensive American postwar economic strategy ascribes too much purpose and cleverness to a nation that had insulated (not isolated) itself from much of the world for so long. From the postwar perspective, American involvement in the Middle East during World War II would seem largely a matter of economics—oil. But that is not the case, at least initially. Despite the efforts of missionaries, consular officials, and a few businessmen, the United States had little interest in that part of the world prior to 1941. Then entry of the Soviet Union into the war as well as the German military/fifth column threat to the area quickly heightened American awareness. Unhappy with British military logistics organization, Roosevelt suggested to Churchill that the U.S. Army take over the Trans-Persian Railway in order to expand the flow of supplies to Russia. Churchill dismissed complaints from his military about the dependence of British Middle East forces on the United States with the comment "In whose hands could we be better dependent?" but that belied his concern. The presence of 30,000 U.S. troops and a full-fledged army Service Command guaranteed greater American knowledge of and interest in that part of the world. By 1944, when military events had made the Middle East and the Persian Gulf supply route a backwater, Americans began to find reasons to continue their involvement there. In October 1944, a committee headed by Assistant Secretary of State Adolf Berle recommended that aid should promote stability and head off problems posed by a "potentially expansionist Soviet policy and a rigid British dog-in-the-manger policy." But attempts to use lend-lease as a lever to improve America's postwar economic position in that area were late and futile, since lend-lease had decreased in importance as the war had moved toward central Europe. Control of oil supplies later became an issue, but during World War II, American strategists concentrated on free access, not exclusive rights. Americans believed that a strong United States presence would enable Middle Eastern countries (and other small nations) to escape the political and economic clutches of both Britain and the Soviet Union, permitting them to stand on their own independent feet.[42]

Perhaps Franklin Roosevelt's letter to Winston Churchill, written about proposals for postwar assistance to Iran but applicable to others, should be taken at face value: "I rather like [the] general approach to the care and education of what used to be called 'backward countries.' . . . The point of all this is that I do not want the United States to acquire a 'zone of influence'—or any other nation for that matter. Iran certainly needs Trustees. It will take thirty or forty years to eliminate the graft and the feudal system. Until that time comes, Iran may be a headache to you, to Russia and to ourselves."[43] This statement becomes even more important when we realize that the differences between Franklin Roosevelt and his advisors on broad economic strategies have been exaggerated. The British found that out when they assumed that American insistence on the dismantling of the Imperial Preference system was merely one of Secretary of State Hull's pet schemes. Told of that assumption, the President quickly disabused Churchill of that notion.[44]

To understand Roosevelt's wartime economic thinking requires an appreciation of his conception of the organization and structure of the postwar world, for that was a major factor in his wartime economic policies.[45] Roosevelt avoided systematic thought and well-defined positions, but his speeches, private conversations, letters, and messages show great consistency regarding his vision of the postwar world. His frequent references to the "four policemen" reflected an attempt to reconcile the nationalism and great power politics of his cousin, Theodore Roosevelt, with the liberal internationalism of his political mentor, Woodrow Wilson. FDR refused to talk in terms of "spheres of influence," yet he regularly referred to the interests and responsibilities of the great powers. Perhaps if we put the two together and speak of "spheres of responsibility" we can better understand what he was thinking. Even though that included certain "police" powers, the concept differed from spheres of influence in that the goal was to assist other nations to develop, not merely to exploit them. More important, none of these "spheres of responsibility" were to be exclusive. He believed that military and political security for the great powers were prerequisites to peace, but each sphere was to be open to the trade, commerce, culture, philanthropy, and ideas of others. Thus American trade opportunities and cultural interests and influence were to be actively protected by the other major powers. Some American business interests wanted the United States to take advantage of the war to protect and expand economic opportunities, but Roosevelt's globalism was more restricted. The problem, of course, is that putting these ideas into a structure creates—and created—enormous tensions, just as Wilson's attempts to articulate and implement his idealism contained self-destructive forces.[46]

World War II, like most wars, cannot be understood as a military event without examining the details of economic strategy and mobilization. Napoleon's quip that an army travels on its stomach was but a colloquial way of saying that economic strength wins wars. Nevertheless, Marx, among others, was right when he wrote of the absolute connection between economics and politics—for both the wartime and the postwar worlds. Roosevelt's postwar planning began even before the United States had entered the war, and wartime economic strategies took postwar goals into consideration. That is not an argument for an American conspiracy or master plan to dominate the world's economy—even if that was the result. It is an argument that those who ignore, dismiss, or downplay the economic dimension for both the wartime and the postwar worlds are condemned to present a flawed picture of a multidimensional history.

NOTES

1. A earlier version of this paper was presented at the Sixteenth International Congress of Historical Sciences, Stuttgart, Germany, 29 August 1985. My thanks to the Rutgers University Research Council for its support on this project and to Ted Wilson of the University of Kansas for his most valuable comments.
2. *New York Times*, 9 May 1985.
3. The war aims of the major belligerents of World War II still await the kind of focused, analytical study that Hans Gatzke did so well for Germany during World War I. See Gatzke, *Germany's Drive to the West: A Study of Western War Aims during the First World War* (Baltimore, 1950).
4. Reactions to situations are also a product of a variety of cultural and political assumptions, as historians like Emily Rosenberg, Lloyd Gardner, Frank Costiglia, and Michael Hunt keep reminding us. But that is a study of intellectual history and beyond the scope of this excursion—even for someone trying to keep in mind that politics and economics are inseparable.
5. Hull's concern about the effects of restrictive trade practices led him to fear that Germany would seek special trading arrangements that would close access for other nations, or, failing that, would resort to war to meet its economic needs. American attempts to ensure German access to raw materials have prompted later historians to label the policy "appeasement"—a misleading use of a much misused word, for Hull's economic policies were not aimed at satiating Hitler's expansionism (as was Neville Chamberlain's appeasement policy) but at the worldwide elimination of restrictive trade agreements. See, for example, Patrick Hearden, *Roosevelt Confronts Hitler* (Dekalb, IL, 1987), chap. 4, "The Quest for Economic Appeasement."
6. See for example, Selig Adler, *The Isolationist Impulse* (New York, 1957); Warren I. Cohen, *The American Revisionists* (Chicago, 1967); Manfred Jonas, *Isolationism in America* (Ithaca, NY, 1966); Justus D. Doenecke, ed., *In Danger Undaunted: The Anti-Interventionist Movement of 1940-1941 as Revealed in the Papers of the America First Committee* (Stanford, CA, 1990); and Wayne S. Cole, *Roosevelt and the Isolationists, 1932-1945* (Lincoln, NE, 1983).
7. Charles A. Beard, *The Idea of National Interest* (New York, 1934).
8. Reliance on economic strategy to the near exclusion of other factors is as old as the American nation. It was the failure of colonial boycotts of British goods—economic coercion—that precipitated the political and military

crisis that became the American Revolution. And as James Field has so perceptively pointed out, early American foreign policy placed a similar emphasis on economic strategies. See Field, "All OEconomists, All Diplomats," in William Becker and Samuel Wells, eds., *Economics and World Power* (New York, 1984), pp. 1-54.

9. See Robert A. Divine, *The Illusion of Neutrality* (Chicago, 1962); Richard P. Traina, *American Diplomacy and the Spanish Civil War* (Bloomington, IN, 1968); Herbert Feis, *Seen From E.A.* (New York, 1966); and especially John Morton Blum, *From the Morgenthau Diaries*, 3 vols. (Boston, 1959-67), vol. I, *Years of Crisis, 1928-1938*, pp. 506-8. For critical views of U.S. policy see David Schmitz, *The United States and Fascist Italy, 1922-1940* (Chapel Hill, NC, 1988), and Douglas Little, *Malevolent Neutrality: The United States, Great Britain, and the Origins of the Spanish Civil War* (Ithaca, NY, 1985).

10. Elliot A. Rosen, "Intranationalism vs. Internationalism: The Interregnum Struggle for the Sanctity of the New Deal," *Political Science Quarterly* 81, no. 2 (1966), pp. 274-97.

11. Blum, *Years of Crisis*, pp. 155-82. A reading of the Morgenthau Diaries and particularly the Presidential Diary, both in the Morgenthau Papers (Franklin D. Roosevelt Library, Hyde Park, NY) for the month of September 1936 drives home the political importance Roosevelt ascribed to the agreement.

12. Blum, *Years of Crisis*, p. 171. Roosevelt's exhortations to the Europeans, particularly to the British, to stand up to Hitler are well summarized in William R. Rock, *Chamberlain and Roosevelt: British Foreign Policy and the United States, 1937-1940* (Columbus, OH, 1988).

13. David Reynolds, *The Creation of the Anglo-American Alliance, 1937-41: A Study in Competitive Co-operation* (Chapel Hill, NC, 1982), p. 44. See James Leutze, *Bargaining for Supremacy: Anglo-American Naval Collaboration, 1937-1941* (Chapel Hill, NC, 1977) for U.S.-U.K. naval discussions.

14. Reynolds persuasively argues for that view, ibid. There is some evidence of a pre-Pearl Harbor commitment by Roosevelt to aid Britain and Holland in the Pacific. See, for example, Edwin T. Layton with John Costello, *And I Was There* (New York, 1985). But, except for a defense of the Philippine Islands, that would not preclude limiting American active participation to air and sea forces.

15. Capital investments by Britain and France are discussed in John Haight, *American Aid to France* (New York, 1970), and Warren F. Kimball, *"The Most Unsordid Act": Lend-Lease, 1939-1941* (Baltimore, MD, 1969). See also the paper presented by G. Ranki, "Economic Strategy in World War II: An Overview," at the Sixteenth International Congress of the Historical Sciences, Stuttgart, Germany, 29 August 1985.

16. The phrase is that of Thomas A. Bailey, *A Diplomatic History of the American People* (8th ed.; New York, 1969), p. 703; the sarcasm we share.

17. See Divine, *Illusion of Neutrality*, pp. 162-99, and Lloyd C. Gardner, *Economic Aspects of New Deal Diplomacy* (Madison, WI, 1964), pp. 97, 107. White was discussing a rate of exchange agreement, but his comment reflects the atmosphere.

18. American fears of a German invasion of Latin America were genuine if exaggerated. See Patrick J. Hearden, *Roosevelt Confronts Hitler: America's Entry into World War II* (DeKalb, IL, 1987), pp. 110-12, 158-69; Stetson Conn and Byron Fairchild, *The Framework of Hemisphere Defense* (Washington, D.C., 1960); Alton Frye, *Nazi Germany and the American Hemisphere, 1933-1941* (New Haven, CT, 1967); Stanley E. Hilton, *Hitler's Secret War in South America* (Baton Rouge, LA, 1981); and Ronald C. Newton, "Disorderly Succession: Great Britain, The United States and the 'Nazi Menace' in Argentina, 1938-47," in Guido di Tella and D. Cameron Watt, eds., *Argentina Between the Great Powers, 1939-46* (Basingstoke, 1989), pp. 111-34. The effect on the Western Hemisphere of Roosevelt's concern about the British fleet is demonstrated in Fred E. Pollock, "Roosevelt, the Ogdensburg Agreement, and the British Fleet: All Done with Mirrors," *Diplomatic History* 5 (Summer 1981), pp. 203-19.

19. The story is told succinctly and well in Theodore A. Wilson, "Leviathan: The American Economy in World War II," in D. J. Reynolds, W. F. Kimball, and A. O. Chubarian, eds., *Allies At War: The American-British-Soviet Experience of World War II* (forthcoming).

20. See, for example, the discussion of the Atlantic Conference in Warren F. Kimball, ed., *Churchill & Roosevelt: The Complete Correspondence* (3 vols.; Princeton, NJ, 1984), I, pp. 227-231. See also Layton, *And I Was There*. The Churchill quotation is from Winston S. Churchill, *The Birth of Britain* (New York, 1956), p. 474.

21. A.J.P. Taylor, *English History, 1914-1945* (New York, 1965). The motives for lend-lease and the later conditions are discussed in Kimball, *The Most Unsordid Act* and "Lend-Lease and the Open Door: The Temptation of British Opulence, 1937-1942," in *The Juggler: Franklin Roosevelt as Wartime Statesman* (Princeton, NJ, 1991), pp. 43-61, and Reynolds, *Creation of the Anglo-American Alliance*, pp. 145-69, 269-80.

22. Hopkins's mission, so crucial to the future of the wartime coalition, is examined in Kimball, *The Juggler*, chap. 2. The decision to aid the Soviet Union is discussed in George Herring, *Aid to Russia, 1941-1946* (New York, 1973), pp. 2-24 and Raymond Dawson, *The Decision to Aid Russia, 1941* (Chapel Hill, NC, 1959). There are indications in the Diary of Admiral William Leahy (Library of Congress, Washington, D.C.) that W. Averell Harriman's report following his trip to Moscow in September also played a key role in Roosevelt's decision to extend lend-lease to the Soviet Union. Harriman's mission can be followed in the books cited above as well as in his papers in the Library of Congress, Washington, D.C.

23. See Richard W. Steele, "American Popular Opinion and the War Against Germany: The Issue of a Negotiated Peace, 1942," *Journal of American History* 65, no. 3 (1978), pp. 704-23; Ranki, "Economic Strategy in World

War II." On Roosevelt's optimistic production goals see Kent Roberts Greenfield, *American Strategy in World War II: A Reconsideration* (Baltimore, MD, 1963); Kimball, *The Juggler*, p. 8, 33-34; and T. A. Wilson. "Leviathan," in *Allies At War*.

24. See the discussion of the Welles Mission in Reynolds, *Creation of the Anglo-American Alliance*, pp. 69-72.

25. See Mark A. Stoler, "From Continentalism to Globalism: General Stanley D. Embick, the Joint Strategic Survey Committee, and the Military View of American National Policy during the Second World War," *Diplomatic History* 6 (Summer 1982), pp. 303-21.

26. See R. Leighton & R. Coakley, *Global Logistics and Strategy, 1940-1943* (Washington, D.C., 1955), esp. chap. 8. "Unconditional Surrender" and the internationalization of the New Deal are widely discussed issues. See, for example, Reynolds, *Creation of the Anglo-American Alliance*, chap. 10, "A New Deal for the World"; Blum, *Years of War*, passim.; Warren F. Kimball, *Swords Or Ploughshares?* (Philadelphia, PA, 1976), pp. 25-34, and Kimball, *The Juggler*, chap. 4. "Unconditional Surrender" is discussed in ibid., pp. 76-77.

27. W. Averell Harriman and Ellie Abel, *Special Envoy to Churchill and Stalin* (New York, 1975), p. 101. Three years later, with the military threat to the Soviet Union ended, Stalin shifted his assessment and told Churchill that "Germany's mistake was that she had wanted to conquer Europe although she had no fleet." The point was that a fleet was needed to carry food and fuel. See Records of the Meetings at the Kremlin, Moscow, 9-17 October 1944 (TOLSTOY), Prime Minister's Operational Files, PREM 3/434/2/61-62 (Public Record Office, London, England).

28. See Blum, *Years of War*, pp. 16-22.

29. See Mark H. Leff, "The Politics of Sacrifice on the American Home Front in World War II," *Journal of American History* 77 (March 1991), pp. 1296-1318.

30. See, for example, Richard Steele, *The First Offensive* (Bloomington, IN, 1973), chap. 4, titled "Mounting Pressure for Action: The Problem of Morale and Unity, January-March 1942." Steele, among others, points to the enormous domestic pressure to concentrate on the war against Japan. Thus the North African invasion became necessary to maintain full American participation in Europe, yet it simultaneously postponed the massive invasion of Europe that Stalin demanded and that American military leaders believed in. See also John M. Blum, *V Was For Victory* (New York, 1976). Even a brief conversation with John Kenneth Galbraith, who headed the Office of Price Administration during the war, buttresses the impression that the Roosevelt administration was greatly concerned about getting the American public involved with the war. The pressures for Pacific-First are further discussed in Mark A. Stoler, *The Politics of the Second Front: American Military Planning and Diplomacy in Coalition Warfare, 1941-1943* (Westport, CT, 1977), pp. 25-26, 28-29, 40-41, and "The 'Pacific-First' Alternative in American World War II Strategy," *The International*

History Review 2 (July 1980), 432-52; and Robert Dallek, *Franklin D. Roosevelt and American Foreign Policy, 1932-1945* (New York, 1979), pp. 331-34. Those fears are most apparent from a reading of the Harry Hopkins papers, FDRL, and Sherwood, *Roosevelt and Hopkins*, for example, p. 594.

31. On financial aid to China see Blum, *Years of War*. George C. Herring, "Experiment in Foreign Aid: Lend-Lease, 1941-1945," (Ph.D. diss., University of Virginia, 1967) treats lend-lease to China. Lloyd Gardner, "The Role of the Commerce and the Treasury Departments," in D. Borg and S. Okamoto, eds., *Pearl Harbor as History* (New York, 1973), pp. 261-86, suggests that the "purchase" of China's resistance to Japan was a long-term policy.

32. See Theodore A. Wilson, "Acceptable Losses: Cultural Determinants of Coalition Strategy in World War II," a paper presented at the Fourth Symposium on US-Soviet Experiences in World War II, Rutgers University, New Brunswick, NJ (October 1990), pp. 14-17.

33. Herring, "Experiment in Foreign Aid," pp. 256, 268-74; Herring, *Aid to Russia*, esp. chaps. 5 and 7.

34. Roosevelt expressed this belief many times. See, for example, U.S. Department of State, *Foreign Relations of the United States (FRUS), Conference at Cairo and Teheran, 1943* (Washington, D.C., 1961), pp. 600-4; Morgenthau memorandum of a conversation with Roosevelt, 19 August 1944, Presidential Diaries, Morgenthau Papers, pp. 1386-88; Morgenthau memorandum of a conversation with Hull, Roosevelt, Stimson, and Hopkins, 9 September 1944, ibid., pp. 1431-32.

35. Morgenthau memorandum of a conference at Red Rice, Andover, England, 15 August 1944, Harry Dexter White papers, box 7, Princeton University.

36. TOLSTOY Conference, PREM 3/434/2/61-62, 92-94 [PRO].

37. See, for example, Gardner, *Economic Aspects*, passim., but esp. pp. 261-91; Reynolds, *Creation of the Anglo-American Alliance*, pp. 251-92; William R. Louis, *Imperialism At Bay* (New York, 1978), esp. pp. 226-28, 538; Christopher Thorne, *Allies of a Kind* (New York, 1978), esp. chap. 27; and Kimball, *The Juggler*, chaps. 7 and 9.

     American faith in economics as a cure-all for international problems is neither new nor abandoned. "American leaders used foreign economic foreign power as the chief instrument of U.S. security from 1945 until the outbreak of the conflict in Korea," argues Robert A. Pollard in "Economic Security and the Origins of the Cold War: Bretton Woods, the Marshall Plan, and American Rearmament, 1944-50," *Diplomatic History* 9, no. 3 (Summer 1985), pp. 271-72.

38. For the initial negotiations on the lend-lease master agreement see Kimball, *The Juggler*, chap. 3, and Reynolds, *Creation of the Anglo-American Alliance*, pp. 274-82; see also Alan P. Dobson, "Economic Diplomacy at the Atlantic Conference," *Review of International Studies* 10, no. 2 (April 1984), pp. 143-63. The various issues of Anglo-American economics relations are discussed in Alan P. Dobson, *US Wartime Aid to Britain, 1940-1946* (London, 1986) and his "'A Mess of Pottage for your Economic

Birthright?' The 1941-42 Wheat Negotiations and Anglo-American Economic Diplomacy," *The Historical Journal* 28, no. 3 (1985), pp. 739-50. See also Randall B. Woods, *A Changing of the Guard: Multilateralism and Internationalism in Anglo-American Relations, 1941-1946* (Chapel Hill, NC, 1989)

The exchange between Churchill and Roosevelt in February 1945 is in Kimball, *Churchill & Roosevelt*, III, R-707/1 (10 February 1945) and C-899/3 (13 February 1945). The war-long debate over the meaning of Article VII of the lend-lease master agreement can be followed in the *FRUS* series. The chapter title is from *FRUS* 1945, VI, p. v. Roosevelt's anticolonialism is treated in Kimball, *The Juggler*, chap. 7.

39.   Kimball, *Churchill & Roosevelt*, I, R-105 (11 February 1942); III, R-655/1, C-836. The entire question of the American search for civil aviation agreements during World War II, an issue that illustrates this complex relationship between economics and politics during the war, has finally found its historian in Alan P. Dobson, *Peaceful Air Warfare: The United States, Britain, and the Politics of International Aviation* (Oxford, 1991). See also the record of the two main protagonists at the Civil Aviation Conference: Adolf A. Berle, Jr., *Navigating the Rapids, 1918-1971: From the Papers of Adolf A. Berle*, B. B. Berle and Travis B. Jacobs, eds. (New York, 1973), and Sir Alexander Cadogan, *The Diaries of Air Alexander Cadogan, 1939-1945*, D. Dilks, ed. (London, 1971).

The importance of cultural influences on American economic strategy is discussed in Emily S. Rosenberg, *Spreading the American Dream: American Economic and Cultural Expansion* (New York, 1982).

40.   See, for example, Pollard, "Economic Security and the Origins of the Cold War," p. 274, and the works cited by Pollard.

41.   Treasury Department memorandum, May 1942, as quoted in Eckes, *A Search for Solvency*, p. 56.

42.   T. H. Vail Motter, *The Persian Corridor and Aid to Russia* (Washington, D.C., 1952); Leighton & Coakley, *Global Logistics and Strategy, 1940-1943*, pp. 574-87; Kimball, *Churchill & Roosevelt*, I, R-166 (15 July 1942), C-135 (22 August 1942); Harriman and Abel, *Special Envoy*, p. 166; Herring, "Experiment in Foreign Aid," pp. 351-55 (the Berle Committee quote is on p. 353).

43.   Kimball, *Churchill & Roosevelt*, III, R-483/2 (29 February 1944).

44.   Hull to Winant, 30 January 1942, and Winant to Hull, 3 February 1942, *FRUS, 1942*, pp. 525-29, and Kimball, *Churchill & Roosevelt*, I, R-80x (4 February 1942).

45.   My study *The Juggler* is an attempt to set forth Roosevelt's thinking about the postwar world.

46.   See Kimball, *The Juggler*, esp. chaps. 5, 6, and 9. A perceptive study of Wilson and his dilemmas is Lloyd C. Gardner, *Safe for Democracy: The Anglo-American Response to Revolution, 1913-1923* (New York, 1984). See especially part III.

9

Genocide Treaty Ratification: Ending an American Embarrassment

William Korey

It was forty years ago, on 16 June 1949, that President Harry S Truman sent the genocide convention to the Senate for its "advice and consent." Few expected any serious resistance to the ratification of this historic treaty, unanimously adopted by the United Nations six months earlier. Nazi aggression and the accompanying Holocaust had not yet disappeared from man's consciousness, and the treaty sought to prevent another example of mass murder against any racial or religious group.

The Senate did not respond then and failed to act until 11 February 1986—almost four decades later. Senator William Proxmire (D-WI) would remind his colleagues that "there is not a single proposal that has been before the Senate as long" as the genocide convention. In the meantime, ninety-seven countries had ratified the treaty, including every major power and every democratic government. The United States remained the single hold-out, much to the embarrassment of its representatives at international forums where the U.S. failure to ratify human rights treaties was often cynically raised by the USSR. Only with the overwhelming 1986 Senate vote in favor of ratification, 83 to 11, had the anomaly and the embarrassment approached an end. The climax would come two years later, in October 1988, with the adoption of required implementation legislation by the U.S. Congress.

What made the failure to ratify especially problematic is the fact that it stands in striking contrast with the emphasis given human rights in American foreign policy. The State Department, in its introduction to the annual evaluation of human rights in most countries of the world, stressed that human rights is the "core" of American foreign policy. Since the genocide treaty was the very first UN human rights accord, preceding even the adoption of the Universal Declaration of Human Rights, failure to ratify it ineluctably raised questions about the commitment of the United States to the principles it espouses.

The Reagan administration, on the eve of its second term, played a critical role in removing this awkwardness and refurbishing the negative image of the United States. If it is often seen as a government reluctant to assume binding international obligations in the human rights field, despite its major leadership role at the Madrid conference of the Helsinki accord signatories, the administration initiated a break in the deadlock. It was spearheaded by Elliott Abrams, assistant secretary of state for human rights and humanitarian affairs. The State Department endorsed ratification and urged the White House to consummate the Truman initiative. In early September 1984, on the eve of a B'nai B'rith convention, which he would address, the president called for ratification.

The problem remained, as it always had been, in the Senate where a two-thirds favorable vote is required. Almost every president since World War II—Dwight Eisenhower was the exception—had supported U.S. ratification, but none had succeeded in obtaining favorable Senate action. At stake was the Reagan administration's ability to demonstrate the extent of its commitment to human rights. The major obstacle to ratification in the Senate was inertia, what some have called a "lingering Brickeritis." What that phrase means, and how the embarrassing impasse had been reached and overcome, require clarification.

The concept of a treaty making genocide a crime had its roots in the struggle against Hitlerism and the overpowering public awareness of what unrestrained racism had wrought. The horrors of the Nazi crematoria and the unprecedented Jewish Holocaust stirred a profound sense of guilt and pricked mankind's uneasy conscience. The inextricable linkage between internal racism and external aggression had never been so terrifyingly demonstrated.

Two postwar sources were to shape the concept. The first was the Nuremberg tribunal, of which the United States was a principal architect. Through the tribunal, the rule of law as applied to criminal violations of human rights was given a firm foundation. President Truman, in November 1946, would observe that the "undisputed gain" of Nuremberg is precisely "the formal recognition that there are crimes against humanity." Recognized among the designated "crimes against humanity" were persecutions on political, racial, or religious grounds, whether or not sanctioned by domestic law.

The tribunal, as one authority later noted, marked a "revolution in international criminal law" for it deeply eroded the earlier-accepted principle of the exclusivity of domestic jurisdiction in the area of human rights. The second source was the UN General Assembly which, on 11 December 1946, legitimized the "revolution." Its famed Resolution 96 (I) formally declared "that genocide is a crime under international law which the civilized world condemns and for the commission of which principals and accomplices are punishable." Again, it was the United States, through its ambassador, Warren R. Austin, that provided the leadership in shepherding the resolution through the assembly.

America's leadership role came into sharp international focus when the genocide convention was adopted by the UN General Assembly in Paris on 9 December 1948. Today, it is all but forgotten that the delegation to the United Nations played a key role in the actual drafting of the text. Anglo-American legal theory was the principal source. Indeed, the formulations were couched in the language of traditional common-law concepts including the very precise wording of common-law crimes long accepted in American jurisprudence. Of critical importance, in this connection, was U.S. insistence that proof of intent to commit genocide must be clearly demonstrated before an offender could be punished. Intent is a central element of U.S. criminal law, as distinct from legal notions in other jurisprudential systems, and it is distinctly placed as the cornerstone in the genocide convention.

American involvement was not limited to mere legal notions in other jurisprudential systems, nor was it limited to mere legal counselling and draftsmanship. It was the U.S. delegation at the General Assembly session in Paris that led the fight from the floor for its adoption. American lobbyists were everywhere promoting a positive vote at the Palais de Chaillot. The head of the delegation, Assistant Secretary of State Ernest A. Gross, would at the time (and as a prominent attorney and churchman in private life for years later) take a personal hand in pushing for decisive and affirmative action. Gross was particularly eloquent and determined just before the 9 December balloting that "in a world beset by many problems and great difficulties, we should proceed with this convention before the memory of recent horrifying genocidal acts has faded from the minds and conscience of man." He demanded that "positive action be taken now." And he noted that the United States "is eager to see the genocide convention adopted at this session of the Assembly and signed by all member states before we quit with our labors now."

The U.S. efforts were impressively successful. Unanimous endorsement was won for the genocide convention, and to testify to its commitment, the American delegation rushed to affix the U.S. signature to the treaty. The signing of a treaty, in the context of international law, is a solemn and formal act by a government. It signifies both a commitment to fulfill the purpose of the treaty and an intent to ratify it. The signature came on 11 December, only two days after the assembly approved the treaty. Although the United States was among the very first to sign, three years later the intent had yet to be fulfilled.

The treaty, formally entitled the Convention on the Prevention and Punishment of the Crime of Genocide, contained nineteen articles, the last ten of which were procedural. The first nine articles were substantive with Article I confirming that genocide is a crime under international law. The second article was the core of the convention. It outlawed "acts committed with an intent to destroy, in whole or in part, a national, ethnic, racial or religious group, as such." Delineated among the "acts" were killing, the causing of serious "mental harm," the inflicting of "conditions of life calculated" to lead to physical destruction, and the imposition of measures intended to prevent reproduction of a group.

The treaty specified what would be subject to punishment: genocide, conspiracy or attempt to commit genocide, direct and public incitement to commit genocide, and complicity in the act of genocide. The convention made clear that no one was immune from punishment, whether rulers, public officials, or private individuals. Persons charged with the crime of genocide were to be tried by a competent tribunal of the state in the territory in which the act was committed. This would require extradition, and the convention stressed that genocide is not, under any circumstances, to be considered a political crime.

The treaty, under Article VI, also conceived of a possible alternative means of rendering judgment. Should an international penal tribunal ultimately be established, and should its jurisdiction be accepted by the particular contracting parties involved in a given case, the genocidist could be tried before it. The formulation became a source of controversy in America as a challenge to the absolute sovereignty of a state. Yet the jurisdiction of such a court—should it ever be established—could not apply to the United States unless the latter, in a totally separate treaty, agreed to accept its jurisdiction.

While trial and punishment of genocidists were left to national courts, the treaty (in Article VIII) permitted a competent organ of the United Nations to take action under the charter, where appropriate, to prevent and suppress genocide. The treaty further specified that disputes about its interpretation, application, or fulfillment may be submitted to the International Court of Justice. The American Bar Association was in the forefront of the effort to reject ratification, although it would reverse itself a quarter of a century later. Two strong objections were vigorously made by the ABA. One argument, taking its inspiration from Charles Evans Hughes's guideline that the treaty-making power of the executive must be used only "with regard to matters of international concern," contended that genocide, along with human rights generally, is essentially a domestic concern. To the extent that it was alleged to be a domestic matter, genocide, it was said, did not meet the relevant test of the Supreme Court as to whether the treaty is "properly the subject of negotiations with a foreign country."

In fact, human rights have been dealt with and protected by international treaties since the sixteenth century. The Treaty of Westphalia, for example, provided for equality of religious rights in Germany. The Congress of Vienna in 1815 advocated the free exercise of religion. And, as part of the settlement following World War I, a number of treaties involving states of Central and Eastern Europe carried elaborate provision for the protection of minorities. During the nineteenth century, the United States itself was a party to dozens of treaties regulating the slave trade.

Moreover, the United States has ratified treaties relating to the activities of its own citizens when those activities have a transnational character: narcotics, public health, or natural conservation. Certainly the critical lesson of World War II, as the Nuremberg tribunal demonstrated, was that genocide was quintessentially an international concern, far more so than even slavery during the nineteenth century.

A second objection sprung from the federal character of the United States. It was argued that ratification would create a constitutional issue by tilting the balance of authority on criminal matters between the federal government and the states to the former. Murder, it was emphasized, is a state crime. The argument failed, however, to take account of the specific constitutional provision that Congress has the power "to define and punish offenses against the law of nations" and of the fact that genocide had been firmly declared to be an offense against international law. Besides, as indicated in various civil rights statutes, which were adopted later, federal authority was recognized as having priority in various human rights fields. The Civil Rights Act of 1957 and 1964 and the Voting Rights Act of 1965 confirmed this authority. Even murder, in certain instances, Congress would later determine following the assassination of President John F. Kennedy, had a distinctive federal concern.

Arguments were also advanced over certain ambiguities in the convention. What constituted the meaning of "in whole or in part" in the crucial Article II of the convention? Fears were apparent in various segregationist circles that the reference to "in part" might be applied to a limited form of race violence, such as lynchings. The phrase "mental harm" also raised concern. Some who pointed to the centrality of civil liberties expressed doubts about reference to direct incitement even though Supreme Court decisions made clear that such activity was not protected by the First Amendment.

In some quarters, the reference to the International Court of Justice aroused concern. Would it not override the Connally amendment, which was designed to protect American sovereignty? The anxiety was misplaced as this amendment applied only to the clause in the World Court's statute providing for an across-the-board compulsory jurisdiction; the amendment was not affected by the genocide treaty. Similar misplaced anxiety characterized the attitude in the same quarters to the projected international penal tribunal. As noted, however, this would necessitate a separate treaty over which the Senate, by a two-thirds vote, could exercise a veto. Besides, the concept of a tribunal was unlikely to be realized in the international community for a very long time.

The ambiguities did not constitute insoluble problems, providing there was goodwill on the part of the critics. They could be handled by clarifications, called "understandings" or, more accurately, "reservations." And, indeed, this is the way the matter would ultimately be handled. The constitutional controversy, on the other hand, was a more serious obstacle. But that kind of resistance involving legitimate questions and concern was reinforced—and complicated—by extremist movements in the political far right. A dozen such organizations were capable of generating a substantial flow of mail and telegrams to the Senate. Among the groups that have led vehement campaigns against the genocide convention are the Liberty Lobby, which dubbed the treaty "fraudulent," and the John Birch Society which called it "pernicious" and a "surrender of the Constitutional rights of American citizens."

However, when President Truman submitted the treaty to the Senate, no serious difficulties were anticipated. The Senate Foreign Relations Committee assigned a subcommittee the task of holding hearings. Promptly held in January and February 1950, the hearings elicited a favorable response from representatives of most public, nongovernmental organizations. And the spokesman for the government, Deputy Undersecretary of State Dean Rusk, was unusually effective in his presentation. He made two principal points.

Ratification was essential to "demonstrate to the rest of the world that the United States is determined to maintain its moral leadership in international affairs." In addition, ratification would show that the United States intended "to participate in the development of international law on the basis of human justice." The two themes—moral leadership and international law—echoed a distinctive strand in American foreign policy, especially since the era of Woodrow Wilson's administration.

In May 1950 the Senate subcommittee, only a few months after the hearings, reported favorably on the genocide convention. Yet, to meet the objections of the legal profession, the subcommittee recommended that four "understandings" and one "declaration" be embodied in the resolution consenting to ratification. One "understanding" (later termed "reservation") dealt with the phrase "in whole or in part." "In part" was interpreted to mean "a substantial portion of the group concerned." A second understanding defined "mental harm" as "permanent physical injury to mental faculties." A third understanding clarified "complicity in genocide" to mean "participation before and after the facts and aiding and abetting in the commission of the crime of genocide." The last understanding was minor. The declaration dealt with the key federal-state balance issue by citing explicitly from Article I of the Constitution the right of Congress to punish "offenses against the law of Nations."

Significantly, the same clarifying statements would appear as "reservations" when the Senate Foreign Relations Committee years later approved the genocide treaty. But in 1950, the entire committee never got the opportunity to vote on the issue. One month after the subcommittee's recommendation, North Korea launched an invasion of South Korea, and a new era was ushered in that profoundly affected the fabric of American society. The war unleashed powerful xenophobic forces which significantly bolstered the earlier anticommunist witch hunt. The genocide convention was perceived in these quarters as undermining American sovereignty.

Paralysis set in among supporters of the genocide treaty. They were simply overwhelmed, less by the arguments of conservative spokesmen or ABA officials as by the resurgent nativist McCarthyite forces. The treaty formally came into force on 12 January 1951 but no action by the United States was even contemplated. Indeed, with the ascendancy of a kind of neo-isolationism, there would appear a movement both in and out of the Senate, under John Bricker's leadership, aimed at limiting the treaty-making authority of the executive. Senator Bricker of Ohio, a pronounced enemy of perceived international authority and of imagined forces threatening American sovereignty, was certain a new danger was beginning to emanate from the United Nations, where the drafting of international covenants on human rights had just started (not until December 1966 would they be completed). Bricker proposed an amendment to the Constitution designed to forever preclude the possibility of the United States being "subverted" through the action of an administration representative at the United Nations. Presidential authority to sign treaties dealing with human rights would simply be forbidden. That such an amendment challenged the intrinsic and traditional power of the president in foreign affairs would be a matter of indifference to the powerful Ohio senator.

The newly elected Eisenhower administration put an end to all further discussion of the genocide treaty and, indeed, of any human rights treaty. The official pronouncement came early in the administration—6 April 1953—and was articulated by its authoritative foreign affairs spokesman, Secretary of State John Foster Dulles. The occasion was a hearing of the Senate Judiciary committee, and Dulles, acutely conscious of the challenge to presidential authority posed by the Bricker movement forces, was anxious to use the opportunity to deprive the movement of its raison d'être. If firm commitments were given to the Senate that the administration would never contemplate signing a human rights treaty, let alone transmitting it to the Senate for action, then the Bricker phenomenon might disintegrate for want of a meaningful rationale.

The administration, Dulles promised, would never "become a party to any covenant or present it as a treaty for consideration by the Senate." If human rights were to be promoted by the United States, it would be accomplished by "methods of persuasion, education and example," and not by "formal undertakings" such as treaties. Indeed, Dulles assured the Senate, the treaty-making power cannot and must not be used "as a way of effectuating reforms, particularly in relation to social matters." In his view, echoing the ABA and at the same time satisfying Bricker as well, there are "traditional limits" of the exercise of treaty making, and those "limits" would be trespassed by striving to effect "internal social changes" through treaties.

If the secretary's assurances caused the Bricker movement to founder and disintegrate, they also erected a virtually impregnable obstacle for Senate action on any human rights treaty. His was, after all, a solemn commitment from the administration. Once formally articulated and accepted, the assurance took on a life of its own and by the very force of inertia prevented new legislative initiatives in the human rights field. Such efforts would ineluctably be compelled to take on a Sisyphean character.

The genocide treaty, to the extent that it, too, was a human rights treaty, was clearly living on borrowed time. Dulles was hesitant about declaring null and void a treaty in which the United States had invested so much and to which it had made the strongest commitments, including the formal signature. To avoid the embarrassment of previously extended solemn obligations, Dulles noted that the USSR had not yet ratified the genocide convention and, therefore, it "could better be reconsidered at a later date." But when the USSR did ratify the treaty in 1954, no notice was taken of the action by the Eisenhower administration. The issue was dead, buried by the Dulles doctrine which had also wrought the internment of those foreign policy goals, given emphasis during and after World War II, that underscored the necessity of extending the rule of law to the world arena.

A glacial silence now settled upon international human rights undertakings generally and the genocide treaty specifically. Not until a decade later would there appear cracks in the monolith of Washington indifference. President John F. Kennedy sounded a renewed hope and vigor with respect to traditional obligations in the human rights field by his historic speech at American University on 10 June 1963. The powerful rhetoric of the address made human rights a critical feature of America's foreign policy thinking a little more than ten years after Dulles's commitment in the Senate. Peace, itself, was declared to be, "in the last analysis a matter of human rights."

Nor was it an uncertain trumpet that had sounded. A month after the American University speech, Kennedy, in a breakthrough move, sent to the Senate three international human rights treaties that had lain dormant for some time. One dealt with practices akin to slavery, a second with forced labor, and the last with the political rights of women. In his message asking for the Senate's consent to ratification, the President wrote: "The United States cannot afford to renounce responsibility for support of the very fundamentals which distinguish our concept of government from all forms of tyranny."

Yet the action was scarcely an example of a profile in particularly unusual courage. Kennedy chose the least controversial of the international treaties. About the genocide convention, he did not urge action, although a White House spokesman publicly noted that "we share the views that prompted President Truman to urge consent of the Senate."

The thrust of the Johnson administration paralleled that of its predecessor, particularly as the embarrassments of nonratification became increasingly difficult to bear. American ambassador to the United Nations Arthur Goldberg articulated the administration's perspective in a public lecture at Columbia University on 19 May 1966. The "establishment of a structure of law" is the "way to peace," he said, and that structure should reflect the concept of "the equality and dignity of all men." The lecture constituted a response to former Secretary of State Dean Acheson who, two weeks earlier at the University of Virginia, rejected the concept of peace through law as "illusory." The use of power, the elder statesman argued, is the only method for preserving peace. Goldberg rebutted by observing that America's influence in the world does not derive from "great physical power" alone; it springs as well from human rights and the "premises" underlying "our basic law and our national outlook." Later that year, Goldberg told the Association of American Law Schools that law must foster in the international realm the same "positive values which nations, at their best, have fulfilled in their domestic life." His point was then underscored: "Law must operate to eliminate discrimination, to assure human rights."

The changed atmosphere was even beginning to erode support for the Dulles doctrine in the legal profession. Virtually every section and committee of the American Bar Association with specialized competence in the area of human rights or the rule of law adopted resolutions calling for ratification of the genocide treaty. These groups included the Section of Individual Rights and Responsibilities; the Section of International and Comparative Law; the Section of Family Law; and the Standing Committee on World Order Under Law. Even several past presidents of the ABA became partisans of ratification. In 1968, a blue-ribbon committee of lawyers, chaired by retired Supreme Court Justice Tom Clark, publicly denounced as "anachronistic" the standard argument of the ABA and its Senate supporters that the treaty-making power of the executive should not be used for human rights purposes.

The year 1968 marked the twentieth anniversary of the Universal Declaration of Human Rights (as well as the genocide convention). Commemoration activity ineluctably brought to the fore a sense of shame and embarrassment surrounding the genocide treaty. Chief Justice Earl Warren captured the altered mood in a moving anniversary address in December. "We, as a nation, should have been the first to ratify the genocide convention. Instead, we may well be near the last." Catharsis, though oratorical breast-beating, undoubtedly was helpful, but no meaningful change appeared to register with the Senate. What some diagnosed as a "lingering Brickeritis" continued to pervade the upper legislative chamber. Senator Proxmire of Wisconsin had initiated in 1967 an educational campaign among his colleagues by delivering a daily appeal for ratification of human rights treaties. His appeal, to a considerable extent, fell on deaf ears. The genocide treaty was tightly wrapped in Senate mothballs. Hope for its removal appeared remote. Neither the Kennedy nor the Johnson administration dared to challenge Senate indifference to genocide.

It was left to a Republican Administration, and a distinctly conservative one at that, to demand a reversal of the Dulles doctrine. On 17 February 1970, Richard M. Nixon, for the first time since President Truman had called for legislative action twenty-one years earlier, formally asked the Senate "to consider anew this important convention." In his message, President Nixon emphasized that ratification was necessary to "demonstrate unequivocally our country's desire to participate in the building of an international order based on law and justice." The language, strikingly, was almost an exact replica of that used by the spokesman of an earlier Truman administration.

What prompted President Nixon to break with the outlook of the Eisenhower administration is probably similar to that which brought about the change with respect to recognition of communist China. Alert and sensitive to emergent public attitudes, and not burdened by fears of possible charges of national "betrayal" from the right, the administration was keenly aware that the altered atmosphere made legitimate a complete break with an anachronistic past posture. Besides, a Republican championing ratification would not go unnoticed and unrewarded in liberal and independent circles. While politically useful, advocacy of a human rights treaty also cloaked the administration in a statesmanlike garb.

Ratification was supported by Secretary of State William Rogers and by the embodiment of Republican conservatism, Attorney General John Mitchell. "No constitutional obstacles" were found by him and his assistants to ratification—a far cry from the traditional ABA argument. It was expected that his opinion would be decisive with the ABA, whose House of Delegates met in Atlanta one week after the Nixon message to the Senate. But after an intense and emotional debate lasting three hours, the citadel of legal rectitude once again rebuffed proposals for change. If the vote was quite close this time, 130 to 126, the 4-vote margin was sufficient to provide a continuing and powerful bulwark for resistance to a two-thirds vote in the Senate.

Remarkably, the arguments of the victors remained the same as they had been twenty-one years earlier: Genocide was largely a domestic matter, not appropriate to the treaty-making power, and ratification would alter unfavorably the balance of authority between the states and the federal government. Antediluvian notions would simply not bow to either change or rationality. Former Attorney General Nicholas deB. Katzenbach warned the delegates: "I remind you, remember who is looking at you. The world is regarding you." The president of the Bar Association also cautioned the delegates that "we stand alone" in not ratifying the genocide treaty since all American allies had already done so.

The warnings were brushed aside. So was the desperate appeal of the Republican administration's top legal expert, solicitor General Erwin N. Griswold, former dean of Harvard Law School. He pleaded that the United States be given the "opportunity to exercise the great function of leadership" in international law. What weighed heavily with the delegates were new additional arguments which emerged from conservative hostility to the continuing youth revolution of the time. It was charged that the Black Panthers would accuse federal officials and police of genocide and, even more fear-provoking, North Vietnam would bring American soldiers to trial on presumed genocide.

But if the administration was unsuccessful in convincing the ABA, it did make important inroads with at least the Senate Foreign Relations Committee. That powerful body, which had failed to act upon the basis of recommendations of its subcommittee in 1950, moved in 1971 to hold hearings and, in May of that year, to render a landmark rejection of the ABA decision. By a decisive vote of ten to four, it announced that "we find no substantial merit in the arguments against the convention" and urged the Senate to "give its advice and consent to ratification of the genocide convention by an overwhelming vote." The decisive committee vote should have resolved the problem and ended a national embarrassment. But the vote failed to take account of technical or procedural considerations which, when buttressed by fierce resistance from extremist forces and by the unanticipated and immeasurable force of inertia, became veritable insuperable obstacles.

In December 1971, Senator Proxmire, joined by another intrepid advocate of ratification, Senator Jacob Javits, asked the Majority Leader, Senator Mike Mansfield to put the treaty on the legislative calendar for action. Mansfield demurred on grounds that "a propitious time has not arisen." He wanted evidence of "sufficient numbers" before he would place it before the Senate. There was some logic to this position for a failure to win a two-thirds vote in the Senate—a form of overt rejection—could prove even more disastrous for America's image than the stigma of nonratification.

What constituted "sufficient numbers"? It was known that various senators were reluctant to tip their hands in advance lest they open themselves up to an endless mail barrage from extremists. The Senate leadership initially decided upon assurances by fifty senators, a definitive list. Senators Proxmire and Javits, along with Frank Church and Hugh Scott (the chairman and the minority leader of the Foreign Relations Committee), on 24 February 1972, sent around a petition asking their colleagues to demonstrate a clear commitment to support ratification. The timing of the petition was deliberate. One week earlier the attorney general transmitted to Congress a formal legislative proposal designed to implement the genocide convention. Such implementing legislation is required by the act of ratification.

Despite the fact that the petition acquired fifty-three signatures and several others orally indicated a willingness to support it—by August, there were sixty definite votes available—a new bottleneck presented itself. A filibuster was threatened by a pillar of the Senate, Sam Ervin of North Carolina. With a determined adherence to the strict construction of the Constitution, Ervin found the arguments of the ABA valid, indeed, unassailable. A filibuster would tie up the Senate calendar and a cloture vote required the same two-thirds (later to be changed to three-fifths or sixty). But a two-thirds vote on cloture was far more difficult to obtain as senatorial courtesy was at stake. In the intimate Senate club, the shutting off of debate evoked the deepest kind of reluctance.

A kind of Catch-22 now prevailed. The Senate leadership would not move without assurances on ratification which in turn required assurances on cloture. But the leadership was profoundly reluctant to support cloture. The paralysis of the vicious circle had set in. Once again, in 1973, the Senate Foreign Relations Committee called for ratification. In 1974, two attempts at invoking cloture for ending the filibuster failed. To resolve the dilemma, the Senate leadership reached a decision that would reject all further debate, let alone action, on the genocide convention without absolute assurances of a two-thirds favorable vote on the treaty as well as a reasonable expectation for cloture. Since such preconditions, in the absence of strong leadership either in the Congress or the White House, were politically almost inconceivable, the question of ratification was back to square one.

Despite the dismal congressional reality, the year 1976 ushered in a new era of hope for the genocide convention. The House of Delegates of the ABA, meeting in Philadelphia, finally voted on 17 February to support ratification. The reversal, after more than a quarter of a century of willful intransigence and resistance, eliminated at long last the aura of respectability in which the opposition to ratification had been enveloped. Jacob Javits, in a joyous mood, rose in the Senate on 4 March to greet "the new propitious conditions" created by the ABA decision which will result in the genocide convention being "ratified as a treaty of the United States as well as of all those other countries in the world." At long last, he said, positive action was certain for "this terribly delayed, almost unbelievably delayed, simple statement of human truth and human decency." If the sharp indictment of the past had to be made—and it was done eloquently—it was deliberately subordinated to the glow of hope and optimism. Even a *New York Times* editorial was convinced that there could be no "doubt about the affirmative outcome of the next Senate vote."

The problem, however, was getting the Senate to vote. The filibuster obstacle remained, even if a significant procedural breakthrough now required only sixty votes for cloture, instead of the earlier two-thirds. Inertia was a crucial consideration. Hope was rekindled when Jimmy Carter became president. No president had addressed himself to the genocide treaty as Carter. Four times he had called for Senate action, the first time in a major UN speech just two months after inauguration and lastly in connection with a special and unusually impressive observance of the Holocaust. His Commission on the Holocaust, chaired by Elie Wiesel, on 27 September 1979 formally joined "in urging the Senate to ratify the Genocide Convention" on grounds that "the knowledge that perpetrators will be held responsible for the crime of genocide can play some role in preventing such acts in the future." But the president's commitment did not translate into strong and effective leadership.

To a senator, the genocide treaty offers little that is conducive to attracting voter support. Earlier constituencies on behalf of ratification have all but dissipated in the face of repeated failure, of apathy, and of frustration. On the other hand, open support for the genocide treaty in states with strong conservative tendencies can evoke powerful opposition. The inevitable inertia and apathy of the Senate underscores the need for presidential leadership. Without a strong administration initiative and a willingness to invest political capital in lobbying and in making the necessary trade-offs, no progress will be made.

"Lingering Brickeritis" has been a costly malaise. The United States has found it difficult to promote any meaningful human rights project in international forums. At the United Nations, for example, the Kennedy and Johnson administrations sought to pursue several important human rights objectives in the area of compliance, only to be thrown onto the defensive by none other than the Soviet Union which, it should be emphasized, had itself always appeared on the defensive on such questions. Indeed, the USSR consistently and vigorously opposed every form of implementation. Once the United States began championing implementation measures, Soviet representatives were quick to strike at America's Achilles' heel.

Thus, in January 1964 when the U.S. expert on the UN Sub-Commission on Prevention of Discrimination and Protection of Minorities, prominent attorney Morris B. Abram, advocated that racial and ethnic discrimination be dealt with through "forceful measures of implementation," the Soviet member of the body had only to remind the subcommission that the United States was not even a contracting party to the genocide convention. The hint of hypocrisy was all that was required to shove the United States on the defensive. The embarrassed American responded with an obvious air of discomfort that he could only "regret, of course, that my country has not ratified the convention on genocide."

Two years later, Abram was serving as the U.S. representative on the parent body, the Commission on Human Rights. On the agenda was an unusually imaginative proposal advanced by Costa Rica that, had it succeeded, could have marked a milestone in UN history. The proposal called for the creation of an independent UN commissioner for human rights, a kind of global ombudsman. Abram, a gifted civil rights lawyer, saw the suggested institution as offering real possibilities for providing essential compliance functions, and he moved to endorse the proposal. The response of Pavel Morozov, a typical hard-nosed apparatchik of the USSR, proved devastating. Noting that the United States had "resolutely refused to accept legal obligations" through treaty ratifications, the Soviet delegate charged that it was "almost indecent" and certainly "hypocritical" for the United States to advocate the creation of special human rights institutions in the international field.

The pointed and sharp critique carried weight with representatives of the nonaligned from Africa and Asia, then beginning to enter the United Nations in large numbers. Within the USSR the charge was used to reinforce anti-American propaganda. *Pravda*, on 24 April 1966, shortly after the UN Commission session, commented that it was "no accident" that the United States has not ratified the genocide convention, for "racial and national oppression is still very wide-spread in the United States of America."

Nonratification of the genocide treaty assured the United States of an extraordinary status, a kind of splendid isolation. Even among its allies and friendly neutrals, there was a unanimity of dismay. Acute embarrassment was the American delegate's lot when the issue was raised, and it was raised often, whether in public or in private meetings.

Embarrassment and defensiveness were especially pronounced at the conference of the Helsinki Final Act signatories which began in Madrid during the second week of November 1980. In the heated human rights debates, the Soviet Union could be expected to exploit its most effective weapon—United States nonratification of human rights treaties, particularly the genocide treaty. On 9 December 1979 Moscow Radio offered a preview of the expected rebuttal by responding, in a special broadcast, to the United States Helsinki Commission report, which had highlighted egregious Soviet abridgements of Helsinki human rights commitments. Another commentator, obviously quite knowledgeable about the American political process, went on to note that President Carter had promised in 1976 to ratify the convention, but that the Senate "has the last word, of course." Pointedly, he added, "the Senate's position speaks quite eloquently . . . of the present American enthusiasm for human rights." Four days later, on 13 December, *Pravda* elaborated upon the theme, clearly signaling how it planned to strike at the American "Achilles' heel."

Opposition in the United States to ratification of the genocide convention has featured a remarkable irony, scarcely noticed by those who have focused upon the constitutional issues of the debate. Extremist critics of ratification have endowed the convention with enormous powers that would somehow be wielded by the international community at the expense of sovereign states. Experience with the genocide convention since its unanimous adoption by the General Assembly on 9 December 1948 in no way conforms with these fears. Indeed, the international community and contracting parties to the convention have been extraordinarily reluctant to use the UN machinery at all, even under the most pressing and tragic of circumstances.

It is perhaps not surprising that the International Court of Justice has never been seized with the issue of genocide even though under Article IX, "disputes" between contracting parties "relating to the interpretation, application or fulfillment" of the treaty could be submitted to the court by a party to the dispute. At least a dozen contracting parties, including the Warsaw Pact powers, have inserted reservations stating that they would not be bound by Article IX. More serious, no United Nations organ has ever taken upon itself the task of investigating a possible case of genocide, despite the fact that Article VIII provides that "any contracting party may call upon the competent organs" of the UN "to take such actions under the Charter . . . as they consider appropriate for the prevention and suppression of acts of genocide." Outer Mongolia, prompted by the USSR, did propose in June 1963, that the General Assembly discuss "the policy of genocide carried out by the Government of the Republic of Iraq against the Kurdish people." But within a few months the obviously politically-motivated proposal was withdrawn.

If, with the mid-1960s, genocide increasingly became an item on the agenda of the world conscience, concern about it found no reflection in the chambers of the United Nations. Egregious examples of wholesale butchery of peoples went unnoticed. When, in the fall of 1965, the Indonesian Army leadership overthrew Sukarno and embarked upon mass killing of communists and urban Chinese, not a single power raised its voice in UN circles. A similar silence blanketed the massacre of Ibos in Nigeria in 1968. Nor was anything said about the ruthless suppression of the blacks of south Sudan by the country's Arab rulers.

Perhaps the classic case of UN indifference was offered in the spring of 1971. Tens of thousands of Bengalis in East Pakistan, particularly the educated elite, were summarily shot by Pakistani government troops. But even as carnage was a subject of passionate discussion in the mass media everywhere, not a word about the Bengali plight was sounded in the UN Commission on Human Rights, then meeting in Geneva. Silence also embraced the mass killing of Christians in Idi Amin's Uganda, of Kurds in Iraq, of Christians in Lebanon, of Eritreans in Ethiopia, and, most recently, of natives in East Timor.

During May and July 1972, a massive form of "selective genocide" was conducted by the Burundi government against Hutu tribesmen leading to the deaths of as many as 225,000 persons. A study published by the Carnegie Endowment for International Peace documents the almost total indifference of governments including those comprising the Organization of African Unity to the tragedy. While former Secretary-General Kurt Waldheim felt moved to dispatch two observer missions to the area and later to report the staggering bloodbath statistics in a press conference, no "audible reaction" occurred elsewhere, the Carnegie study noted, and most governments avoided having the issue raised "in the UN or in any other forum." Similar UN indifference largely characterized the vast and appalling killings in Cambodia by the Pol Pot regime. The "auto-genocide" destroyed between one and one-half to three million persons—a mind-boggling figure.

To cope with the growing and unimpeded numbers of genocidal acts, an Indian expert on the UN Sub-Commission on Prevention of Discrimination and Protection of Minorities, Arcot Krishnaswami, several years ago had proposed the creation of an international body "which would endeavor to prevent the crime of genocide before it actually occurred on a massive scale. Such a body should be able to investigate and assess allegations of genocide, and to take the steps necessary to halt at its outset the deliberate destruction of a national, racial, religious or ethnic group."

The need for creative initiatives utilizing the resources and institutions of the international community is precisely that which should attract the imagination of the United States. It launched the United Nations on an adventure to prevent genocide as early as 1946. The task remains unfulfilled. Nothing is more urgent. For genocide goes to the very heart of elemental human rights—the right to survive. But ratification of the treaty was the indispensable first step. It was time to end the shame and embarrassment and to consummate the hope of President Truman when he first sent it to the Senate thirty-five years ago.

The necessity for administration action became increasingly apparent in the context of the East-West struggle for the minds and hearts of mankind. If the United States was to assert international leadership championing human rights, especially in Eastern Europe, it had to cope with and remove the stain of nonratification of the genocide treaty. That was precisely the position of Assistant Secretary of State Elliott Abrams. He successfully encouraged the State Department to move in the direction of urging ratification.

On the eve of the 1984 national election, President Reagan decided to call for Senate action, as almost all of his predecessors had done. Just prior to an address to the B'nai B'rith Biennial Convention, the president announced to the press on 6 September that positive Senate action was essential to assist "our efforts to expand human freedom and fight human rights abuses around the world." Shortly afterward, Elliott Abrams, in testimony, told the Senate Foreign Relations Committee that "we have all delayed too long" and that ratification would "add America's moral and political prestige to this landmark in international law."

The leadership provided by the administration was crucial. In view of its conservative ideology, opposition from traditional right-wing sources was certain to be less intense and less shrill than it might have been for a liberal or moderate Democratic administration. Still, the right-wing refused to relent. If early in October 1984 the Senate Foreign Relations unanimously approved ratification, 17 to 0, a rare legislative endorsement of the treaty, the resistance had only begun to be marshalled.

Old conservative fears surfaced about the weakening of American sovereignty, particularly in terms of imagined powers that might be exercised by the World Court. Anxieties among the Senate leadership that filibuster might ensue, holding up all legislation at a moment when the political election campaigns were heating up, promoted an unprecedented vote not on ratification but on the principles of the genocide treaty. By a huge, lopsided vote of 87 to 2, the Senate adopted a resolution approving the "principles" of the treaty and pledging to act "expeditiously" on the ratification question at the next legislative session beginning in late January 1985. As interpreted by a key Senator involved in the negotiating process, Rudy Boschwitz (R-MN), the vote on the resolution "commits us to early action in the next Congress."

But "early action" in 1985 was not forthcoming. Conservative Senators, under the leadership of Senator Jesse Helms (R-NC), insisted upon the acceptance of eight amendments before they might accede. Six of the amendments covering clarifications that had been agreed to in 1950 and 1971 were quickly accepted by the State Department and by other Senators. Little dispute centered on the seventh which held that the United States Constitution must be implemented in conformity with Constitutional precepts.

What created conflict was the right-wing insistence that the World Court not be given any authority under the treaty provisions (Article IX) except with formal United States approval. Since the United States had already given notice that it would not participate in a case brought to the World Court by Nicaragua against the United States, the perspective of the conservatives on the genocide treaty appeared to find a positive echo. While the State Department initially opposed with considerable vigor the proposed amendment, it finally agreed to accept what had been considered an unnecessary weakening of the treaty text. Strikingly, the amendment on the World Court was exactly similar to "reservations" made by the Soviet Union and its communist allies when they ratified the treaty.

Yet, even when acquiescence was reached on the World Court amendment, Senate leadership was reluctant to take the plunge and decisively call for a vote. The rear-guard action of the Right appeared to carry political ramifications. It was believed in some quarters that in some tight Senate election races in 1986, a favorable vote on the genocide issue would compromise a conservative candidate.

Senate Majority Leader Robert Dole (R-KS), at a groundbreaking ceremony in October 1985 for a Holocaust museum to be created by the U.S. Holocaust Council, gave public assurances that he would bring the genocide treaty issue to a vote. It was patently evident to him that the official national focus upon the trauma of the Holocaust was scarcely consonant with the failure to ratify the only international treaty expressly designed to prevent another Holocaust. Senator Dole reiterated his commitment in November to a large assembly of Jewish communal leaders.

However, on 5 December, when the majority leader sought unanimous consent to bring up the genocide treaty, two Senators objected: Senator Helms and Senator Chic Hecht (R-NV). This killed the issue for 1985 despite the firm commitment made by the entire Senate on 11 October 1984. A new argument was advanced by the two objecting senators: that Israel would be the first to be targeted were the treaty to be activated. What this supposition had to do with United States ratification was not made clear. Besides, the supposition was itself open to question as Israel had been one of the very first countries to ratify the treaty. This it did on 9 March 1950, which made it the seventh country to accede, and its support for the treaty has never wavered since.

With the onset of the new Senate session in 1986, the determination to finally act on the genocide treaty issue had grown. The administration was pressing for action. The ABA, now in the forefront of a national effort of a broad-based coalition of major organizations, was intensely lobbying for a vote. Careful nose-counting indicated that close to 80 percent of the Senate would support ratification and that should a filibuster be launched, sufficient votes for cloture were at hand.

"We have waited long enough", said Majority Leader Dole on 11 February. Firmly calling for a vote on the treaty (along with the eight amendments), he added: "As a nation which enshrines human dignity and freedom ... we must correct our anomalous position on this basic rights issue." The vote was indeed overwhelming, 83 to 11. It was solid endorsement of the treaty with opposition coming only from conservatives mainly from several western states and a few from a couple of southern states.

The Senate vote had ended the long night of American embarrassment in international meetings and regional conferences. Two more years, however, would elapse before the ratification process was completed. As the genocide treaty is not self-executing, but rather, under Article V, requires enactment of implementing legislation, both houses of Congress had to adopt a special statute which makes genocide a federal crime and imposes appropriate penalties. In April 1988—the month was appropriate, for it commemorated the Holocaust—the house of Representatives overwhelmingly approved such legislation, and the Senate Judiciary Committee provided its support. On 14 October, the Senate formally adopted the implementing legislation. With the signature of the president placed on the new law on 4 November 1988, ratification was now consummated.

The United States could again reassert its leadership in the international human rights field without being challenged for its failure to ratify the genocide treaty. More pertinently, in a world in which the possibilities for genocide continue to constitute a clear and present danger, the United States can now more effectively "blow the whistle" on practitioners and advocates of genocide. Validated is America's tradition of advancing the rule of law in the international field.*

---

* This kind of treaty is not "self-executing" but required implementing legislation making genocide a crime in the U.S. Such legislation was adopted in October 1988 by Congress and signed by President Reagan on 4 November 1988. At that point, the United States became, in the full legal sense, a contracting party to the genocide convention.

BIBLIOGRAPHY

Ferencz, B. B. *Enforcing International Law*, 2 vols. New York, 1983.

———. *A Common Sense Guide to World Peace*. New York, 1985.

———. "The Future of Human Rights in International Jurisprudence," *Hofstra University Law Review* 10, no. 2 (Winter 1982).

Kaufman, Natalie Henever. *Human Rights Treaties and the Senate: A History of Opposition*. Chapel Hill, NC, 1990.

NOTES ON CONTRIBUTORS

WARREN F. KIMBALL is Professor of History at Rutgers University, The State University of New Jersey and was Pitt Professor of History at Cambridge University for 1988-89. He organized the conference that generated most of these papers and is the editor of this volume. He has published a number of works on the foreign policy of Franklin Roosevelt including *The Most Unsordid Act: Lend-Lease, 1939-1941* (1969), *Swords Or Ploughshares? The Morgenthau Plan for Defeated Nazi Germany* (1976), *Churchill & Roosevelt: The Complete Correspondence* (3 vols., 1984), and *The Juggler: Franklin Roosevelt as Wartime Statesman* (1991).

WILLIAM KOREY is Director of International Policy Research for B'nai B'rith. He is the author of *The Soviet Cage: Anti-Semitism in Russia* (1973) and *Human Rights and the Helsinki Accord* (1983). His articles have appeared in numerous scholarly and popular publications including the *New York Times*, the *Wall Street Journal*, the *Los Angeles Times*, and *The Christian Science Monitor*. He has been a guest scholar at the Woodrow Wilson International Center and, most recently, received a three-year Ford Foundation grant for research on the Helsinki process.

WALTER LaFEBER is Noll Professor of American History at Cornell University. Among his many publications are *The New Empire* (1967), *America, Russia, and the Cold War* (6th ed., 1990), *The American Age: U.S. Foreign Policy at Home and Abroad since 1750* (1989), and *Inevitable Revolutions: The United States in Central America* (1984).

HAYDEN B. PEAKE is a former intelligence officer with the U.S. Army and the Central Intelligence Agency. He is a graduate of Rochester Institute of Technology (B.S.) and Georgetown University (M.A. in international relations). Currently he is Executive Director of the National Intelligence Study Center and an adjunct professor at the Defense Intelligence College, where he teaches courses in counterintelligence and the history of intelligence.

DAVID REYNOLDS is a fellow of Christ's College and a university lecturer at the University of Cambridge. He is author of the prize-winning study, *The Creation of the Anglo-American Alliance, 1937-1941: A Study in Competitive Co-operation* (1982) and co-author of *An Ocean Apart: The Relationship between Britain and America in the Twentieth Century* (1988), as well as numerous articles on international history since World War I.

BRADLEY F. SMITH lectures at Cabrillo College. He is the author of a long list of books on World War II. Among them are *Adolph Hitler, His Family, Childhood, and Youth* (1967), *Heinrich Himmler* (1971), *Operation Sunrise* (co-author, 1979), *The Shadow Warriors: OSS and the Origins of the CIA* (1983), and *The War's Long Shadow* (1986). He is currently studying intelligence exchanges between the United States, Britain, and the Soviet Union during World War II.

RUSSELL F. WEIGLEY is Distinguished University Professor at Temple University. The recipient of the 1989 American Military Institute's Samuel Eliot Morison Prize for military history, he has written an array of books and articles on military history. These include *The American Way of War* (1973), *Eisenhower's Lieutenants: The Campaign of France and Germany, 1944-1945* (1981), and *The Age of Battles: The Quest for Decisive Warfare from Breitenfeld to Waterloo* (1990). He is currently working on a second volume of *The Age of Battles*.

DONALD CAMERON WATT, Stevenson Professor of International History at the London School of Economics and Political Science, has written numerous books and articles on international history in the twentieth century. Among them are *Personalities and Policies: Studies in the Formulation of British Foreign Policy in the Twentieth Century* (1965), *Too Serious a Business: European Armed Forces and the Approach of the Second World War* (1975), *Succeeding John Bull: America in Britain's Place, 1900-1975* (1984), and *How War Came: The Immediate Origins of the Second World War* (1989).

INDEX